THE

WRITER'S

LEGAL GUIDE

AN AUTHORS GUILD DESK REFERENCE

THIRD EDITION

TAD CRAWFORD and KAY MURRAY

ALLWORTH PRESS
NEW YORK

AUTHORS GUILD

Copublished with The Authors Guild, Inc.

Published by Allworth Press, an imprint of Allworth Communications, Inc., 10 East 23rd Street, New York, NY 10010.

Cover design by Leah Lococo

Book design/typography by Jennifer Moore, Leah Lococo Ltd.
Page composition by SR Desktop Services, Ridge, NY
Printed in Canada

Library of Congress Cataloging-in-Publication Data
Crawford, Tad, 1946–
The writer's legal guide : an authors guild desk reference /
Tad Crawford and Kay Murray.—3rd ed.
p.   cm.
Includes bibliographical references and index.
ISBN 1-58115-230-2
1. Authors—Legal status, laws, etc.—United States—Popular works.
2. Copyright—United States—Popular works.   I. Murray, Kay.   II. Title.
KF390.A96 C734 2002
346.7304'82—dc21
2002002450

10 09 08 07 06   7 6 5 4 3

For Elsie B. Meyer and Elsie K. Mills,
whose standards and generosity to a young writer were,
I now understand, gifts that last a lifetime.
— T.C.

For Taylor Skye, Jack Christopher, Zachary Michael,
Craig Joseph, F. John, and Andrea Michelle.
— K.M.

OTHER BOOKS BY TAD CRAWFORD

The Artist-Gallery Partnership (coauthored with Susan Mellon)

AIGA Professional Practices in Graphic Design (editor)

Business and Legal Forms for Authors and Self-Publishers

Business and Legal Forms for Crafts

Business and Legal Forms for Fine Artists

Business and Legal Forms for Graphic Designers
(coauthored with Eva Doman Bruck)

Business and Legal Forms for Illustrators

Business and Legal Forms for Interior Designers
(coauthored with Eva Doman Bruck)

Business and Legal Forms for Photographers

Legal Guide for the Visual Artist

The Money Mentor: A Tale of Finding Financial Freedom

The Secret Life of Money: How Money Can Be Food for the Soul

CONTENTS

ACKNOWLEDGMENTS

I would like to express my appreciation to Kay Murray for her excellent work in reshaping and updating the third edition of *The Writer's Legal Guide.* I am also thankful that Paul Aiken, Executive Director of the Authors Guild, supported the Guild's endorsement of the book and Kay's participation in its revision. As always, I'm appreciative to the Allworth Press staff for their support in all aspects of publishing this book.

In prior editions, I received assistance from many people. I would especially like to thank Tony Lyons, the Publisher for The Lyons Press, for his work as coauthor on the second edition. In addition, I'm thankful to the many professionals who gave generously of their time and expertise in reviewing portions of the second edition of *The Writer's Legal Guide:* Paul Basista, Executive Director, Graphic Artists Guild; James R. Cohen, Esquire, of Kleinberg, Kaplan, Wolff & Cohen; John Johnson, Esquire, of Heslin & Rothenberg; Ralph E. Lerner, Esquire, of Sidley & Austin; Charles Lyons, Ph.D., of Mud Pony Productions/The Walt Disney Company; Jennifer Lyons, M.A., of Writer's House; Nick Lyons, Ph.D., of Lyons & Burford, Publishers; Philip Mattera, National Book Grievance Officer, National Writers Union; Daniel Y. Mayer, Esquire, Executive Director, Volunteer Lawyers for the Arts (NYC); Kay Murray, Esquire, Director of Legal Services, Ed McCoyd, Esquire, Staff Attorney, and Carol Williams, Esquire, Staff Attorney, of the Authors Guild; Michael D. Remer, Esquire, of Cowan, Gold, DeBaets, Abrahams & Gross; Kirk T. Schroder, Esquire, of LeClair Ryan; and Eric Schwartz, Esquire, of Proskauer Rose Goetz & Mendelsohn.

Nor would this book would have been possible without those who offered constructive criticism in the development of the first edition: Arthur F. Abelman, Esquire; Alan Berlin, Esquire; Jeffrey Cooper, Esquire; Professor Jack Crawford, Jr.; Darcie Denkert, Esquire; Donald C. Farber, Esquire; Eileen Farley; James L. Garrity, Esquire; Paul Jacobs, Esquire; Professor John Kernochan; Elsie K. Mills; Jean V. Naggar; Professor Joseph M. Perillo; Nelson Richardson; Carolyn Trager; and Carl Zanger, Esquire.

—Tad Crawford

I am grateful to Tad Crawford for allowing me to work on a revised edition of this book. The people most responsible for the contents of my contribution are the thousands of members of the Authors Guild, its governing council, and its unsurpassed professional staff: Paul Aiken, Executive Director; Anita Fore,

Director of Legal Services; and Michael Gross, staff attorney (who contributed to the chapters on taxes). Their questions and insights, our collective struggles, accomplishments, and disappointments, have taught me more about law, business, and the writing life than school and law firm practice combined. Former colleagues and current friends Ed McCoyd, Carol Williams Lally, and Tania Zamorsky also added more than they know. Ms. Zamorsky provided much of the material underlying Chapter 13.

In addition, two most excellent assistants, Bianca Hidalgo and Abby Bender, made sense of my always-confusing, never-ending revisions. This book would not exist were it not for their cheerful, unflagging competence.

Finally, my heartfelt thanks go to Mary, Herb, Roger, Jean, Scott, Nick, Nicky, Letty, Judy, Jim, and most of all to Sidney. It has been a great honor to work with and for you.

—Kay Murray

CHAPTER 1

THE BUSINESS

OF WRITING

A re you writing for publication? If so, congratulations. You are in business—literally. Like any business owner, small or large, for-profit or nonprofit, you must protect your assets and earn adequate income from selling your valuable products. This book is intended to show you how to do so.

Writing and business might seem to you unrelated concepts, especially if you have a literary agent. Knowing the law might seem even more irrelevant, involved as you are in the creative process. These suppositions are just what many publishers are counting on in their business dealings with authors. As businesspeople, publishers hope their authors will simply sign the "standard" publishing contract as is, without questioning (or even reading) its many complex terms. They also hope, even assume, that you will passively accept royalty statements that make little sense or raise more questions than they answer, and that you will give up all the rights to new media uses of your work that they ask for. In short, publishers want you to sell your writing for as little as possible and then disappear (until, that is, you write a valuable new work).

Unfortunately, this is exactly what many professional writers do, to the detriment of their pocketbooks, their writing careers, even their artistic freedom, not to mention their peace of mind. The tendency is naturally more acute in a writer who has yet to be published. Elated by the first offer from a publisher, many writers become psychologically incapable of negotiating. Sometimes this happens from fear that the deal will fall through. Other times, authors simply do not have the skills and information they need to hold their own in a business negotiation. Learn this simple fact: Publishing contracts are *always* biased in favor of the publisher and against the author. If you sign the "boilerplate" contract form your publisher presents to you, without negotiating, there is a good chance you will regret it someday.

Every writer, whatever his or her motivation to write, can and should be capable of resolving business and legal issues. A better understanding of law and the publishing business will prevent you from being intimidated, helpless, or victimized in a business context. While no book can solve the unique problems of every writer, learning the general legal principles governing your intellectual property will help you avoid risks and earn proper rewards from your work.

Even if you have a good literary agent, you should learn how to protect your interests and to license your intellectual property. Some agents are lawyers, and others are so good at negotiating contracts that they do not need to be lawyers to get you a good deal. But many agents are better at selling a book than negotiating a contract or confronting a publisher about a questionable practice. An agent might not know copyright or contract law well enough to advise you when you need to get a release from a third party or to negotiate hard for a certain change to a contract. Even if your agent is terrific in all such matters, it is never wise to give too much control of one's property and career interests to another person. Unless you are your agent's only client, he or she has an interest beyond, or even in conflict with, yours: his or her own relationship with publishers, for the sake of other clients. Furthermore, agency relationships have been known to end, cordially or badly, but always under circumstances that require you to know something about your rights and obligations to both the agent and your publisher(s).

The laws that protect writers' rights have always been closely connected to commerce. Domestic copyright protection, for example, is the result of an implacable economic tension between the right of creators to benefit from the fruits of their talent and labor, and society's need to enjoy and build on their creations. The law's attempt to balance those interests is the fundamental principle underlying U.S. and international intellectual property law. Increasingly, that principle favors protecting creators' interests. The United States Supreme Court has said explicitly that the copyright laws are based on the economic philosophy: that the "sacrificial days" devoted to creativity ultimately benefit the general public and must be encouraged by commensurate personal profit.

This third edition of *The Writer's Legal Guide* has a broad scope and uses the term "writer" to include creators of nonfiction books and articles, journalists, novelists, poets, playwrights, screenwriters, and all others who put pen to paper—or fingers to keyboard—for profit, conviction, or pleasure. All types of writers can benefit from the business and legal information offered here.

Five years have passed since the second edition of *The Writer's Legal Guide*. In the interim, the dramatic evolution of technology—networked computers, digital imaging, print-on-demand and electronic publishing, and of course, the World Wide Web—has transformed the ways information can be processed and disseminated to the public. Among other topics, this book will explain how the current copyright law and savvy negotiating can be used to protect authors' increasingly valuable electronic rights.

The Writer's Legal Guide seeks to deal with each of the sequence of issues that arise as soon as an author contemplates creating a written work, including copyright, publishing contracts, freedom of expression, liability, taxes, and estate planning. Most writers reading this book will be writing to earn all or part of their livelihood. This book can help you earn what your work is worth by helping you know how and what to negotiate, while preserving your relationship with your publishers. If you are writing for purely creative reasons, you still owe it to yourself, and to your readers, to protect your work from piracy and distortion and to realize your work's economic value.

DISCLAIMER

Every attempt has been made to ensure that the information in this book is thorough, accurate, and current, but the publishers, the authors, their agents, employees, and representatives cannot warrant or guarantee that this is the case. This book is not a substitute for the advice of a lawyer, accountant, literary agent, or any other expert who has examined the specific facts of a given situation. The publishers, authors, and their agents, employees, and representatives disclaim all liability for any loss arising out of or in connection with anything that appears or fails not appear in this book.

WRITERS GROUPS

Membership in writers' organizations can increase your awareness of the legal and business environment in which you work and sometimes significantly advance your negotiating position. Some groups provide a valuable support network. If you are a published author, or if you have been offered a book-publishing contract, you should seriously consider joining the Authors Guild. No other professional writers' group offers so many benefits and services for so little money. The Authors Guild is a copublisher of this edition of *The Writer's Legal Guide*. It offers members individual business and legal advice (including contract reviews) and advocacy from experienced publishing attorneys at no additional charge. It has published a Recommended Tradebook Contract and Guide, complete with negotiating lessons. Its quarterly *Bulletin* and frequent Advocacy Alerts keep authors up to date on key legal and business developments. The Guild frequently lobbies for legislation favorable to writers. It offers health and life insurance at group rates, an online bookstore with a print-on-demand republishing service, and superior and economical Web site design software to members.

The online edition of this book is available exclusively to Authors Guild members at *www.authorsguild.org*. If you qualify, and if you want to run your writing business well, you should join the Authors Guild.

The Authors Guild, Inc.
31 East 28th Street, 10th Floor, New York, New York 10016
(212) 563-5904
www.authorsguild.org
(online application available)

Other major writers groups include the following:

American Society of Journalists and Authors
1501 Broadway, Suite 302, New York, New York 10036
(212) 997-0947
www.asja.org

The ASJA is the nation's leading organization of independent non-fiction writers. It offers extensive benefits and services focusing on professional development, including regular confidential market information, meetings with editors and other field professionals, an exclusive referral service, seminars and workshops, discount services, and the opportunity for members to explore professional issues and concerns with their peers.

The Authors Registry
31 East 28th Street, New York, New York 10016
(212) 563-6920
www.authorsregistry.org

The Authors Registry is a nonprofit organization formed to help expedite the flow of royalty payments and small reuse fees to authors, particularly for new-media uses. As a payment clearinghouse for certain categories of royalties and fees, the Registry lifts the burden from publishers and delivers checks to freelancers. The Registry also distributes to U.S. authors fees paid for photocopying of their work in the United Kingdom. The Registry's services are crucial to authors' continuing control of rights to their works and will help ensure receipt of income due under those rights that might otherwise be lost.

The Dramatists Guild
234 West 44th Street, New York, New York 10036
(212) 398-9366
www.dramaguild.com

The Dramatists Guild of America is the only professional association for playwrights, composers, and lyricists working to advance the rights of its members spanning the globe. Membership is open to all dramatic writers, regardless of their production history. Any writer who has completed a dramatic script may become a member of the Dramatists Guild of America and receive a wide range of benefits, including business affairs advice and contract reviews.

The National Writers Union
873 Broadway, Suite 203, New York, New York 10003
(212) 254-0279
www.nwu.org

The NWU is a trade union for freelance writers of all genres who work for American publishers or employers. It is committed to improving the economic and working conditions of freelance writers through the collective strength of 6,500 members in 17 local chapters throughout the country. It offers grievance resolution, industry campaigns, contract advice, health and dental plans, member education, job banks, and networking.

Novelists, Inc.
PO Box 1166, Mission, Kansas 66222-0166
(913) 262-6435
www.ninc.com

Novelists, Inc. is dedicated to serving the needs of multipublished writers of popular fiction. Novelists, Inc. not only keeps its members connected, communicating, and well informed, but also is actively striving to better the status of fiction writers. It is a coalition of working writers dedicated to serving the professional needs of its members.

The Science Fiction and Fantasy Writers of America
PO Box 877, Chestertown, Maryland 21620
www.sfwa.org

Over 1,200 science fiction and fantasy writers, artists, editors, and allied professionals are members of SFWA. The SFWA Grievance Committee investigates claims of illegal or unethical contracts, assertions of plagiarism, evidence of contract violation by editors and publishers, misuse of royalty statements and funds, and other complaints of professional concern.

The Society of Children's Book Writers and Illustrators
8271 Beverly Boulevard, Los Angeles, California 90048
(323) 782-1010
www.scbwi.org

The SCBWI serves as a voice for professional writers and illustrators across the world. As a unified body, the SCBWI acts as a powerful force to effect important changes within the field of children's literature. The SCBWI serves an advisory function for all of its members. Individual advice, information, and counsel are gladly provided.

Text and Academic Authors Association
University of South Florida, 140 Seventh Avenue S., St. Petersburg,
  Florida 33701
(727) 553-1195
http://taa.winona.msus.edu/TAA/

TAA represents text and academic authors in professional matters including taxes, copyright, and better appreciation of their work within academe. It is also committed to improving the quality of educational materials. Members qualify for a free initial legal consultation and discounted legal fees with the law offices of Michael R. Lennie.

Outdoor Writers Association of America
2017 Cato Avenue, State College, Pennsylvania 16801-1011
(814) 234-1011
www.owaa.org

The mission of Outdoor Writers Association of America is to improve the professional skills of members, set the highest ethical and communications standards, encourage public enjoyment and conservation of natural resources, and be mentors for the next generation of professional outdoor communicators.

P.E.N. American Center
568 Broadway, New York, New York 10012
(212) 334-1660
www.pen.org

P.E.N. is a membership association of prominent literary writers and editors. As a major voice of the literary community, the organization seeks to defend the freedom of expression and promote and encourage the recognition and reading of contemporary literature. A membership committee elects members of P.E.N.

The Writers Guild of America—East
555 West 57th Street, New York, New York 10019
(212) 767-7800
www.wgaeast.org

The Writers Guild of America—West
8955 Beverly Blvd., Los Angeles, California 90048
(310) 550-1000
www.wga.org

The Writers Guild of America is made up of two unions—the Writers Guild, East and the Writers Guild, West. Together they consist of some 11,000 professionals who are the primary creators of what is seen or heard on television and film in the United States. The Guild answers agent, lawyer, and member questions and reviews private contracts, notices of hire, work lists, and other data that is provided to ensure that it knows who is working, when, and under what terms. The Guild also administers the credits provisions of its contracts.

DO AUTHORS NEED LAWYERS?

The Writer's Legal Guide encourages authors to think in a new way—like a lawyer. It will help you to better your business practices, increase your income, and protect your work. It will *not* make you a legal expert on copyright or any of the areas covered. It is not meant to substitute for the advice of a lawyer on specific issues. In fact, there is no substitute for the advice of a knowledgeable attorney who can carefully evaluate an author's unique legal query. Throughout this book, you will be advised when you should consult with a lawyer, literary agent, tax or royalty accountant, or any other professional.

For questions about the meaning of a contract term, help with reviewing an entire contract, and concerns about your royalty statements or your publisher's behavior, check first with the Authors Guild's Contract Services staff (if you are a member of the Guild). It can answer your questions and offer advice on how to proceed, and it can send demand letters to publishers and other parties on your behalf. If your matter requires a private lawyer, the Guild can refer you to one who is qualified.

You should consider consulting a lawyer if:

- ✍ You are negotiating or facing an issue in a contract (signed or unsigned), and you feel you cannot conduct the negotiation on your own behalf.
- ✍ You are being threatened with suit or termination of a contract or a withholding of royalties.
- ✍ You are ever unsure about the consequences of a document you are asked to sign.
- ✍ Whenever a large amount of money or other valuable property is at stake in a transaction or dispute.

The search for a lawyer can be time-consuming and disheartening. Not only are fees high, but most general practitioners are not knowledgeable about the special issues facing writers. Standard techniques for finding a lawyer include asking friends or family who used a lawyer for a similar problem, calling a local bar association's referral service, or searching the Martindale Hubbell Lawyer Locator *(www.martindale.com).* Some of the author organizations listed previously offer lawyer referrals.

Fortunately, lawyers' interest in the amount of literature and the number of educational programs that deal with authors' legal issues has increased substantially. Law schools now offer publishing law courses and are integrating issues affecting writers into their intellectual property courses. Along with this increased interest is an increase in the number of lawyers across the country volunteering to help authors and artists. If you cannot afford legal assistance, consider contacting one of these groups. Even if they cannot provide free or low-cost legal services in a specific matter, many of them offer general advice and referrals to knowledgeable attorneys. A current list of nonprofit legal services organizations for artists appears as an appendix to this book.

VALUE OF *THE WRITER'S LEGAL GUIDE*

Many people call the most successful working writers lucky, and most of those writers would agree. Remember, though, that "chance favors the prepared mind." Authors who learn to protect their rights and negotiate effectively are likely to earn more money from writing, save time by avoiding time-consuming legal problems, maintain more control over their careers and their work, and suffer less stress because knowing more allows them to worry less. We hope this third edition of *The Writer's Legal Guide* will give you greater self-reliance, confidence, and peace of mind as you build your writing career.

CHAPTER 2

COPYRIGHT: GAINING

AND KEEPING

PROTECTION

One of the top priorities of our nation's governing blueprint, the United States Constitution, is the legal recognition of intellectual property: "The Congress shall have the power . . . To promote the Progress of Science and useful Arts, by securing for limited Times to Authors and Inventors the exclusive Right to their respective Writings and Discoveries" (Article 1, Section 8, Clause 8). Historically, laws protecting literary property rights evolved under English judge-made law and legislation. In 1790, Congress responded to its constitutional prerogative by enacting the first federal copyright law. In its current incarnation, the Copyright Act covers virtually every kind of original work in written or other perceptible form (electronic symbols, magnetic tape, photographs, CD-ROM, film, videotape, canvas, and so on). The most recent major amendment to the statute, the Digital Millennium Copyright Act of 1998, added the transmission of works in digital form (for example, over the Internet) to its governance.

THE VALUE OF COPYRIGHT

Virtually all the economic value a written work has comes from ownership of the copyright in the work. The Copyright Act gives to the author exclusively all rights to exploit his or her written work through reproduction, distribution, public display, public performance, and the creation of derivative works, any or all of which the author can choose to use, to allow others to use, or to prevent others from using. The author's agreement to authorize others to enjoy any of these rights is the mechanism by which he or she earns compensation from the written work. This chapter will explain how to obtain and keep the benefits and protections of the copyright law.

Copyright law has historically proven remarkably adaptable to technological advances that have altered the way we create, store, and deliver literary works. Some commentators have argued recently that copyright cannot meet future technological challenges or have advocated for a more flexible reading of copyright law because of the difficulty of enforcing it in the so-called Digital Age. Arguing that the ease of copying online will destroy copyright is a bit premature, however, in view of the many technologies (such as computer programs, sound recordings, film, and television) for which copyright protection has survived. In fact, the United States is a net exporter of intellectual property, and its protection is vital to our gross national product. In order to maintain the needed incentives for creativity, copyright law will become more vital as it is adjusted to technological innovation.

The federal administrator of the Act is the Copyright Office, a part of the Library of Congress. One helpful free aid that every writer should obtain is a Copyright Information Kit, which can be obtained from the Copyright Office, Library of Congress, Washington, D.C. 20559. This kit includes the Copyright Office's regulations, registration forms, and "Copyright Office Circulars" that explain the law in detail and the operation of the Copyright Office. These items can also be downloaded individually from the Copyright Office Web site at *www.loc.gov/copyright/*. The Web site offers numerous circulars explaining specific provisions of the Act, frequently asked questions about copyright, the complete text of the Copyright Act, pending and final legislation, regulations, announcements, and press releases. Circular 1, *Copyright Basics,* and Circular 2, *Publications on Copyright,* are especially helpful overviews.

If you are not online, you can obtain a paperback copy of the Copyright Act current to April 2000 (Circular 92 or stock #030-002-

00182-9) for $14 from the Superintendent of Documents, P.O. Box 371954, Pittsburgh, Pennsylvania 15250-7954, (202) 512-1800. You can call a hotline number, (202) 707-9100, to request expedited mailing of registration forms, and the Authors Guild has registration forms and various circulars for members. The Copyright Office's public information number is (202) 707-3000.

THE GOVERNING COPYRIGHT LAW

Until January 1, 1978, copyright in the United States existed in two distinct forms: common-law and statutory. Common-law copyright derived from judge-made precedent, while statutory copyright derived from federal legislation. Common-law copyright protected works as soon as they were created, without copyright notice or registration; statutory copyright protected works only when registered with the Copyright Office or published with copyright notice. Common-law copyright lasted forever if the work was unpublished or unregistered; statutory copyright lasted for a finite time.

On January 1, 1978, an entirely revised federal copyright law, known as the Copyright Act of 1976, replaced the federal law that had been in effect since 1909 and preempted all common law copyright. The 1976 Act, with continuous amendments and judicial interpretations, is the sole law of copyright in the United States today. The 1976 Act (with later amendments) generally favors the creator, but some provisions of the Act that maximize the benefits of copyright protection are fairly intricate, and every writer should understand them. The 1976 Act is constantly evolving, as courts and Congress attempt to address the effect of new technologies and new economic realities on the balance of competing interests that the Act must sustain.

Most of the 1976 Act became effective on January 1, 1978, and all works created on or after that date are covered by that law. If copyright in a pre-1978 work had not expired as of January 1, 1978, the 1976 Act governs the treatment of that copyright. Note, however, that certain copyright transactions (including grants, licenses, registrations, and renewal registrations) made before January 1, 1978 are still governed by the federal Copyright Act of 1909. If a work entered the public domain (which means that it has no copyright and can be freely exploited by anyone) under the 1909 Act, the 1976 Act did not revive the expired copyright, even if the work would not have gone into the public domain had the 1976 Act been in effect when the work was created.

The 1976 Act explicitly eliminated all common-law copyright, a reform that substantially simplified the copyright system. Federal copyright law now protects all works from the moment they "are first fixed in a tangible medium of expression, now known or later developed, from which they can be perceived, reproduced or otherwise communicated, either directly or with the aid of a machine or device." That means that your work is governed by the Copyright Act as soon as you write it, type it, store it in a computer file, tape record it, or otherwise fix it in a tangible medium of expression. You need not comply with any formalities in order to obtain copyright protection (although the formalities of registration are not difficult or expensive and provide valuable legal and economic advantages). This immediate copyright protection, regardless of registration or publication with copyright notice, revolutionized U.S. copyright law and made it consistent with the more creator-friendly copyright laws of many other nations.

WHAT WORKS MAY BE COPYRIGHTED?

A writer has a copyright only in an original work. "Originality" under the Act simply means that the writer created the work and did not copy it from another copyrighted work. The work need not be brilliant, unique, or even good to be entitled to copyright, so long as it originated with the writer. To be legally "original," a work has only to show a minor level of creativity or minimal artistic qualities.

To illustrate, it is the actual copying and not the similarity to another work that makes a work unoriginal (and, therefore, an infringement of the other work's copyright). If two writers, by some unlikely turn of fate, happened independently to create identical works, both would be entitled to copyright. As Judge Learned Hand wrote, "Borrowed the work must indeed not be, for a plagiarist is not himself pro tanto an 'author'; but if by some magic a man who had never known it were to compose anew Keats's 'Ode on a Grecian Urn,' he would be an 'author,' and . . . others might not copy that poem, though they might of course copy Keats's [because it is in the public domain]," *Sheldon v. Metro-Goldwyn Pictures Corporation,* 81 F.2d 49, 55 (2d Cir. 1936). Two writers choosing the same subject matter, such as a historical event or well-known person, would each own the copyright in their respective writings.

What is not covered by copyright? Ideas, facts, concepts, principles, discoveries, titles, names, slogans, short phrases, blank forms, general topics, common plots or themes, stock characters, and processes or procedures are not eligible for copyright (although some of these might be protected under other legal theories discussed in chapter 7). It is the creative *expression* of any of these items, the writer's original realization of the subject, that is copyrightable. Thus, the description of an idea is copyrightable, as is the selection and arrangement of facts and computer programming code. Common themes and stock characters can be fleshed out to create copyrighted works. But the underlying ideas, facts, processes, themes, and stock characters remain forever in the public domain, free for the taking by anyone.

Although copyright protection does not extend to the discovery of what is objectively true, it does protect the original way objective facts are presented. In 1985, the U.S. Supreme Court articulated the minimum level of originality required for copyright in the presentation of facts. In *Feist Publications, Inc. v. Rural Telephone Service Company, Inc.,* 499 U.S. 346 (1991), the Supreme Court held that a white pages telephone directory is not a copyrightable compilation because its selection, arrangement, and coordination—it contained nothing more than an alphabetical listing of all the names and addresses in a particular area code—failed to meet constitutional standards of originality.

The *Feist* ruling is clearly consistent with general copyright principles, but it overturned a long-standing rule known as "the sweat of the brow doctrine." Under that doctrine, courts "handed out proprietary interests in facts and declared that authors are absolutely precluded from saving time and effort by relying upon the facts contained in prior works." The Supreme Court, noting that not all copying amounts to infringement, concluded in *Feist* that even an exact copy, which included names that were added specifically to detect copying (called "franking"), did not infringe the copyright of the compiler because there was no copyright in the work.

Since *Feist,* copyright no longer protects raw data, regardless of the time and effort involved in finding it. Writers can freely copy the bare facts from prior works without infringing copyright, although they must verify those facts and be sure to select, coordinate, and arrange them independently. Remember, however, that many compilations of individually uncopyrightable elements remain protected by copyright. A protected compilation is a work formed by the collection and assembling of preexisting material that is selected, coordinated, and arranged in such a way that the resulting work is in some sense original. Examples range from the yellow pages of the phone book (in contrast to the white pages in *Feist*) to annotated listings of the best restaurants in New York City. Whether the copyright in such a compilation has been infringed depends on the nature of the collected material, the manner in which it is presented, and the nature of the appropriation.

The increasing prevalence of sequels, spin-offs, and "retellings" raises the issue of whether a specific character can be copyrightable apart from the story containing that character. The Copyright Act states that stock characters or literary types—the "riotous knight" or "a vain and foppish steward"—are not copyrightable, but there are many cases in which a character is copyrightable. The test of copyright for characters is not an easy one. As one court put it: "The less developed the characters, the less they can be copyrighted: that is the penalty an author must bear for marking them too indistinctly," *Nichols v. Universal Pictures Corp.,* 45 F.2d 119, 121 (2d Cir. 1930), *cert denied,* 282 U.S. 902 (1931). Subsequently, another court, in a case involving Sam Spade of *Maltese Falcon* fame, enunciated a different test in noting that a character in a piece of writing would be independently copyrightable if that character actually "constitut[ed] the story being told," *Warner Bros. Pictures, Inc. v. Columbia Broadcasting System, Inc.,* 216 F.2d 945, 950 (9th cir. 1954), *cert. denied,* 298 U.S. 669 (1956). Cases involving the copyrightability of characters will generally require detailed jury determinations of fact as well as a consideration of the equities involved.

The fact that part of a work infringes someone else's copyright, or contains public domain material, will not prevent the author from securing copyright in the remainder of the work. For example, if an author writes a group of articles to appear in a book but also includes someone else's copyrighted piece without permission, the original contribution of the writer, but only that, would still be copyrightable.

Derivative works, which are distinguishable variations of existing works, can be copyrighted in appropriate circumstances. The author of the original work has the exclusive right to make derivative works based on the original or to authorize others to do so. An author who owns a copyright can add new elements to the previously copyrighted work and copyright those new elements. If a work is in the public domain, anyone can create a copyrightable work by adding original elements to it. For example, a writer could create a copyrightable work by adding new elements to Keats's "Ode on a Grecian Urn." The new author would only be able to prevent copying of the new elements; others could still take freely from Keats's poem. Derivative works such as abridgments, adaptations, and translations all require original effort and are copyrightable in their own right. If the derivative work is based on copyrighted material, the consent of the copyright owner must be obtained. If consent is not obtained, the maker of the derivative work will be liable for infringement.

The Copyright Office can refuse to register a work on the ground that it is not copyrightable, but the courts can review this exercise of the Copyright Register's discretion. It is the federal courts, not the Copyright Office, that interpret the Copyright Act, and the federal courts are the final arbiter of what is and is not copyrightable.

WHAT WORKS DOES U.S. LAW COVER?

If a work is published, U.S. copyright law protects it if one or more of its authors is:

- A national or permanent resident of the United States
- A stateless person
- A national or a permanent resident of a nation covered by a copyright treaty with the United States or by a presidential proclamation

If a work is unpublished, the U.S. copyright law protects it regardless of the author's nationality or place of residence. The Copyright Act treats published works differently from unpublished works in several situations. "Publication" under the Act means public distribution, which occurs when one or more copies of a work are distributed to people who are not restricted from disclosing the work's content to others. Distribution can take place by sale, rental, lease, lending, or other transfer of copies to the public. Also, offering copies to a group of people for the purpose of review, further distribution, public performance, or public display constitutes "publication" under the Act.

What about copyright protection in other countries? The United States is a party to several treaties (called "conventions") in which the signing nations agree to apply their copyright protection to works published in the other parties' countries. Authors automatically obtain protection in the participating nations under these treaties when they publish a work in the United States. The Universal Copyright Convention, which dates from 1955, provides that publication in any nation that is a party to it will bestow copyright in the United States, and vice versa. There is one special requirement: The works must contain a copyright notice that includes the symbol ©, the author's full name, and the year of first publication. The author's initials will not suffice when protection is sought under the Universal Copyright Convention. For an older treaty, the Buenos Aires Convention, which covers many Western Hemisphere countries, the notice must also contain the phrase "All rights reserved."

The United States joined the larger Berne Convention as of March 1, 1989. As a result, it is no longer necessary for U.S. writers to publish simultaneously in a Berne Union country to gain protection under the Berne Convention. In fact, the Berne Convention forbids member countries from imposing copyright formalities—such as publication with copyright notice—as a condition of copyright protection for the works of foreign writers, which has led to a number of favorable changes in U.S. copyright law. (These changes will be described in relation to the appropriate sections of the text.) Details of the international copyright relations of the United States can be obtained from the Copyright Office in Circular 38a, *International Copyright Relations of the United States.* Circular 38a, covering copyright relations as of October 31, 1999, lists every nation and the copyright conventions to which they belong. Many belong to both major treaties, and some to one or the other, but not both. Keep in mind that you are automatically protected under both conventions when you publish a work in the United States.

TERM OF COPYRIGHT

Copyright in a work exists for a limited time. After that time, the work enters the public domain, where it belongs to everyone. Nobody can control how others exploit a public domain work (think of the works of Shakespeare). Today, under an amendment to the 1976 Act that passed in 1998 and is currently under Supreme Court review, the term of copyright for works published on or after January 1, 1923 is the length of the writer's life plus seventy years. The amendment extended the term by twenty years, matching most Berne Convention nations' term of copyright. For works created anonymously, under a pseudonym, or as a work made for hire on or after 1923, the term is either ninety-five years from first publication of the work or one hundred twenty years from its creation, whichever period is shorter. The Copyright Office maintains records as to when a writer dies, but a presumption exists that a copyright has expired if ninety-five years have passed and the records disclose no information indicating the copyright term might still be in effect. This does not mean, however, that copyright has expired; the presumption can be rebutted with evidence of the author's continued existence or date of death. If the name of the author of an anonymous or pseudonymous work is recorded with the Copyright Office, the copyright term runs for the writer's life plus seventy years.

The term of copyright for a joint work is the life of the last surviving writer plus seventy years. A "joint work" is defined in the Act as a work created by two or more writers with the intention that their contributions be merged into inseparable or interdependent parts of a unitary whole.

The 1909 copyright law had an original twenty-eight–year term and a second term, called the "renewal term," of twenty-eight years. The renewal term was so called because it came into existence only if the author filed a renewal registration in the twenty-eighth year of the first term. If the author failed to do so, the work entered the public domain. As a rule, the terms of copyrights that existed on January 1, 1978, are extended to ninety-five years from first publication (twenty-eight years in the first term, sixty-seven years in the renewal term). All works copyrighted between January 1, 1964, and December 31, 1977 automatically have their terms extended to ninety-five years.

Since common-law copyright was eliminated by the 1976 Act, all works protected by common-law copyright as of January 1, 1978, now have a statutory copyright term of the writer's life plus seventy years. In no event, however, will a copyright previously protected under common law expire prior to December 31, 2002, and, if the work has been published, the copyright will extend until at least December 31, 2047. All copyright terms run through December 31 of the year in which they are scheduled to expire.

The 1998 extension of the term of copyright protection by twenty years was strongly criticized by many who claim it vitiates the Constitutional mandate that copyright exist "for limited times." Recently, the U.S. Supreme Court decided to review this important issue in Eldred v. Ashcroft, and it should rule by Fall 2002.

EXCLUSIVE RIGHTS

Only the owner of a copyright has the exclusive rights to exploit the work's value by doing, or authorizing others to do, any of the following: reproduce the work, sell and distribute the work, perform the work publicly, display the work publicly, and prepare derivative works. (A derivative work adapts or transforms an earlier work, such as making a film from a novel, adding new chapters to a nonfiction book, or translating a work into a different language.)

Before the 1976 Act became law, the strict notice required of the 1909 Act meant that a copyright owner could transfer only the entire copyright, not selected parts of it, to another. This restriction led to notoriously unfair results for authors, as when a short story published in a magazine transferred the entire copyright to the magazine. If that story was purchased to make a motion picture, it was bought from the magazine, the owner of the copyright, not from the author. The most important change made by the 1976 Act was to make copyright divisible and the exclusive rights of copyright subdivisible. Copyright is now often described as a bundle of rights, each of which may be licensed separately by the owner. For example, the exclusive rights to reproduce (and to sell and distribute copies of) an article might be licensed to *Harper's* magazine, while all other exclusive rights remain the author's. *Harper's* rights could be subdivided further into "first North American serial rights," which is still an exclusive right, because it gives the magazine the right to be first to publish the work in the given geographical area. Second serial rights and foreign publication rights still belong to the author in this scenario. It is crucial that you understand how to subdivide your rights, because this is how you can limit the rights that are transferred to one party and retain the other rights for future licenses with others.

There are some limited exceptions to the exclusive rights of the copyright owner. The most important of these is "fair use," which in special cases allows others to use a copyrighted work without the owner's permission. Fair use is discussed in chapter 5. Another exception is the "first sale" doctrine, which allows one who has purchased a lawfully made copy to resell that copy. Also, the exclusive right to display a work does not prevent the owner of a copy of the work from displaying the copy directly or with the aid of a projector to people present at the place of display, such as exhibiting a beautifully designed novel at a lecture on book design. For an audiovisual work, including a motion picture, a "display" is defined as showing its images nonsequentially. The owner of a copy of an audiovisual work, such as a motion picture, may lawfully display the copy publicly. *Performing* an audiovisual work, however, means to show its images sequentially, and the owner of the copy may do so only in private. As you read at the beginning of most movie videotapes, one may not perform the work publicly, either in a public place or before an audience of a substantial number of people, without permission of the copyright owner. Despite these limited exceptions, copyright is completely separate and distinct from ownership of a physical manuscript (or a computer disk containing the manuscript, or a painting, photograph, or sound recording). An author can sell the physical work or a copy of it with or without a written agreement, and this sale alone does not grant any of the rights under copyright to the purchaser.

As the movie videotape notice also warns, anyone who uses a work in violation of the copyright owner's exclusive rights is liable for copyright infringement and subject to substantial money damages, a restraining order from continuing the infringement, and even, in severe cases, criminal penalties. Chapter 5 explains infringement claims and penalties in detail.

TRANSFERS AND LICENSES

The Act requires that all transfers and licenses of any of the exclusive rights of copyright be made in a writing signed by the licensor (that is, the owner of the rights). An exclusive license grants to the licensee a right that no one else may exercise. Book publishers rarely accept any rights that are not exclusive. The scope of the exclusive rights granted could be varied by the duration of the license, the geographic extent of the license and other factors that the writer believes are useful and can be obtained through negotiation. The Act specifically requires an exclusive license to be signed by the licensor—assent will not suffice. The requirement of a written transfer is clearly an important protection for the writer.

Nonexclusive licenses need not be made in writing. Nonexclusive licenses allow two or more parties to exploit a work in the same way, at the same time, in the same place, and are consequently less valuable than exclusive rights. For example, a writer could give two magazines "simultaneous rights" to publish an article. Something similar to this occurs when newspapers are granted syndication rights. The effect is a kind of simultaneous license under which many newspapers can run a story or article as long as they pay a licensing fee to the syndicator (which could be the original publisher, a syndication agency, or even an unusually enterprising author). The syndicator in turn pays a set fee to the writer for each time the work runs.

Because nonexclusive licenses can be granted verbally, vigilance is needed to ensure that an implied and/or unwanted license is not created. Be wary of verbal statements, unsigned writings (such as a memorandum on a publisher's letterhead), or e-mail that suggests a party has a right to exploit your work in certain ways. Licenses and transfers of rights under copyright, whether exclusive or nonexclusive, should spell out what rights are granted or transferred and explicitly reserve to the writer all rights not specifically granted. Later chapters of this book will explain in greater detail how to do so.

Your exclusive licensee (the purchaser of the rights) may file copies of documents recording transfers of copyrights or exclusive licenses with the Copyright Office. Whether or not the licensee does so, however, will not affect your copyright or the validity of the license.

THE AUTHOR'S TERMINATION RIGHTS

An important new right was bestowed on authors by the 1976 Act. Any author may terminate his or her grant of exclusive or nonexclusive rights after many years (thirty-five years for post-1978 works; fifty-six years for pre-1978 works). The purpose of the right of termination is to give creators a second chance to share in the unexpected increase in the value of rights that were transferred years before the work's value was known. The right to terminate a grant exists "notwithstanding any agreement to the contrary," in the words of the Act. Even if an author agrees in writing and for compensation not to exercise this right, he or she may do so when the time comes. Only if the work was done "for hire" or if the transfer was made in a will can the author's right to terminate a grant be defeated. After January 1, 1978, any author who grants exclusive or nonexclusive rights in a copyright may terminate the grant(s) during a five-year period starting at the end of thirty-five years after the execution of the grant or, if the grant includes the right of publication, during a five-year period beginning at the end of thirty-five years from the date of publication or forty years from the date of execution of the grant, whichever term ends earlier. Similarly, if before January 1, 1978, an author (or his or her surviving family members) made a grant of the renewal term of a copyright, that grant may be terminated during a five-year period starting fifty-six years after the copyright was first obtained.

The mechanics of termination involve giving notice from two to ten years prior to the termination date and complying with requirements listed in Copyright Office Circular 96, "Notice of Termination of Transfers and Licenses." Do not forget that this right exists and is inalienable. Should your work succeed beyond your expectations, the termination right could prove extremely valuable to you or your family many years from now.

SPECIAL COPYRIGHT CONCERNS WHEN LICENSING RIGHTS TO PERIODICALS AND OTHER COLLECTIVE WORKS

Magazines, newspapers, anthologies, encyclopedias—anything in which a number of separate contributions are combined—are defined in the Act as "collective works." The law explicitly provides that the copyright in each contribution is distinct from the copyright in the entire collective work. The copyright in a contribution belongs to the author of the contribution, who may grant to the collective work owner the right to include it in the collective work. Until a few years ago, it was not uncommon for newspapers and magazines to publish freelance contributions without an express agreement over what rights were being licensed. The law deals with this situation by providing that where there is no express agreement, the collective work publisher has only the privilege to reproduce the contribution in (1) the issue of the collective work for which it was contributed, (2) any revision of that collective work, or (3) any later collective work in the same series.

For example, where a freelance article is contributed to a magazine based only on an editor's verbal assignment, the magazine may use the article in one issue and again in later issues, but it cannot publish that work in a different magazine. Magazines are not usually revised, but anthologies and encyclopedias are. In that case, the article may be used in the original issue of the anthology or encyclopedia and any later revisions, but it may not be included in a new anthology or different encyclopedia. In the absence of a written agreement, only nonexclusive rights are transferred to the magazine or other collective work, so a writer could contribute the work elsewhere at the same time. Unless they approve of this, however, both publishers are likely to see this as a breach of professional ethics and pass you over for future assignments.

Rather than allowing your sale to be governed by a law that might not satisfy either party's needs, it might be better to have the sale governed by terms understood and negotiated by both parties, such as a grant of "first North America serial rights." A signed written transfer can be accomplished by a simple letter stating:

> This is to confirm that in return for your agreement to pay me $_____, I grant to [Publisher] exclusive first North American rights to reproduce my work titled _____ described as follows: _____ for publication in your magazine titled: _____. All other rights, including but not limited to electronic rights, are reserved to me.

If the publisher wants to use your contribution in another way, such as in an online edition, an additional fee and appropriate usage limitation might be negotiated.

If you are a freelance contributor to newspapers or magazines, you need to read chapter 12 for important developments in the respective rights and contract practices of contributors and collective works publishers. Electronic rights are at the heart of these developments.

WRITING CONTESTS AND COPYRIGHT

Writing contests sponsored by publications or professional organizations are popular, especially among aspiring writers. Closely scrutinize the application form and all contest literature with an eye to the reproduction and other rights the proprietor wants. Does winning, or even entering, the contest require that the writer transfer the copyright, or some part thereof, to the sponsor? If so, unless you will be paid fairly for the grant, it might be unwise to enter that contest.

Consider entering a contest only after deciding that the impact of winning the contest on your ownership rights in the work is fair and ethical. If the contest requires that exclusive rights in the winning work be transferred to the sponsor, then you should evaluate whether this transfer of rights is reasonable. The sponsor should seek only limited rights, such as the right to publish the submission in a book of contest winners. If the sponsor seeks more than limited rights, you should require fair compensation for additional rights that appear unnecessary to fulfill the purpose of the contest. Remember that this must be done *before* signing any documents, including the contest application, that contain the grant of additional rights.

If the sponsor is seeking free articles or works of fiction to use for commercial purposes, such as promoting or advertising products, then reconsider entering. Not only does this situation appear very similar to working on speculation, which should be anathema to all writers, but also could be fair only if the sponsor awarded a reasonable fee for the use made of the work.

PUBLICATION WITH COPYRIGHT NOTICE

Due to the United States joining the Berne Convention, as of March 1, 1989, U.S. copyright law no longer requires copyright notice to be placed on published works for protection. Most copyright proprietors, however, continue to use copyright notice. The notice warns potential infringers of the copyright, so the infringers could not ask a court to lower damages on the grounds that the infringement was innocent. Also, the Universal Copyright Convention still requires copyright notice and has a number of member countries that are not signatories of the Berne Convention.

FORM OF COPYRIGHT NOTICE

The proper form of copyright notice is: Copyright or Copr. or ©, the author's name or an abbreviation by which that name can be recognized or an alternative designation by which the writer is known, and the year of publication (or the year of creation, if the work is unpublished). Although valid notice could be © ZM 2002, if the writer's initials were Z.M., the Copyright Office takes the position that initials are insufficient unless the author is well known by them. If the writer is not well known by his or her initials, the Copyright Office will treat the notice as lacking a name. If a work was primarily authored by the U.S. government, a statement indicating this fact must be included with the copyright notice. (Works created by the U.S. government are always in the public domain.) If the notice fails to do so, the work will be treated as if notice had been completely omitted. Copyright Office Circular 3, *Copyright Notice,* discusses in detail the proper form and placement of copyright notice.

DEFECTIVE NOTICE

Works published before March 1, 1989 without proper copyright notice might have entered the public domain. There are two categories of works at issue: those that were published before January 1, 1978 and those published between January 1, 1978 and March 1, 1989. Prior to 1978, a missing or defective notice usually caused the loss of copyright protection. If, for example, a year later than the year of first publication was placed on the notice, copyright protection was lost. There are some exceptions to this harsh rule. The use of a year prior to that of first publication reduces the copyright term but does not invalidate the copyright. If notice was omitted from a relatively small number of copies, the copyright would continue to be valid, although an inno-cent-infringer would not be liable for the infringement.

For works published between January 1, 1978 and March 1, 1989, copyright is not necessarily lost if the copyright notice was incorrect or omitted when authorized publication took place. For example, if the wrong name appeared on the notice, the copyright is valid. Therefore, if a writer contributed to a magazine or other collective work but there was no copyright notice in the writer's name published with the con-tribution, the copyright remains protected by the copyright notice in the front of the magazine. Notice in the publisher's name does not, however, protect advertisements that appeared without separate notice (unless the publisher was also the advertiser). If an earlier date than the actual date of publication appeared on the notice, the term of copyright is computed from the earlier date, but the copyright remains. In the case of a book or freelance contribution, computing the copyright term from the earlier date makes no difference because the term of copyright is measured by the author's life plus seventy years, not by a fixed time period that can be shortened. If the name or date was omitted from the notice or if the date was more than one year later than the actual date of publication, the work is treated as if notice was completely omitted. In those cases, the copyright is valid and the work has not entered the public domain if any one of the following three tests can be met:

- The notice was omitted from only a relatively small number of copies distributed to the public
- The notice was omitted from more than a relatively small number of copies, but copyright registration was made within five years of publication and a reasonable effort was made to add notice to the copies distributed in the United States
- The notice was omitted despite the author's written instructions that notice appear on the work

An innocent infringer who proves he was misled by incorrect or omitted notice would not be liable for damages for infringement com-mitted before receiving notice.

CHAPTER 3

COPYRIGHT: REGISTRATION

AND DEPOSIT

All works may be registered with the United States Copyright Office, the official repository for copyright registrations, whether or not they have been published. Because copyright exists from the moment a work is fixed in tangible form, whether or not it is ever registered, many authors question why one should register her work. There are several excellent reasons to do so, chief among them the great advantages you have if your work is infringed. The right to sue, evidentiary advantages, even attorneys' fees and statutory damages are available to the owner of a timely registered work. The cost of registration is not great (in most cases $30), the application forms are short and straightforward, and groups of works can often be registered for one fee. The Copyright Office continues to liberalize its group registration rules. New rules make it much easier to register groups of photographs. Book publishers routinely agree to register a work in the author's name within three months of publication, so the author need not do so to have full protection, though it is always a good idea to make sure the publisher has kept its promise.

ADVANTAGES OF REGISTRATION

Your certificate of registration, if issued either before or within five years of first publication, is presumptive proof of the validity of the copyright and the facts stated on the form. More important, registration is necessary in order to bring a suit for infringement of copyright (unless the infringed work is protected under the Berne Convention and its country of origin is not the United States). If registration is made before an infringement occurs or within three months of publication, the copyright holder will be eligible to receive his or her attorneys' fees and "statutory" damages (a special kind of damages that an author may elect to receive if actual damages are difficult to prove). With respect to works published from January 1, 1978 to March 1, 1989, registration cuts off certain defenses that an innocent infringer could claim due to defective copyright notice.

Although works originating in a Berne Union country other than the United States do not have to be registered before suing, the other advantages of registration make it a good idea for authors of foreign works.

There are important legal benefits to renewing pre-1978 works by filing Form RE and paying the $45 fee for renewal, including that the renewal certificate is considered proof that the copyright is valid and the facts stated in the certificate are true. As shown on Form RE, it may be possible to make a group renewal for a number of copyrights expiring in the same year. Circular 15, *Renewal of Copyright,* offers additional information about copyright renewal and Circular 15t, *Extension of Copyright Terms,* discusses the extended terms of copyrights in existence on January 1, 1978, whether the copyright was in its first twenty-eight–year term or in its renewal term.

CHOOSING THE COPYRIGHT FORM

Form TX (for "text") is the correct registration form for all non-dramatic literary works, including books, articles, and short stories. Periodicals or serial issues, not to be confused with contributions to periodicals, should be registered on Form SE. Works meant to be performed, such as songs, scripts, or plays, should be registered on Form

PA. All the registration forms are available for downloading at the Copyright Office Web site *(www.loc.gov/copyright/forms/)*. Form TX is a simple two-page form with step-by-step instructions for completion. Along with the completed form, the filing fee of $30 and "deposit" copies of the work being registered must be mailed in one package to the Copyright Office. In the event of litigation, it is important that the work deposited with the Copyright Office show all of the features for which the copyright is claimed. Also, make sure that the deposit copies are not likely to fade or alter with time. Circular 1c, *Make Sure Your Application Will Be Acceptable,* helps you do what its title suggests.

Upon processing, the Office will mail to you the official copyright certificate. Although it might take several months to receive the certificate, the effective date of registration is the date on which the Copyright Office receives the acceptable application, deposit, and fee. For this reason, it is a good idea to send it by certified mail and request a return receipt. Should the examiner assigned to process your registration detect problems with the registration, you will be contacted. Depending on the problem and your response to it, the official registration date should date back to the Copyright Office's original receipt of the application.

To correct a mistake or amplify information contained in a completed registration, Form CA for supplementary registration may be used, but only after a registration certificate has been obtained for the work.

GROUP REGISTRATION

A group registration of unpublished works can be made under a single title for a thirty-dollar registration fee using Form GR/CP. Registering an unpublished collection can sharply reduce the cost of registering each work in the collection (and no copyright notice need be placed on unpublished work). To qualify for group registration, the following conditions must be met:

- ✏ The deposit materials are assembled in an orderly form
- ✏ The collection bears a single title identifying the work as a whole, such as "Collected Writing of Jane Author, January, 2002"

✏ The person claiming copyright in each work forming part of the collection is also the person claiming copyright in the entire collection

✏ All the works in the collection are by the same person or, if by different persons, at least one of them has contributed copyrightable material to each work in the collection

There is no limit to the number of works that one may include in a collective registration of unpublished works. Also, a work registered when unpublished need not be registered again when published (although if new material is added to the work or it is published in a new medium, creating a substantial variation from the registered work, the changed version should be registered to protect it fully).

If works have already been published in a newspaper or magazine, the writer may register as a group all contributions to collective works published within a twelve-month period, as long as each contribution has the same copyright claimant (and, if published before March 1, 1989, it also had proper copyright notice). In this case, Form GR/CP is used along with the basic application on Form TX. As with all other registration forms, Form GR/CP and its instructions are available at the Copyright Office Web site.

Freelancers should register their contributions even if their publishers register the periodical as a collective work. Registration of a collective work does not confer the benefits of registration on each individual contribution. Also, even though you may register an entire year's works at a time, it is wiser to register your works every three months in order to qualify for attorneys' fees and statutory damages in case of infringement, as explained previously. At $30 for each group registration, the total cost of $120 and some paperwork affords you complete copyright protection for your life plus seventy years for an entire year's work. That's quite a bargain.

DEPOSIT COPIES

With the registration form and fee, one complete copy of an unpublished work or two copies of the "best edition" of a published work must be sent to the Copyright Office. If editions of differing quality have been published, Copyright Office guidelines explain which edition is to be considered the "best" (Circular 7b). For works first published outside of the United States, one complete copy of the work must be deposited. If a work is published simultaneously in the United States and abroad, it is treated as if first published in the United States.

For group registration of contributions to periodicals, the deposit materials can be one copy of any of the following:

- ➯ One complete copy of each periodical or section of a newspaper in which the work appeared
- ➯ The entire page(s) containing the contribution
- ➯ The contribution clipped from the collective work
- ➯ One photocopy of the contribution

For a multimedia work first published in the United States, the required deposit is one complete copy of the best edition. Circular 55, *Copyright Registration for Multimedia Works,* discusses the deposit requirements and the forms for the different combinations of works that a multimedia work may comprise.

The deposit for works fixed in CD-ROM format is one complete copy, which includes a copy of the disk, a copy of any accompanying operating software and instructional manual, and, if the work is in print as well as on the CD-ROM, a printed version of the work.

ALTERNATE DEPOSIT

In certain cases, such as the publication of limited editions or fine printings, it is possible to make an alternate deposit in place of a valuable copy of the actual work. This alternative might save substantial money. Make a special request to the Copyright Office for permission to submit identifying material rather than copies of the work. The Copyright Office rules on requests for "special relief" on a case-by-case basis, so a clear, written request is advisable. Generally, regardless of whether a work is published or unpublished, only one set of alternate deposit materials must be sent.

DEPOSIT FOR THE LIBRARY OF CONGRESS

In addition to depositing copies for copyright registration, copies must be deposited with the Library of Congress for works published in the

United States on or after March 1, 1989 (or if the work was published with a copyright notice in the United States from January 1, 1978 to March 1, 1989). For a published work, sending the correct deposit copies for registration with the application form and fee within three months of publication satisfies the Library of Congress deposit requirement. For works that were previously registered as unpublished, within three months of publication two copies of the best edition of the work should be deposited for the Library of Congress.

Many works are exempt from the Library of Congress deposit requirement, including contributions to collective works; lectures, speeches, and addresses when published individually and not as a collection; greeting cards, picture postcards, and stationery; prints, labels, advertising catalogs, and other advertising matter published in connection with renting, leasing, lending, licensing or selling merchandise, works of authorship, or services; and any works published only on jewelry, dolls, toys, plaques, floor coverings, wallpaper, textiles, and other fabrics, packaging, or useful articles.

The Library of Congress deposit requirement does not affect copyright protection already in effect. If a writer registered a work when unpublished and failed to send in the required copies upon publication, the Register of Copyrights could request copies from the writer or publisher for the Library of Congress. If the copyright owner failed to comply with this request within three months, he or she could be subject to fines and other penalties, but the copyright would remain valid.

FILLING OUT THE COPYRIGHT FORMS

The application forms come with simple directions. Several of these forms are reproduced here. To simplify the process even further, the following types of answers are most likely to be given to the questions asked in the copyright forms, assuming that an individual author working under his or her own name created a work and now wants to register it:

1. **Unpublished non-dramatic literary work—Form TX**
   Space I—Fill in the title of the work and the nature of the work, such as fiction, nonfiction, poetry, textbook, advertising copy, or computer program.

Space 2—State the author's name and indicate that the work is not a work-for-hire. Give the date of the author's birth, nation of citizenship or permanent residence, and indicate that the work is neither anonymous nor written under a pseudonym. Where it asks "Nature of Authorship," briefly explain the author's particular contribution (e.g., "entire text").

Space 3—For an unpublished work, give the year the work was finished; leave blank the date and nation of first publication.

Space 4—The writer's name and address should be shown for the copyright claimant. A claimant is either the writer or the owner of *all* rights who obtained rights from the writer; it is *not* a licensee or an owner of *some* exclusive rights.

Space 5—Answer no, if the writer did not previously register the work, or yes, if the author were registering new material to a work that had been previously registered.

Space 6—If the writer has added new material to a previously registered work, explain what material the writer added to the old work to make a derivative work (e.g., "new text" or "revisions"). The registration will protect the new elements of the derivative work.

Space 7—Fill in the information about a deposit account, if the writer has one. Give the writer's name and address for correspondence purposes.

Space 8—Check the box for author, sign your name, and then print or type it.

Space 9—Enter the writer's name and address for mailing of the certificate of registration.

2. Group registration for unpublished non-dramatic literary works—Form TX

Fill out the form exactly as you would for an unpublished non-dramatic literary work, except for the following changes:

Space 1—The collection must have its own title, and it is this title that is used here.

Space 3—The year in which creation of the work was completed is the year in which the most recently completed work contained in the collection was completed.

3. Published non-dramatic literary works—Form TX

Fill out the form exactly as you would for an unpublished non-dramatic literary work, except for the following change:

Space 3—In addition to giving the date of creation, give the date and nation of first publication of the work.

4. Group registration of published contributions to periodicals—Form TX

Use form TX if the contributions are non-dramatic literary works, along with the adjunct Form GR/CP. To qualify, the contributions must meet the criteria listed on page 38. Form TX is filled out exactly as for a published non-dramatic literary work, except for the following changes:

Space 1—In the space for the title, write "See Form GR/CP, attached" and leave the other parts of Space 1 blank.

Space 3—Give the year of creation of the last work completed and leave blank the date and nation of first publication. Next, fill out **Form GR/CP.**

Space A—Mark Form TX as the basic application and give the appropriate name(s) as both writer and copyright claimant.

Space B—For each box, fill in the requested information about the title of the contribution, the title of and other information about the periodical, and the date and nation of first publication. Mail Form GR/CP together with Form TX, the deposit copies, and the filing fee.

5. Unpublished works in the performing arts—Use Form PA
Includes works intended to be performed for an audience that is physically present at the performance and also works delivered indirectly to an audience by means of a device or process. This form is filled out in essentially the same way as for an unpublished non-dramatic work.

6. Published works in the performing arts—Use Form PA
This is filled out essentially the same way as for a published non-dramatic literary work.

✒ **Application Form TX** ✒

Detach and read these instructions before completing this form.
Make sure all applicable spaces have been filled in before you return this form.

BASIC INFORMATION

When to Use This Form: Use Form TX for registration of published or unpublished nondramatic literary works, excluding periodicals or serial issues. This class includes a wide variety of works: fiction, nonfiction, poetry, textbooks, reference works, directories, catalogs, advertising copy, compilations of information, and computer programs. For periodicals and serials, use Form SE.

Deposit to Accompany Application: An application for copyright registration must be accompanied by a deposit consisting of copies or phonorecords representing the entire work for which registration is to be made. The following are the general deposit requirements as set forth in the statute:

   Unpublished Work: Deposit one complete copy (or phonorecord)
   Published Work: Deposit two complete copies (or one phonorecord) of the best edition.
   Work First Published Outside the United States: Deposit one complete copy (or phonorecord) of the first foreign edition.
   Contribution to a Collective Work: Deposit one complete copy (or phonorecord) of the best edition of the collective work.
   The Copyright Notice: Before March 1, 1989, the use of copyright notice was mandatory on all published works, and any work first published before that date should have carried a notice. For works first published on and after March 1, 1989, use of the copyright notice is optional. For more information about copyright notice, see Circular 3, "Copyright Notices."

For Further Information: To speak to an information specialist, call (202) 707-3000 (TTY: (202) 707-6737). Recorded information is available 24 hours a day. Order forms and other publications from the address in space 9 or call the Forms and Publications Hotline at (202) 707-9100. Most circulars (but not forms) are available via fax. Call (202) 707-2600 from a touchtone phone. Access and download circulars, forms, and other information from the Copyright Office Website at www.loc.gov/copyright.

> **PRIVACY ACT ADVISORY STATEMENT Required by the Privacy Act of 1974 (P.L. 93-579)**
> The authority for requesting this information is title 17, U.S.C., secs. 409 and 410. Furnishing the requested information is voluntary. But if the information is not furnished, it may be necessary to delay or refuse registration and you may not be entitled to certain relief, remedies, and benefits provided in chapters 4 and 5 of title 17, U.S.C.
> The principal uses of the requested information are the establishment and maintenance of a public record and the examination of the application for compliance with the registration requirements of the copyright code.
> Other routine uses include public inspection and copying, preparation of public indexes, preparation of public catalogs of copyright registrations, and preparation of search reports upon request.
> NOTE: No other advisory statement will be given in connection with this application. Please keep this statement and refer to it if we communicate with you regarding this application.

LINE-BY-LINE INSTRUCTIONS

Please type or print using black ink. The form is used to produce the certificate.

1 SPACE 1: Title

   Title of This Work: Every work submitted for copyright registration must be given a title to identify that particular work. If the copies or phonorecords of the work bear a title or an identifying phrase that could serve as a title, transcribe that wording *completely* and *exactly* on the application. Indexing of the registration and future identification of the work will depend on the information you give here.
   Previous or Alternative Titles: Complete this space if there are any additional titles for the work under which someone searching for the registration might be likely to look or under which a document pertaining to the work might be recorded.
   Publication as a Contribution: If the work being registered is a contribution to a periodical, serial, or collection, give the title of the contribution in the "Title of This Work" space. Then, in the line headed "Publication as a Contribution," give information about the collective work in which the contribution appeared.

2 SPACE 2: Author(s)

   General Instructions: After reading these instructions, decide who are the "authors" of this work for copyright purposes. Then, unless the work is a "collective work," give the requested information about every "author" who contributed any appreciable amount of copyrightable matter to this version of the work. If you need further space, request Continuation Sheets. In the case of a collective work, such as an anthology, collection of essays, or encyclopedia, give information about the author of the collective work as a whole.
   Name of Author: The fullest form of the author's name should be given. Unless the work was "made for hire," the individual who actually created the work is its "author." In the case of a work made

for hire, the statute provides that "the employer or other person for whom the work was prepared is considered the author."
   What is a "Work Made for Hire"? A "work made for hire" is defined as (1) "a work prepared by an employee within the scope of his or her employment"; or (2) "a work specially ordered or commissioned for use as a contribution to a collective work, as a part of a motion picture or other audiovisual work, as a translation, as a supplementary work, as a compilation, as an instructional text, as a test, as answer material for a test, or as an atlas, if the parties expressly agree in a written instrument signed by them that the works shall be considered a work made for hire." If you have checked "Yes" to indicate that the work was "made for hire," you must give the full legal name of the employer (or other person for whom the work was prepared). You may also include the name of the employee along with the name of the employer (for example: "Elster Publishing Co., employer for hire of John Ferguson").
   "Anonymous" or "Pseudonymous" Work: An author's contribution to a work is "anonymous" if that author is not identified on the copies or phonorecords of the work. An author's contribution to a work is "pseudonymous" if that author is identified on the copies or phonorecords under a fictitious name. If the work is "anonymous" you may: (1) leave the line blank; or (2) state "anonymous" on the line; or (3) reveal the author's identity. If the work is "pseudonymous" you may: (1) leave the line blank; or (2) give the pseudonym and identify it as such (for example: "Huntley Haverstock, pseudonym"); or (3) reveal the author's name, making clear which is the real name and which is the pseudonym (for example, "Judith Barton, whose pseudonym is Madeline Elster"). However, the citizenship or domicile of the author **must** be given in all cases.
   Dates of Birth and Death: If the author is dead, the statute requires that the year of death be included in the application unless the work is anonymous or pseudonymous. The author's birth date is optional but is useful as a form of identification. Leave this space blank if the author's contribution was a "work made for hire."

Author's Nationality or Domicile: Give the country of which the author is a citizen or the country in which the author is domiciled. Nationality or domicile **must** be given in all cases.

Nature of Authorship: After the words "Nature of Authorship," give a brief general statement of the nature of this particular author's contribution to the work. Examples: "Entire text"; "Coauthor of entire text"; "Computer program"; "Editorial revisions"; "Compilation and English translation"; "New text."

SPACE 3: Creation and Publication

General Instructions: Do not confuse "creation" with "publication." Every application for copyright registration must state "the year in which creation of the work was completed." Give the date and nation of first publication only if the work has been published.

Creation: Under the statute, a work is "created" when it is fixed in a copy or phonorecord for the first time. Where a work has been prepared over a period of time, the part of the work existing in fixed form on a particular date constitutes the created work on that date. The date you give here should be the year in which the author completed the particular version for which registration is now being sought, even if other versions exist or if further changes or additions are planned.

Publication: The statute defines "publication" as "the distribution of copies or phonorecords of a work to the public by sale or other transfer of ownership, or by rental, lease, or lending." A work is also "published" if there has been an "offering to distribute copies or phonorecords to a group of persons for purposes of further distribution, public performance, or public display." Give the full date (month, day, year) when, and the country where, publication first occurred. If first publication took place simultaneously in the United States and other countries, it is sufficient to state "U.S.A."

SPACE 4: Claimant(s)

Name(s) and Address(es) of Copyright Claimant(s): Give the name(s) and address(es) of the copyright claimant(s) in this work even if the claimant is the same as the author. Copyright in a work belongs initially to the author of the work (including, in the case of a work made for hire, the employer or other person for whom the work was prepared). The copyright claimant is either the author of the work or a person or organization to whom the copyright initially belonging to the author has been transferred.

Transfer: The statute provides that, if the copyright claimant is not the author, the application for registration must contain "a brief statement of how the claimant obtained ownership of the copyright." If any copyright claimant named in space 4 is not an author named in space 2, give a brief statement explaining how the claimant(s) obtained ownership of the copyright. Examples: "By written contract"; "Transfer of all rights by author"; "Assignment"; "By will." Do not attach transfer documents or other attachments or riders.

SPACE 5: Previous Registration

General Instructions: The questions in space 5 are intended to show whether an earlier registration has been made for this work and, if so, whether there is any basis for a new registration. As a general rule, only one basic copyright registration can be made for the same version of a particular work.

Same Version: If this version is substantially the same as the work covered by a previous registration, a second registration is not generally possible unless: (1) the work has been registered in unpublished form and a second registration is now being sought to cover this first published edition; or (2) someone other than the

author is identified as copyright claimant in the earlier registration, and the author is now seeking registration in his or her own name. If either of these two exceptions applies, check the appropriate box and give the earlier registration number and date. Otherwise, do not submit Form TX. Instead, write the Copyright Office for information about supplementary registration or recordation of transfers of copyright ownership.

Changed Version: If the work has been changed and you are now seeking registration to cover the additions or revisions, check the last box in space 5, give the earlier registration number and date, and complete both parts of space 6 in accordance with the instructions below.

Previous Registration Number and Date: If more than one previous registration has been made for the work, give the number and date of the latest registration.

SPACE 6: Derivative Work or Compilation

General Instructions: Complete space 6 if this work is a "changed version," "compilation," or "derivative work" and if it incorporates one or more earlier works that have already been published or registered for copyright or that have fallen into the public domain. A "compilation" is defined as "a work formed by the collection and assembling of preexisting materials or of data that are selected, coordinated, or arranged in such a way that the resulting work as a whole constitutes an original work of authorship." A "derivative work" is "a work based on one or more preexisting works." Examples of derivative works include translations, fictionalizations, abridgments, condensations, or "any other form in which a work may be recast, transformed, or adapted." Derivative works also include works "consisting of editorial revisions, annotations, or other modifications" if these changes, as a whole, represent an original work of authorship.

Preexisting Material (space 6a): For derivative works, complete this space **and** space 6b. In space 6a identify the preexisting work that has been recast, transformed, or adapted. The preexisting work may be material that has been previously published, previously registered, or that is in the public domain. An example of preexisting material might be: "Russian version of Goncharov's 'Oblomov.'"

Material Added to This Work (space 6b): Give a brief, general statement of the new material covered by the copyright claim for which registration is sought. **Derivative work** examples include: "Foreword, editing, critical annotations"; "Translation"; "Chapters 11-17." If the work is a **compilation**, describe both the compilation itself and the material that has been compiled. Example: "Compilation of certain 1917 Speeches by Woodrow Wilson." A work may be both a derivative work and compilation, in which case a sample statement might be: "Compilation and additional new material."

SPACE 7,8,9: Fee, Correspondence, Certification, Return Address

Deposit Account: If you maintain a Deposit Account in the Copyright Office, identify it in space 7a. Otherwise leave the space blank and send the fee of $30 (effective through June 30, 2002) with your application and deposit.

Correspondence (space 7b): This space should contain the name, address, area code, telephone number, fax number, and email address (if available) of the person to be consulted if correspondence about this application becomes necessary.

Certification (space 8): The application cannot be accepted unless it bears the date and the **handwritten signature** of the author or other copyright claimant, or of the owner of exclusive right(s), or of the duly authorized agent of author, claimant, or owner of exclusive right(s).

Address for Return of Certificate (space 9): The address box must be completed legibly since the certificate will be returned in a window envelope.

FEE CHANGES
Fees are effective through June 30, 2002. After
that date, check the Copyright Office Website
at www.loc.gov/copyright or call (202) 707-
3000 for current fee information.

FORM TX
For a Nondramatic Literary Work
UNITED STATES COPYRIGHT OFFICE

REGISTRATION NUMBER

TX   TXU

EFFECTIVE DATE OF REGISTRATION

Month   Day   Year

DO NOT WRITE ABOVE THIS LINE. IF YOU NEED MORE SPACE, USE A SEPARATE CONTINUATION SHEET.

1 TITLE OF THIS WORK ▼

PREVIOUS OR ALTERNATIVE TITLES ▼

PUBLICATION AS A CONTRIBUTION If this work was published as a contribution to a periodical, serial, or collection, give information about the collective work in which the contribution appeared. **Title of Collective Work ▼**

If published in a periodical or serial give: Volume ▼   Number ▼   Issue Date ▼   On Pages ▼

2 a NAME OF AUTHOR ▼

DATES OF BIRTH AND DEATH
Year Born ▼   Year Died ▼

Was this contribution to the work a "work made for hire"? ☐ Yes ☐ No   AUTHOR'S NATIONALITY OR DOMICILE Name of Country OR ⎰ Citizen of ▶ ⎱ Domiciled in▶   WAS THIS AUTHOR'S CONTRIBUTION TO THE WORK Anonymous? ☐ Yes ☐ No Pseudonymous? ☐ Yes ☐ No   If the answer to either of these questions is "Yes," see detailed instructions.

NATURE OF AUTHORSHIP Briefly describe nature of material created by this author in which copyright is claimed. ▼

NOTE
Under the law, the "author" of a "work made for hire" is generally the employer, not the employee (see instructions). For any part of this work that was "made for hire" check "Yes" in the space provided, give the employer (or other person for whom the work was prepared) as "Author" of that part, and leave the space for dates of birth and death blank.

b NAME OF AUTHOR ▼

DATES OF BIRTH AND DEATH
Year Born ▼   Year Died ▼

Was this contribution to the work a "work made for hire"? ☐ Yes ☐ No   AUTHOR'S NATIONALITY OR DOMICILE Name of Country OR ⎰ Citizen of ▶ ⎱ Domiciled in▶   WAS THIS AUTHOR'S CONTRIBUTION TO THE WORK Anonymous? ☐ Yes ☐ No Pseudonymous? ☐ Yes ☐ No   If the answer to either of these questions is "Yes," see detailed instructions.

NATURE OF AUTHORSHIP Briefly describe nature of material created by this author in which copyright is claimed. ▼

c NAME OF AUTHOR ▼

DATES OF BIRTH AND DEATH
Year Born ▼   Year Died ▼

Was this contribution to the work a "work made for hire"? ☐ Yes ☐ No   AUTHOR'S NATIONALITY OR DOMICILE Name of Country OR ⎰ Citizen of ▶ ⎱ Domiciled in▶   WAS THIS AUTHOR'S CONTRIBUTION TO THE WORK Anonymous? ☐ Yes ☐ No Pseudonymous? ☐ Yes ☐ No   If the answer to either of these questions is "Yes," see detailed instructions.

NATURE OF AUTHORSHIP Briefly describe nature of material created by this author in which copyright is claimed. ▼

3 a YEAR IN WHICH CREATION OF THIS WORK WAS COMPLETED This information must be given ◀Year in all cases. **b** DATE AND NATION OF FIRST PUBLICATION OF THIS PARTICULAR WORK Complete this information ONLY if this work has been published. Month ▶ _____ Day ▶ _____ Year ▶ _____ ◀ Nation

4 COPYRIGHT CLAIMANT(S) Name and address must be given even if the claimant is the same as the author given in space 2. ▼

TRANSFER If the claimant(s) named here in space 4 is (are) different from the author(s) named in space 2, give a brief statement of how the claimant(s) obtained ownership of the copyright. ▼

See instructions before completing this space.

DO NOT WRITE HERE OFFICE USE ONLY

APPLICATION RECEIVED

ONE DEPOSIT RECEIVED

TWO DEPOSITS RECEIVED

FUNDS RECEIVED

MORE ON BACK ▶ • Complete all applicable spaces (numbers 5-9) on the reverse side of this page.
• See detailed instructions. • Sign the form at line 8.

DO NOT WRITE HERE
Page 1 of _____ pages

EXAMINED BY	FORM TX
CHECKED BY	
☐ CORRESPONDENCE Yes	FOR COPYRIGHT OFFICE USE ONLY

DO NOT WRITE ABOVE THIS LINE. IF YOU NEED MORE SPACE, USE A SEPARATE CONTINUATION SHEET.

PREVIOUS REGISTRATION Has registration for this work, or for an earlier version of this work, already been made in the Copyright Office?

☐ Yes ☐ No If your answer is "Yes," why is another registration being sought? (Check appropriate box.) ▼

a. ☐ This is the first published edition of a work previously registered in unpublished form.

b. ☐ This is the first application submitted by this author as copyright claimant.

c. ☐ This is a changed version of the work, as shown by space 6 on this application.

If your answer is "Yes," give: **Previous Registration Number** ▶   **Year of Registration** ▶

5

DERIVATIVE WORK OR COMPILATION

Preexisting Material Identify any preexisting work or works that this work is based on or incorporates. ▼

a   **6**

Material Added to This Work Give a brief, general statement of the material that has been added to this work and in which copyright is claimed. ▼

b

See instructions before completing this space.

DEPOSIT ACCOUNT If the registration fee is to be charged to a Deposit Account established in the Copyright Office, give name and number of Account.

Name ▼   **Account Number** ▼

a   **7**

CORRESPONDENCE Give name and address to which correspondence about this application should be sent.   Name/Address/Apt/City/State/ZIP ▼

b

Area code and daytime telephone number ▶   Fax number ▶

Email ▶

CERTIFICATION* I, the undersigned, hereby certify that I am the

Check only one ▶

☐ author
☐ other copyright claimant
☐ owner of exclusive right(s)
☐ authorized agent of _____

of the work identified in this application and that the statements made by me in this application are correct to the best of my knowledge.

Name of author or other copyright claimant, or owner of exclusive right(s) ▲

8

Typed or printed name and date ▼ If this application gives a date of publication in space 3, do not sign and submit it before that date.

          Date ▶

Handwritten signature (X) ▼

X _

Certificate will be mailed in window envelope to this address:	Name ▼	YOU MUST: • Complete all necessary spaces • Sign your application in space 8	**9**
	Number/Street/Apt ▼	SEND ALL 3 ELEMENTS IN THE SAME PACKAGE: 1. Application form 2. Nonrefundable filing fee in check or money order payable to *Register of Copyrights* 3. Deposit material	As of July 1, 1999, the filing fee for Form TX is $30.
	City/State/ZIP ▼	MAIL TO: Library of Congress Copyright Office 101 Independence Avenue, S.E. Washington, D.C. 20559-6000	

*17 U.S.C. § 506(e): Any person who knowingly makes a false representation of a material fact in the application for copyright registration provided for by section 409, or in any written statement filed in connection with the application, shall be fined not more than $2,500.

June 1999—200,000   ⟳ PRINTED ON RECYCLED PAPER   ☆U.S. GOVERNMENT PRINTING OFFICE: 1999-454-879/49

WEB REV: June 1999

◉ Instructions for Short Form TX ◉

For nondramatic literary works, including fiction and nonfiction, books, short stories, poems,
collections of poetry, essays, articles in serials, and computer programs

USE THIS FORM IF—

1. You are the **only** author and copyright owner of this work, *and*
2. The work was **not** made for hire, *and*
3. The work is completely new (does not contain a substantial amount of material that has been previously published or registered or is in the public domain).

If any of the above does not apply, you must use standard Form TX.
NOTE: *Short Form TX is not appropriate for an anonymous author who does not wish to reveal his or her identity.*

HOW TO COMPLETE SHORT FORM TX

■ Type or print in black ink.

■ Be clear and legible. (Your certificate of registration will be copied from your form.)

■ Give only the information requested.

NOTE: You may use a continuation sheet (Form __/CON) to list individual titles in a collection. Complete Space A and list the individual titles under Space C on the back page. Space B is not applicable to short forms.

1 Title of This Work

You must give a title. If there is no title, state "UNTITLED." If you are registering an unpublished collection, give the collection title you want to appear in our records (for example: "Joan's Poems, Volume 1"). Alternative title: If the work is known by two titles, you also may give the second title. If the work has been published as part of a larger work (including a periodical), give the title of that larger work in addition to the title of the contribution.

2 Name and Address of Author and Owner of the Copyright

Give your name and mailing address. You may include your pseudonym followed by "pseud." Also, give the nation of which you are a citizen or where you have your domicile (i.e., permanent residence).

Please give daytime phone and fax numbers and email address, if available.

3 Year of Creation

Give the latest year in which you completed the work you are registering at this time. A work is "created" when it is written down, stored in a computer, or otherwise "fixed" in a tangible form.

4 Publication

If the work has been published (i.e., if copies have been distributed to the public), give the complete date of publication (month, day, and year) and the nation where the publication first took place.

5 Type of Authorship in This Work

Check the box or boxes that describe your authorship in the copy you are sending with the application. For example, if you are

registering a story and are planning to add illustrations later, check only the box for "text."

A "compilation" of terms or of data is a selection, coordination, or arrangement of such information into a chart, directory, or other form. A compilation of previously published or public domain material must be registered using a standard Form TX.

6 Signature of Author

Sign the application in black ink and check the appropriate box. The person signing the application should be the author or his/her authorized agent.

7 Person to Contact for Rights and Permissions

This space is optional. You may give the name and address of the person or organization to contact for permission to use the work. You may also provide phone, fax, or email information.

8 Certificate Will Be Mailed

This space must be completed. Your certificate of registration will be mailed in a window envelope to this address. Also, if the Copyright Office needs to contact you, we will write to this address.

9 Deposit Account

Complete this space only if you currently maintain a deposit account in the Copyright Office.

■■■■■■■ MAIL WITH THE FORM ■■■■■■■

■ A $30 (effective through June 30, 2002) filing fee in the form of a check or money order (*no cash*) payable to "Register of Copyrights," **and**

■ One or two copies of the work. If the work is unpublished, send one copy. If published, send two copies of the best published edition. (If first published outside the U.S., send one copy either as first published or of the best edition.) **Note:** Inquire about special requirements for works first published before 1978. Copies submitted become the property of the U.S. Government.

Mail everything (**application form, copy or copies, and fee**) *in one package* to:

Library of Congress
Copyright Office
101 Independence Avenue, S.E.
Washington, D.C. 20559-6000

QUESTIONS? Call (202) 707-3000 [TTY: (202) 707-6737] between 8:30 a.m. and 5:00 p.m. eastern time, Monday through Friday. For forms and informational circulars, call (202) 707-9100 24 hours a day, 7 days a week, or download them from the Internet at www.loc.gov/copyright. Selected informational circulars but not forms are available from Fax-on-Demand at (202) 707-2600.

FEE CHANGES
Fees are effective through June 30, 2002. After that date, check the Copyright Office Website at www.loc.gov/copyright or call (202) 707-3000 for current fee information.

SHORT FORM TX

For a Nondramatic Literary Work
UNITED STATES COPYRIGHT OFFICE

Registration Number

_____

TX _____ TXU _____

Effective Date of Registration

_____

Examined By _____

Application Received

_____

Deposit Received
One _____ | Two _____

Correspondence ☐

Fee Received

TYPE OR PRINT IN BLACK INK. DO NOT WRITE ABOVE THIS LINE.

1 Title of This Work:

Alternative title or title of larger work in which this work was published:

2 Name and Address of Author and Owner of the Copyright:

Nationality or domicile:
Phone, fax, and email:

Phone ( ) Fax ( )
Email

3 Year of Creation:

4 If work has been published, Date and Nation of Publication:

a. Date _____ Month _____ Day _____ Year _____ (Month, day, and year all required)

b. Nation

5 Type of Authorship in This Work:

Check all that this author created.

☐ Text (includes fiction, nonfiction, poetry, computer programs, etc.)
☐ Illustrations
☐ Photographs
☐ Compilation of terms or data

6 Signature:

Registration cannot be completed without a signature.

I certify that the statements made by me in this application are correct to the best of my knowledge.* Check one:
☐ Author ☐ Authorized agent

X _____

7 Name and Address of Person to Contact for Rights and Permissions:

Phone, fax, and email:

OPTIONAL

☐ Check here if same as #2 above.

Phone ( ) Fax ( )
Email

8
Certificate will be mailed in window envelope to this address:

Name ▼
Number/Street/Apt ▼
City/State/ZIP ▼

Complete this space only if you currently hold a Deposit Account in the Copyright Office.

9
Deposit Account # _____
Name _____

DO NOT WRITE HERE Page 1 of _____ pages

*17 U.S.C. § 506(e): Any person who knowingly makes a false representation of a material fact in the application for copyright registration provided for by section 409, or in any written statement filed in connection with the application, shall be fined not more than $2,500.
June 1999—100,000
WEB REV: June 1999

☆ PRINTED ON RECYCLED PAPER

☆U.S. GOVERNMENT PRINTING OFFICE: 1999-454-879/53

Adjunct Application Form GR/CP

Detach and read these instructions before completing this form.
Make sure all applicable spaces have been filled in before you return this form.

When to Use This Form: Form GR/CP is the appropriate adjunct application form to use when you are submitting a basic application on Form TX, Form PA, or Form VA for a group of works that qualify for a single registration under section 408(c)(2) of the copyright statute.

This Form:
- Can be used solely as an adjunct to a basic application for copyright registration.
- Is not acceptable unless submitted together with Form TX, Form PA, or Form VA.
- Is acceptable only if the group of works listed on it all qualify for a single copyright registration under 17 U.S.C. § 408 (c)(2).

When Does a Group of Works Qualify for a Single Registration Under 17 U.S.C. §408 (c)(2)? For all works first published on or after March 1, 1989, a single copyright registration for a group of works can be made if **all** of the following conditions are met:

(1) All of the works are by the same author, who is an individual (not an employer for hire); and

(2) All of the works were first published as contributions to periodicals (including newspapers) within a 12-month period; and

(3) All of the works have the same copyright claimant; and

(4) One copy of the entire periodical issue or newspaper section in which each contribution was first published; or a photocopy of the contribution itself; or a photocopy of the entire page containing the contribution; or the entire page containing the contribution cut or torn from the collective work; or the contribution cut or torn from the collective work; or photographs or photographic slides of the contribution or entire page containing the contribution as long as all contents of the contributions are clear and legible are (is) deposited with the application; and

(5) The application identifies each contribution separately, including the periodical containing it and the date of its first publication.

> **NOTE:** For contributions that were first published prior to March 1, 1989, in addition to the conditions listed above, each contribution as first published must have borne a separate copyright notice, and the name of the owner of copyright in the work (or an abbreviation or alternative designation of the owner) must have been the same in each notice.

How to Apply for Group Registration:

First: Study the information on this page to make sure that all of the works you want to register together as a group qualify for a single registration.

Second: Read through the **Procedure for Group Registration** in the next column. Decide which form you should use for the basic registration (Form TX for nondramatic literary works; Form PA for musical, dramatic, and other works of the performing arts; or Form VA for pictorial and graphic works). Be sure that you have all of the information you need before you start filling out both the basic and the adjunct application forms.

Third: Complete the basic application form, following the detailed instructions accompanying it **and the special instructions on the reverse of this page.**

Fourth: Complete the adjunct application on Form GR/CP and mail it, together with the basic application form and the required copy of each contribution, to:

Library of Congress
Copyright Office
101 Independence Avenue, S.E.
Washington, D.C. 20559-6000

Unless you have a Deposit Account in the Copyright Office, your application and copies must be accompanied by a check or money order payable to *Register of Copyrights.*

Procedure for Group Registration

Two Application Forms Must Be Filed
When you apply for a single registration to cover a group of contributions to periodicals, you must submit two application forms:
(1) A basic application on either Form TX, Form PA, or Form VA. It must contain all of the information required for copyright registration except the titles and information concerning publication of the contributions.
(2) An adjunct application on Form GR/CP. The purpose of this form is to provide separate identification for each of the contributions and to give information about their first publication, as required by the statute.

Which Basic Application Form To Use
The basic application form you choose to submit should be determined by the nature of the contributions you are registering. As long as they meet the statutory qualifications for group registration (outlined above), the contributions can be registered together even if they are entirely different in nature, type, or content. However, you must choose which of three forms is generally the most appropriate on which to submit your basic application:

Form TX: for nondramatic literary works consisting primarily of text. Examples are fiction, verse, articles, news stories, features, essays, reviews, editorials, columns, quizzes, puzzles, and advertising copy.

Form PA: for works of the performing arts. Examples are music, drama, choreography, and pantomimes.

Form VA: for works of the visual arts. Examples are photographs, drawings, paintings, prints, art reproductions, cartoons, comic strips, charts, diagrams, maps, pictorial ornamentation, and pictorial or graphic material published as advertising.

If your contributions differ in nature, choose the form most suitable for the majority of them.

Registration Fee for Group Registration
If a published serial has not been assigned an ISSN, application forms and additional information my be obtained from Library of Congress, National Serials Data Program, Serial Record Division, Washington, D.C. 20540-4160. Call (202) 707-6452. Or obtain information via the Internet at www.loc.gov/issn/. Unless you maintain a Deposit Account in the Copyright Office, the registration fee must accompany your application forms and copies. Make your remittance payable to: *Register of Copyrights.*

What Copies Should Be Deposited for Group Registration?
The application forms you file for group registration must be accompanied by one complete copy of each published contribution listed on Form GR/CP. The deposit may consist of the entire issue of the periodical containing the contribution. Or, if the contribution was first published in a newspaper, the deposit may consist of the entire section in which the contribution appeared. Tear sheets or proof copies are also acceptable for deposit. Additional acceptable deposits for a GR/CP registration include a photocopy of the contribution itself; a photocopy of the entire page containing the contribution; the entire page containing the contribution cut or torn from the collective work; the contribution cut or torn from the collective work; and photographs or photographic slides of the contribution or entire page containing the contribution as long as all contents of the contributions are clear and legible.

> **NOTE:** Since these deposit alternatives differ from the current regulations, the Office will automatically grant special relief upon receipt. There is no need for the applicant to request such relief in writing. This is being done to facilitate registration pending a change in the regulations.

The Copyright Notice: Before March 1, 1989, the use of a copyright notice was mandatory on all published works, and any work first published before that date should have carried a notice. Furthermore, among the conditions for group registration of contributions to periodicals for works first published prior to March 1, 1989, the statute establishes two requirements involving the copyright notice: (1) Each of the contributions as first published must have borne a separate copyright notice; and (2) "The name of the owner of copyright in the works, or an abbreviation by which the name can be recognized, or a generally known alternative designation of the owner" must have been the same in each notice. For works first published on and after

continued ▶

March 1, 1989, use of the copyright notice is optional. For more information about copyright notice, request Circular 3, "Copyright Notice."

For Further Information: To speak to an information specialist, call (202) 707-3000 (TTY: (202) 707-6737). Recorded information is available 24 hours a day. Order forms and other publications from Library of Congress, Copyright Office, 101 Independence Avenue, S.E., Washington, D.C. 20559-6000 or call the Forms and Publications Hotline at (202) 707-9100. Most circulars (but not forms) are available via fax. Call (202) 707-2600 from a touchtone phone. Access and download circulars, forms, and other information from the Copyright Office Website at **www.loc.gov/copyright.**

> **NOTE:** The advantage of group registration is that it allows any number of works published within a 12-month period to be registered "on the basis of a single deposit, application, and registration fee." On the other hand, group registration may also have disadvantages under certain circumstances. If infringement of a published work begins before the work has been registered, the copyright owner can still obtain the ordinary remedies for copyright infringement (including injunctions, actual damages and profits, and impounding and disposition of infringing articles). However, in that situation—where the copyright in a published work is infringed before registration is made—the owner cannot obtain special remedies (statutory damages and attorney's fees) unless registration was made within 3 months after first publication of the work.

INSTRUCTIONS FOR THE BASIC APPLICATION FOR GROUP REGISTRATION

In general, the instructions for filling out the basic application (Form TX, Form PA, or Form VA) apply to group registrations. In addition, please observe the following specific instructions:

1 SPACE 1: Title

Do not give information concerning any of the contributions in space 1 of the basic application. Instead, in the block headed "Title of this Work," state: "See Form GR/CP, attached." Leave the other blocks in space 1 blank.

2 SPACE 2: Author

Give the name and other information concerning the author of all of the contributions listed in Form GR/CP. To qualify for group registration, all of the contributions must have been written by the same individual author.

3 SPACE 3: Creation and Publication

In the block calling for the year of creation, give the year of creation of the last of the contributions to be completed. Leave the block calling for the date and nation of first publication blank.

4 SPACE 4: Claimant

Give all of the requested information, which must be the same for all of the contributions listed on Form GR/CP.

Other Spaces

Complete all of the applicable spaces and be sure that the form is signed in the certification space.

HOW TO FILL OUT FORM GR/CP

Please type or print using black ink.

A PART A: Identification of Application

• **Identification of Basic Application:** Indicate, by checking one of the boxes, which of the basic application forms (Form TX, Form PA, or Form VA) you are filing for registration.

• **Identification of Author and Claimant:** Give the name of the individual author exactly as it appears in line 2 of the basic application, and give the name of the copyright claimant exactly as it appears in line 4. These must be the same for all of the contributions listed in Part B of Form GR/CP.

B PART B: Registration for Group of Contributions

General Instructions: Under the statute, a group of contributions to periodicals will qualify for a single registration only if the application "identifies each work separately, including the periodical containing it and its date of first publication." Part B of the Form GR/CP provides enough lines to list 19 separate contributions; if you need more space, use additional Forms GR/CP. If possible, list the contributions in the order of their publication, giving the earliest first. Number each line consecutively.

• **Important:** All of the contributions listed on Form GR/CP must have been published within a single 12-month period. This does not mean that all of the contributions must have been published during the same calendar year, but it does mean that, to be grouped in a single application, the earliest and latest contributions must not have been published more than 12 months apart. Example: Contributions published on April 1, 1978, July 1, 1978, and March 1, 1979, could be grouped together, but a contribution published on April 15, 1979, could not be registered with them as part of the group.

• **Title of Contribution:** Each contribution must be given a title that identifies that particular work and can distinguish it from others. If the contribution as published in the periodical bears a title (or an identifying phrase that could serve as a title), transcribe its wording completely and exactly.

• **Identification of Periodical:** Give the overall title of the periodical in which the contribution was first published, together with the volume and issue number (if any) and the issue date.

• **Pages:** Give the number of the page of the periodical issue on which the contribution appeared. If the contribution covered more than one page, give the inclusive pages, if possible.

• **First Publication:** The statute defines "publication" as "the distribution of copies or phonorecords of a work to the public by sale or other transfer of ownership, or by rental, lease, or lending"; a work is also "published" if there has been an "offering to distribute copies or phonorecords to a group of persons for purposes of further distribution, public performance, or public display." Give the full date (month, day, and year) when, and the country where, publication of the periodical issue containing the contribution first occurred. If first publication took place simultaneously in the United States and other countries, it is sufficient to state "U.S.A."

ADJUNCT APPLICATION
for Copyright Registration for a
Group of Contributions to Periodicals

- Use this adjunct form only if you are making a single registration for a group of contributions to periodicals, and you are also filing a basic application on Form TX, Form PA, or Form VA. Follow the instructions, attached.
- Number each line in Part B consecutively. Use additional Forms GR/CP if you need more space.
- Submit this adjunct form with the basic application form. Clip (do not tape or staple) and fold all sheets together before submitting them.
- **Fees are effective through June 30, 2002. After that date, check the Copyright Office Website at www.loc.gov/copyright or call (202) 707-3000 for current fee information.**

FORM GR/CP

For a Group of Contributions to Periodicals
UNITED STATES COPYRIGHT OFFICE

REGISTRATION NUMBER

TX	PA	VA

EFFECTIVE DATE OF REGISTRATION

Month	Day	Year

FORM GR/CP RECEIVED

Page _____ of _____ pages

DO NOT WRITE ABOVE THIS LINE. FOR COPYRIGHT OFFICE USE ONLY

A
Identification of Application

IDENTIFICATION OF BASIC APPLICATION:
• This application for copyright registration for a group of contributions to periodicals is submitted as an adjunct to an application filed on: (Check which)

☐ Form TX   ☐ Form PA   ☐ Form VA

IDENTIFICATION OF AUTHOR AND CLAIMANT: (Give the name of the author and the name of the copyright claimant in all of the contributions listed in Part B of this form. The names should be the same as the names given in spaces 2 and 4 of the basic application.)

Name of Author _____

Name of Copyright Claimant _____

B
Registration for Group of Contributions

COPYRIGHT REGISTRATION FOR A GROUP OF CONTRIBUTIONS TO PERIODICALS: (To make a single registration for a group of works by the same individual author, all first published as contributions to periodicals within a 12-month period (see instructions), give full information about each contribution. If more space is needed, use additional Forms GR/CP.)

☐ Title of Contribution _____
Title of Periodical _____ Vol.____ No._____ Issue Date _____ Pages _____
Date of First Publication _____ Nation of First Publication _____
(Month)   (Day)   (Year)   (Country)

☐ Title of Contribution _____
Title of Periodical _____ Vol.____ No._____ Issue Date _____ Pages _____
Date of First Publication _____ Nation of First Publication _____
(Month)   (Day)   (Year)   (Country)

☐ Title of Contribution _____
Title of Periodical _____ Vol.____ No._____ Issue Date _____ Pages _____
Date of First Publication _____ Nation of First Publication _____
(Month)   (Day)   (Year)   (Country)

☐ Title of Contribution _____
Title of Periodical _____ Vol.____ No._____ Issue Date _____ Pages _____
Date of First Publication _____ Nation of First Publication _____
(Month)   (Day)   (Year)   (Country)

☐ Title of Contribution _____
Title of Periodical _____ Vol.____ No._____ Issue Date _____ Pages _____
Date of First Publication _____ Nation of First Publication _____
(Month)   (Day)   (Year)   (Country)

☐ Title of Contribution _____
Title of Periodical _____ Vol.____ No._____ Issue Date _____ Pages _____
Date of First Publication _____ Nation of First Publication _____
(Month)   (Day)   (Year)   (Country)

☐ Title of Contribution _____
Title of Periodical _____ Vol.____ No._____ Issue Date _____ Pages _____
Date of First Publication _____ Nation of First Publication _____
(Month)   (Day)   (Year)   (Country)

FORM GR/CP

DO NOT WRITE ABOVE THIS LINE. FOR COPYRIGHT OFFICE USE ONLY.

B
Continued

Title of Contribution _____
Title of Periodical _____ Vol.____ No.____ Issue Date _____ Pages _____
Date of First Publication _____ Nation of First Publication _____
(Month)   (Day)   (Year)   (Country)

Title of Contribution _____
Title of Periodical _____ Vol.____ No.____ Issue Date _____ Pages _____
Date of First Publication _____ Nation of First Publication _____
(Month)   (Day)   (Year)   (Country)

Title of Contribution _____
Title of Periodical _____ Vol.____ No.____ Issue Date _____ Pages _____
Date of First Publication _____ Nation of First Publication _____
(Month)   (Day)   (Year)   (Country)

Title of Contribution _____
Title of Periodical _____ Vol.____ No.____ Issue Date _____ Pages _____
Date of First Publication _____ Nation of First Publication _____
(Month)   (Day)   (Year)   (Country)

Title of Contribution _____
Title of Periodical _____ Vol.____ No.____ Issue Date _____ Pages _____
Date of First Publication _____ Nation of First Publication _____
(Month)   (Day)   (Year)   (Country)

Title of Contribution _____
Title of Periodical _____ Vol.____ No.____ Issue Date _____ Pages _____
Date of First Publication _____ Nation of First Publication _____
(Month)   (Day)   (Year)   (Country)

Title of Contribution _____
Title of Periodical _____ Vol.____ No.____ Issue Date _____ Pages _____
Date of First Publication _____ Nation of First Publication _____
(Month)   (Day)   (Year)   (Country)

Title of Contribution _____
Title of Periodical _____ Vol.____ No.____ Issue Date _____ Pages _____
Date of First Publication _____ Nation of First Publication _____
(Month)   (Day)   (Year)   (Country)

Title of Contribution _____
Title of Periodical _____ Vol.____ No.____ Issue Date _____ Pages _____
Date of First Publication _____ Nation of First Publication _____
(Month)   (Day)   (Year)   (Country)

Title of Contribution _____
Title of Periodical _____ Vol.____ No.____ Issue Date _____ Pages _____
Date of First Publication _____ Nation of First Publication _____
(Month)   (Day)   (Year)   (Country)

Title of Contribution _____
Title of Periodical _____ Vol.____ No.____ Issue Date _____ Pages _____
Date of First Publication _____ Nation of First Publication _____
(Month)   (Day)   (Year)   (Country)

Title of Contribution _____
Title of Periodical _____ Vol.____ No.____ Issue Date _____ Pages _____
Date of First Publication _____ Nation of First Publication _____
(Month)   (Day)   (Year)   (Country)

CHAPTER 4

COPYRIGHT: WORKS

MADE FOR HIRE,

JOINT WORKS, AND

COMMUNITY PROPERTY

As you know, the "author" of an original work owns the copyright initially. But two special situations can make the identity of the "author" someone other than the primary creator. In a "work made for hire" situation, the party for whom the work is prepared—the writer's employer or other commissioning party—is the considered legal "author" of the work and owns the copyright as if it, in fact, created the work. This means that the writer has no right to terminate a grant of rights in the work after thirty-five years because there was no grant—the writer never owned the copyright. Should the work go out of print, the writer has no recourse to retrieve the rights. Furthermore, if the writer reused all or part of the work he or she created as a work-for-hire, even if it is out of print, he or she would be an infringer of the legal "author's" rights. Because of these severe legal consequences to the creator of a work-for-hire, the Copyright Act recognizes it in only two cases: (1) when an employee creates copyrightable work within the course and scope of his or her employment, such as newspaper staff writers and advertising agency copywriters, or (2) when a writer creates a specific kind of specially ordered or commissioned work *and* both parties agree in writing that it is a work made for hire.

Traditional book authors, short story writers, and freelance journalists are rarely asked, and even more rarely agree, to write works for hire, and they should not. There are some cases, however, when a writer has no need or desire to own the copyright to a specially commissioned work, such as a foreword or afterword to another's work, a compilation of a corporation's financial data, or an instruction booklet, and is willing for the right price to sign away all present and future copyright interests in the work.

The second situation that raises the question of the "author's" identity is when the work constitutes a "joint work." A joint work is defined in the Act as one that is created by two or more writers with the intention, at the time the work is created, that their contributions be merged into inseparable or interdependent parts of a unitary whole. Regardless of who did the majority of the work, coauthors of a joint work own equal shares in the copyright (unless they agree otherwise). Each coauthor of a joint work may license nonexclusive (but not exclusive) rights in the work without the other's consent, although royalties must be shared equally (again, unless they agree otherwise).

For obvious reasons, both work-for-hire and joint-work situations require professional writers to protect their interests carefully. This chapter explains how to do so. It also addresses copyright ownership questions in divorce cases.

WHO IS AN "EMPLOYEE" FOR COPYRIGHT PURPOSES?

If an employee creates copyrightable work in the course of his or her employment, the employer is automatically deemed the author of the work and the owner of the copyright. What distinguishes an employee who creates work-for-hire and an independent contractor who owns copyright? Someone who is paid a salary for working from 9:00 A.M. to 5:00 P.M., Monday through Friday, under the control, direction, and supervision of an employer and at that employer's office is certainly an employee. This type of employee will typically have state and federal tax payments withheld from the paycheck and receive employee benefits. These perquisites of traditional employment are a fair trade-off, in Congress's eyes, for copyright ownership in the works created. At the other end of the spectrum, a freelancer who receives an assignment and writes it in his or her home office in exchange for a fee, who is generally free to accept assignments from others and typically does not receive employee benefits, and who is considered an independent contractor, is not an employee.

Many fall somewhere on the spectrum between these clear cases. What about a "contributing editor" to a periodical, who works as a freelancer in her own space and buys her own health insurance, pays her own taxes, but makes a regular submission of the same length for each issue that is regularly published for a set fee? This is a more difficult question, but over the years, the courts have refined the relevant indicia of the parties' relationship in distinguishing an employee from an independent contractor for copyright purposes. Today, authors and publishers have fairly clear and consistent guidance in this matter.

In the 1980s, a writer working under the direction and supervision of another, creating a work at the "instance and expense" of a commissioning party or where that party was the motivating force behind the work, might well have been ruled an employee of the commissioning party. Many courts had adopted the rationale of the 1909 Act, that when the commissioning party exercises sufficient control and direction over a project, the writer becomes an employee for purposes of copyright. Under the 1976 Act, the disagreement among the courts over the definition of an employee for hire finally led to a 1989 Supreme Court decision that comprehensively laid out the relevant factors. In *Community for Creative Non-Violence v. Reid,* 490 U.S. 730 (1989), a sculptor was commissioned to create a sculpture for the Community for Creative Non-Violence (CCNV). CCNV's founder, who envisioned a modern Nativity scene with the Holy Family replaced by a homeless couple and infant, conceived the idea. Titled *Third World America,* the tableau was set on a steam grate with a legend reading "and still there is no room at the inn."

Reid grafted the sculpture without charging a fee, receiving payment only for his expenses. CCNV built the pedestal in the form of the steam grate and gave Reid ideas and some direction as the work progressed (such as insisting that the family have its belongings in a shopping cart rather than bags or suitcases). After the work was finished, a dispute over copyright ownership arose. No contract had been made between the parties.

The Supreme Court decided that whether someone is an "employee" under the Copyright Act depends on the law of agency, which is primarily concerned with determining when one party's actions should be legally attributed to another party (that is, to an employer). Under the law of agency, a key factor is "the hiring party's right to control the manner and means by which the product is accomplished." The Court went on to list the other factors relevant to its inquiry:

- The skill [of the creator] required
- The source of the instrumentalities and tools
- The location of the work
- The duration of the relationship between the parties
- Whether the hiring party has the right to assign additional projects to the hired party
- The extent of the hired party's discretion over when and how long to work
- The method of payment
- The hired party's role in hiring and paying assistants
- Whether the work is part of the regular business of the hiring party
- Whether the hiring party is in business
- The provision of employee benefits
- The tax treatment of the hired party

Using these factors, Mr. Reid was ruled an independent contractor, and the owner of the copyright to *Third World America.* By the same token, a freelance writer who writes an assigned article for a magazine is not legally an employee. A later court pointed out that not all the *Reid* factors are significant in every case, and suggested that courts should consider only the factors that are actually indicative of an agency relationship in the particular circumstances. However, five of the factors are considered most important and will almost always be significant:

- The hiring party's right to control the manner and means of creation
- The skill required of the hired person
- The provision of employee benefits

- The tax treatment of the hired party
- Whether the hiring party has the right to assign additional projects to the hired party. *Aymes v. Bonelli,* 980 F.2d 857 (2d Cir. 1992)

Even under this refined test, which other courts have used, the "contributing editor's" status remains uncertain. As always, the parties to this arrangement would do well to define their relationship in a written agreement to avoid the cost and uncertainty of a dispute over ownership of the writers' works.

SPECIALLY COMMISSIONED OR ORDERED WORKS

An independent contractor can create a work-for-hire only if the work meets the second definition under the Act. For specially commissioned or ordered works, the parties must agree in a writing signed by both that the work is made for hire. Also, the work must fall into one of the following categories:

- A contribution to a collective work, such as a magazine, newspaper, encyclopedia, or anthology.
- A contribution used as part of a motion picture or other audiovisual work.
- A translation.
- A compilation, which is a work formed by collecting and assembling preexisting materials or data.
- An instructional text.
- A test.
- Answer material for a test.
- An atlas.
- A supplementary work, defined as a work used to supplement a work by another author for such purposes as illustrating, explaining, or assisting generally in the use of the writer's work. Examples of supplementary works are forewords, afterwords, pictorial illustrations, maps, charts, tables, editorial notes, appendixes, and indexes.

Note that a freelance contribution to a collective work, including a magazine or newspaper, is one of the eligible categories. Remember that even if an assignment falls into one of these categories, it cannot be a work-for-hire unless the parties agree in writing. Therefore, it is crucial that writers, especially freelance contributors, understand precisely what they are agreeing to. The effect of contractual language other than "work-for-hire" is unclear, so be wary of any agreement (including check legends) with language similar to "work-for-hire," "specially commissioned or ordered" work, or work to be done at the "instance and expense" of the publisher. Some courts have ruled that the requisite writing need not precede the creation of the work but can memorialize, after the fact, the intentions of the parties to create a work-for-hire. That means you should take care not to cash a check unwittingly with an endorsement saying the payment is for a "work-for-hire" or similar language. Always try to clarify all contractual terms before starting work, and insist that any check endorsement conform to your understandings.

If a writer creates a specially ordered or commissioned work that is outside of the listed categories, technically it cannot be a work-for-hire (unless, of course, the writer is an employee). If work falling into one of the categories is created independently (that is, not specially ordered or commissioned) and submitted to a potential buyer, it too falls outside the definition. Even so, you must use caution in your dealings with commissioning parties. Even if a contract is technically not a work-for-hire contract, a court might still find a way to make a writer live up to the bargain struck. Therefore, take care not to sign an agreement that could be reasonably read as creating a work-for-hire, unless you intend to give up your copyright.

Of course, in some cases, you might be perfectly willing to agree to create a commissioned work in one of the enumerated categories as a work-for-hire. If so, remember to consider the consequences of not being the legal author when negotiating your fee for the work. Unless you specifically agree to royalties or secondary use fees, your initial payment will be the only compensation you will ever receive for the work. No rights will revert to you even if the work goes, and stays, out of print. If you are willing to give up copyright, keep in mind the principle of every copyright negotiation: The greater the scope of rights the other party wants from you, the more it should have to pay. Other negotiating points to consider:

- ✑ Be sure that only one particular work is included in the contract, and not any future or past works created for the commissioning party.
- ✑ Limit the work the commissioning party is taking as much as possible. You can do this by describing the work specifically in terms of its length, medium, intended use, and any other distinguishing factors.
- ✑ Reserve the right, if applicable, to make sequels and other supplementary works related to the primary work and rights in other media, such as television or movies.
- ✑ Consider providing that, should the commissioning party reject the work for any reason, the author retains the copyright. This will prevent the possibility of an unscrupulous commissioning party being able to cancel the project at the last minute and obtain the copyright to the complete or almost complete work without tendering full payment to the author.
- ✑ If authorship attribution is important to you, even if someone else owns the copyright, request that it be included in your contract.

JOINT WORKS

After the 1989 *CCNV v. Reid* decision placed restrictions on the right of commissioning parties to claim authorship of commissioned works, some began to assert joint authorship with the writers they had hired. Actually, the question of joint authorship can arise in all kinds of authors' working relationships, with commissioning parties, freelance editors (or "book doctors"), research assistants, dramaturges, producers, even overly ambitious typists. Authors of some great successes have faced claims of joint copyright from such professionals. In recent years courts have had to elaborate on the rather stark definition of "joint work" in the Act, giving some guidance to parties who make the grave mistake of collaborating on a work without agreeing on ownership rights beforehand.

Keep in mind that the Copyright Act defines a "joint work" as "a work prepared by two or more authors with the intention that their contributions be merged in inseparable or interdependent parts of a unitary whole." Authors who create a joint work are co-owners of the undivided copyright in the work. Thus, each owns all the rights in the work, but shares them with the other. Each may license nonexclusive rights without the other's consent, subject only to the obligation to share all proceeds from licensing equally with the other. But as co-owners of the copyright, neither joint author is able to license *exclusive* rights to the joint work without the other's written agreement. The equality of the ownership rights of each joint author exists despite any difference in the authors' respective contributions. One person's minuscule contribution as compared to the other author's, if joint authorship exists, entitles that person to the same reward as the greater contributor. Joint authorship in a work does not confer joint author status in derivative works based on the joint work, although the joint author should be entitled to compensation for the use of the original.

Examples of "inseparable parts" of the work are joint contributions to a single novel or painting. Examples of "interdependent parts" are the lyrics and music of a song or the text and illustrations of a children's picture book. Should the lyrics or the illustrations alone be licensed, both authors would, unless they agreed otherwise, be entitled to share equally in the proceeds.

THE CHILDRESS RULE

Nowhere does the Copyright Act define an "author," and courts have had to grapple with whether a person claiming a joint copyright must have contributed independently copyrightable elements to the work. If so, collaborators who added extensive ideas and research to a work would have no copyright share in it. If not, then editors, peer reviewers who offered ideas and comments, and even research assistants could conceivably claim an equal interest in the primary author's copyright.

In 1991, the influential Second Circuit Court of Appeals chose the copyrightable contribution requirement, reasoning that the spirit of the copyright law was better served by obliging any joint author to make copyrightable contributions and leaving those with noncopyrightable contributions to protect their rights through contract. In

Childress v. Taylor, the defendant, an actress, performed independent historical research for a play based on the life of "Moms" Mabley, but then hired the plaintiff to write the play for a fee. They discussed the play and the scenes together, and Ms. Taylor shared her research with Ms. Childress, but Childress actually wrote the script. Later, Taylor produced a play written by another person on the same subject, and Childress claimed that the subsequent script infringed the copyright of her work.

When Taylor claimed to be a joint author of the first script, the lower court and the Second Circuit on appeal held that she could not be a joint author because she had contributed only general ideas and research, neither of which are copyrightable. The so-called Childress Rule has become the law in most jurisdictions. *Childress v. Taylor,* 945 F.2d 500 (2d Cir. 1991); *Seshadri v. Kasraian,* 130 F.3d 798 (7th Cir. 1997); *M.G.B. Homes, Inc. v. Ameron Homes, Inc.* 903 F.2d 1486 (11th Cir. 1990). But the courts have also held overwhelmingly that although each contribution must be copyrightable, they need not be qualitatively or quantitatively equal to create a joint work.

The second sine qua non of joint authorship is what the Second Circuit has called its "crucial aspect:" The intent of "*each* putative joint author at the time the contribution of each was created" to regard themselves as joint authors. *Childress,* 945 F.2d at 508. All parties must share this intention at this time, although they need not understand the legal effects of joint authorship. An editor, for example, might meet the first test by contributing copyrightable material to a work, but neither she nor her author is likely to intend a joint author relationship.

In some cases, intent can be inferred from the coauthors' relatively equal contributions to the work (such as a song with lyrics by one person, music by another). When the respective contributions of each are very unequal, courts must consider other factors that illuminate collaborators' intent. The recent case of *Thomson v. Larson,* 147 F.3d 195 (2d Cir. 1998) involves that analysis. The plaintiff was a dramaturge who worked intensively with playwright Jonathan Larson on revising his book and libretto for the musical *Rent.* Larson died suddenly, just before the play opened to great acclaim and commercial success. Thomson then claimed she had contributed copyrightable material to the work amounting to 9 percent of the work, and as such was entitled to share the copyright with Larson's heirs.

The Second Circuit agreed with the trial court that Thomson had contributed significantly to the work, but that Larson had not intended to share authorship with the dramaturge. The court considered four factors in ascertaining the parties' intent. First was the contributors' decision-making authority over what changes were made and what was included in the work. Larson alone indisputably had this authority. The parties' billing or credit is another significant, though not decisive, indicator of their intent, and that too named Larson as author in every listing, Thomson as "dramaturge." A third factor is the parties' agreements, such as licenses, with third parties. Larson had entered several agreements as the sole author of *Rent* with the theater that had hired Thomson to help him. Finally, additional testimony and documents proved that Larson steadfastly intended *Rent* to remain entirely his own project. For all these reasons, Thomson's joint authorship claim failed. *Thomson,* 147 F.3d at 202–205.

It should be obvious from this chapter that writers must do their best to avoid the kinds of disputes that lead to the lawsuits described here. Aside from the tremendous cost in time and money and the uncertainties of a lawsuit, litigation signifies a costly failure to protect your rights and interests at the right time—when your business relationships begin. In any collaboration on a work, authors should make sure they own what they believe they own. If you are working with another independent contractor, you need a collaboration agreement (See chapter 16).

DIVORCE AND COPYRIGHT

Community property laws have been adopted by nine states— Arizona, California, Idaho, Louisiana, Nevada, New Mexico, Texas, Washington, and Wisconsin. While there are variations from state to state, community property laws make both spouses equal owners of property acquired during the marriage (with some exceptions, such as gifts or bequests). If you are or were married and now live or previously lived in one of these nine states, any property you acquired while living in one of these states is probably community property. The remaining states all provide for some form of "equitable distribution" of property acquired during a marriage upon divorce, which might be more or less than 50 percent of any asset to either party. If you should divorce, the question whether the copyright in your works acquired during the marriage are either community property or are subject to equitable distribution will arise. The issue is complicated by the special nature of copyright ownership and the fact that the Copyright Act preempts conflicting state laws. Can a divorcing author be forced to become a joint copyright owner with the estranged spouse? Who would control the licensing and management of the work?

A California case examined the issue for the first time when a husband argued that books he wrote during the marriage were not community property. He lost that argument. An appellate court ruled:

> Our analysis begins with the general proposition that all property acquired during marriage is community property. Thus, there seems little doubt that any artistic work created during the marriage constitutes community property. . . . Since the copyrights derived from the literary efforts, time and skill of husband during the marriage, such copyrights and related tangible benefits must be considered community property. *In re Marriage of Worth*, 195 Cal. App. 3d 768, 773 (1987).

The court rejected the argument that the federal copyright law, which vests copyright in the author (rather than in the author and the author's spouse), preempts state community property laws. *Worth* left unresolved such questions as who has the right to renew a copyright or terminate a grant of rights once a copyright is designated community property. Most recently, a federal appeals court resolved those questions in *Rodrigue v. Rodrigue*, 218 F.3d 432 (5th Cir. 2000). It held that the creator of copyrighted works can maintain all the ownership rights of copyright—that is, control and management of the works—but that the spouse must be awarded the ownership right to receive half of all the economic rewards from the works (including any derivative works). Whether other courts will agree with the Fifth Circuit's analysis remains to be seen. These and other complex issues are explored in "Copyright Ownership by the Marital Community: Evaluating *Worth*," by David Nimmer, 36 *UCLA Law Review* 383 (1988).

CHAPTER 5

COPYRIGHT:

INFRINGEMENT,

FAIR USE,

AND PERMISSIONS

With few exceptions, anyone who exploits one or more of the exclusive rights of copyright without the owner's permission commits copyright infringement. All lawsuits involving copyright must be brought in federal court. The Copyright Act allows judges and juries to punish infringement harshly. Possible penalties include judicial restraint from further use of the work, impounding and/or destruction of unauthorized copies, and money damages covering the copyright owner's actual damages *plus* the profits earned from the unauthorized use and, if the copyright was registered within three months of publication, for special "statutory" damages in lieu of actual damages and the plaintiff's attorneys' fees. Respect for copyright is, in its deepest sense, self-protective. No writer wants her work copied without the opportunity to know about it, receive payment and proper attribution, and to control or veto alterations to it. Respect for the underlying purpose of copyright—the advancement of human achievement through creativity—requires compliance with the law. For writers, not only is infringement unethical, it probably also constitutes a breach of their publishing contracts, leaving them liable for their publishers' damages and attorneys' fees, as well as for their own.

On the other hand, one should not confuse the appearance of similar plot elements, stock characters, and so-called *scènes à faire* with infringement. Many writers who have sued for infringement of their work have learned the hard way that the elements of their works that appear in a second work are unprotected ideas, not protected expression.

THE ELEMENTS OF INFRINGEMENT

In order for a court to find infringement, it must determine that (1) the alleged infringer actually copied the protected work, and (2) the allegedly infringing work is "substantially similar" to the copyrightable elements of the work. Proof that copying occurred is only half the battle. The court must then decide whether the allegedly infringing work is substantially similar enough to the original work to warrant infringement liability.

OWNERSHIP

The claimant in an infringement suit must prove ownership of the copyright or one of the rights thereof. If the owner registered the copyright within five years of first publication, the certificate of registration serves as presumptive proof of the validity of the owner's copyright and the facts stated on the certificate.

ACTUAL COPYING

Copyright protects against copying but not against the independent creation of a similar or even identical work, so infringement is impossible unless the defendant came into contact with and actually copied the work (either deliberately or unconsciously). If there is no direct evidence of copying, courts may infer copying from evidence of the defendant's access to the original work and similarities between the works that are probative of copying.

ACCESS TO THE ORIGINAL WORK

In some cases, access is easy enough to prove. If the original work was a bestseller, a Broadway production, a widely broadcast television program, or a Hollywood movie, a court would be hard pressed to accept that a defendant living in the United States at the time did not have access to the work. If there is no direct proof of access, courts will consider indirect evidence of access, such as correspondence to or from a publisher or producer (for example, submission or rejection letters) or the masthead of a publication, to infer who might have seen the work. Courts have sometimes found access based solely on a striking similarity in the works. The reasoning is that, if two works are enough alike so that the similarities can be explained only by copying rather than by independent creation, the infringer must have had access.

PROBATIVE AND SUBSTANTIAL SIMILARITY

Probative similarity is needed to show that actual copying took place. Substantial similarity is needed to prove infringement (that is, copying of protected expression as opposed to unprotected ideas). Establishing "probative similarity" can be a challenge when the work is not either strikingly similar to the other work or copied verbatim. The test for substantial similarity is as follows: Will an ordinary observer, looking at the two works, believe one has copied copyrightable elements of the other? For written works, courts look for similarities in the text, format, structure, sequence, and other protected elements. Altering some parts of an original work—10, 25, or even 75 percent—will not avoid infringement if the ordinary-observer test leads to the conclusion that more than a trivial amount of the original work has been copied.

The ordinary-observer test has undergone some refinement due to the increasing complexity of some copyrightable works. Courts increasingly allow expert testimony on the issue of the intended audience on the theory that where a specialized group, not the general public, was the intended audience, the "ordinary observers" should have the same expertise in the relevant field as the intended audience. *Dawson v. Hinshaw Music, Inc.*, 905 F.2d 731 (4th Cir. 1990), *cert. denied,* 111 S. Ct. 511 (1991).

Why is substantial similarity, not just verbatim reproduction, the test of infringement? In the classic explanation of the substantial similarity test, Judge Learned Hand held that copyright protection for literary works cannot be limited to protecting merely the literal text of the work but also must not give an author a monopoly on the ideas inherent in the work. Every work can be abstracted on several levels, from the most general statement of what the work is about to the pure reproduction of the work. Between these abstractions lies the boundary between uncopyrightable ideas and their copyrightable expression and, by the same token, between an original new work and a substantially similar infringing work. As Judge Hand described it:

> Upon any work, and especially upon a play, a great number of patterns of increasing generality will fit equally well, as more and more of the incident is left out. The last may perhaps be no more than the most general statement of what the play is about, and at times might consist of only its title; but there is a point in this series of abstractions where they are no longer protected, since otherwise the playwright could prevent the use of his "ideas," to which, apart from their expression, his property is never extended. *Nichols v. Universal Pictures Co.*, 45 F.2d 119, 121 (2d Cir. 1930), *cert. denied* 282 U.S. 902 (1931).

CONTRIBUTORY INFRINGEMENT AND VICARIOUS LIABILITY

The Act makes copyright infringement a strict liability tort, so that the intent of the infringing party is irrelevant to its liability (although it is certainly relevant to damages calculations). Therefore, a party who knowingly helps another party infringe copyright is equally liable, as is one who infringes unknowingly if it receives a financial benefit from the infringement.

DAMAGES FOR INFRINGEMENT

The owner of an infringed copyright is entitled to recover his or her actual damages caused by the infringement, plus any profits earned by the infringing work and not included in the actual damages. If the claimant registered the work within three months of publication or, for unpublished works, before the infringement, he or she has the right to choose statutory damages in lieu of actual damages, which are often low or difficult to prove. Statutory damages of $750 up to $30,000 for each infringed work may be awarded in the court's discretion. A court has discretion to limit statutory damages to as little as $200, if the infringement was innocent, or increase them to not more than $150,000, if the infringement was willful. A defendant has the right to have a jury determine statutory damages. Willful copyright infringement can also result in criminal penalties, including fines, imprisonment, or both for each act of infringement.

In addition to damages, the Act specifically allows an injunction to prevent additional infringement, impounding and disposal or destruction of infringing copies (including stopping the importation of and seizing infringing copies at Customs agencies), criminal penalties, awards for court costs, and attorneys' fees for timely registered works. Because attorneys' fees can be substantial, sometimes wiping out awards entirely, this is major inducement to register copyrights within three months of publication. A court will generally order an injunction, such as a ban on distribution and sale of an infringing work, when the plaintiff would otherwise suffer irreparable injury.

STATUTE OF LIMITATIONS

The statute of limitations for a copyright infringement claim is three years from the time the claim accrued. This means that plaintiffs are barred from suing infringers who have been able to elude detection for that period of time, except that the statute is "tolled," which means extended, in certain cases. For example, the statute is tolled when a defendant fraudulently conceals the infringement. A few jurisdictions will toll the statute if the copyright owner could not, in the exercise of reasonable care and diligence, have discovered the infringement.

Where an infringement is continuing, courts differ on when the statute of limitations should begin to run. Some hold that the statute does not begin to run until all aspects of the continuing infringement are completed, while others allow relief only for acts that occurred within the three-year window immediately prior to the date the plaintiff brought suit. This different treatment of the accrual date of a claim can make a world of difference in damage calculations when an infringement continued for many years.

WHO IS LIABLE FOR INFRINGEMENT?

Liability for infringement damages is generally joint and several, making each defendant, including contributory and vicarious infringers, liable for the full amount of the award, including any other defendants' shares. Contributory or vicarious infringers will generally not be liable for the other defendants' profits, however. Four defendants who owe damages totaling $600,000 might each pay $150,000, but if one or more of the defendants cannot satisfy their shares, the remaining defendant(s) can be required to pay the entire judgment. In one case, a publisher and a printer were found jointly and severally liable for all damages when the publisher wrongfully authorized the reprint of a book for which it did not own a valid copyright. *Fitzgerald Pub. Co. v. Baylor Pub. Co.,* 807 F.2d 1110 (2d Cir. 1986).

The limited liability normally gained by forming a corporation might not prove a shield against individual liability in a copyright infringement lawsuit. Particularly if a corporate officer participates in the infringement, uses the corporation for the purposes of carrying out an infringement, or is the dominant influence over the corporation, courts might impose personal liability. Likewise, an employee who, in exercising discretion, commits or causes the employer to commit an infringement can be held personally liable with the employer facing contributory or vicarious liability.

STATES AND STATE ENTITIES IMMUNE

A very troubling series of decisions by the U.S. Supreme Court has vastly increased states' rights by making them immune from lawsuits by private parties to enforce federal rights, including copyright. In *College Savings Bank v. Florida Prepaid Postsecondary Educ. Expense Bd.,* 527 U.S. 666 (1999), a sharply divided Court ruled that unless states explicitly agree to be sued by private citizens to enforce federal claims—including copyright and other intellectual property rights—the concept of sovereign immunity embodied in the Eleventh Amendment to the Constitution shields the states from such lawsuits, in both state and federal courts.

Chavez v. Arte Publico Press, 204 F.3d 601 (5th Cir. 2000), a copyright infringement lawsuit against the University of Houston Press brought by author Denise Chavez, was thrown out by the federal Court of Appeals for the Fifth Circuit following the *College Savings Bank* decision. The rulings mean that states, state-owned entities (including state university presses and educational institutions), and their employees cannot be sued for damages. They may be brought to court only for injunctive relief for infringement. The Senate Judiciary Committee is currently studying ways to subject states to federal laws within the Court's new doctrine, and the Authors Guild is supporting this effort.

FAIR USE

Not every unauthorized appropriation of a copyright is an infringement. Several very specific activities are exempted in Sections 108 through 120 of the 1976 Act. The "fair use" doctrine is the most important limitation on the owner's exclusive rights. A long-standing tenet of common law, the doctrine was codified in the 1976 Act: The use of a copyrighted work "for purposes such as criticism, comment, news reporting, teaching (including multiple copies for classroom use), scholarship or research, without the consent of the copyright owner" is not an infringement of copyright. Technically, fair use is a defense to an infringement claim.

Every fair use claim is decided on its particular facts in a statutory test that is easy to state but very difficult to apply, much less to predict. One court called fair use "so flexible as virtually to defy definition." One thing is certain: Quantifying the amount of an original work used in a second work does not provide safe harbor. Fair use has been rejected as a defense when as few as three hundred words of a 200,000-word manuscript were copied. Yet fair use was credited as a defense when a famous photograph was copied almost in its entirety in a movie advertisement for the purpose of parody. In the common law the key question was "the degree in which the use may prejudice the sale, or diminish the profits, or supersede the objects, of the original work." *Folsom v. Marsh,* 9 F.Cas. 342, 348 (C.C.D. Mass. 1841). Today, though the analysis in any given case can be complex, this basic inquiry seems to remain the cornerstone of the fair use doctrine.

The Copyright Act directs courts to weigh the following four factors to determine whether a use (that is, copying) is "fair":

➡ The purpose and character of the use, including whether the use is of a commercial nature or for nonprofit educational purposes

✏ The nature and character of the copyrighted work

✏ The amount and substantiality of the portion used in relation to the copyrighted work as a whole (and sometimes in relation to the defendant's work)

✏ The effect of the unauthorized use on the market for or value of the copyrighted work

Courts may also consider any other factors they deem relevant. No one factor automatically trumps the others. The weight given to any particular factor in the endless possible variety of fact situations is left to the courts' discretion.

Fair use questions might arise for writers in a number of situations. They might want to use historical works as background for their own historical works. They might want to punctuate their novel or essays with song lyrics or other quotations. They might want to quote text from a work to illustrate its style, criticize its content, or compare it to another work. They might want to parody another work. Whether or not these sorts of uses amount to fair use can only be resolved through common sense application of the four fair use factors. To help illustrate how a court might analyze a given fair use issue, the following are discussions of the leading judicial decisions about specific kinds of uses.

QUOTING OTHER WORKS

For a review or scholarly article, an entire work might be reproduced verbatim without infringing. On the other hand, beware of copying the heart of a work to appropriate any part of its audience or market. A landmark case involved the memoirs of President Gerald Ford, which Ford had agreed to publish with Harper & Row. Harper & Row in turn granted *Time* magazine the exclusive first serial right to publish a 7,500-word excerpt from the memoirs prior to book publication. Before *Time*'s intended publication date, *The Nation* magazine obtained a copy of the book and published an article that copied approximately three hundred words verbatim from the memoirs, preempting the impact of the *Time* excerpt. *Time* decided not to publish the excerpt and refused to pay Harper & Row. Harper & Row sued *The Nation* for copyright infringement. The district and appellate courts disagreed about whether *The Nation*'s excerpt was fair use. The U.S Supreme Court ruled that it had infringed. *Harper & Row Publishers, Inc. v. Nation Enterprises,* 471 U.S. 539 (1985). The Court analyzed the four fair use factors as follows:

1. **Purpose and Character of Defendant's Use:** Although the Court noted that the defendant's purpose was reporting news, which is socially beneficial, the use was still clearly for profit and the defendant profited from its exploitation of the copyright without paying the customary license fee. Furthermore, the court found that the intended purpose of the reporting was not purely the dissemination of news, which would have come out soon anyway. The purpose was to scoop the competition, which might not necessarily be a socially beneficial goal. Therefore, the first factor weighed against fair use.

2. **Nature of the Copyrighted Work:** Fair use is more likely to be found when works such as factual compilations or historical nonfiction works are copied than it is with more creative works, such as fiction. Nonetheless, the Court noted that there are limits to the right to copy even factual works. Here, Ford's memoirs were essentially factual, a compilation of historical events that would normally possess only "thin" copyright protection. Where works are unpublished, however, their creators should have the right to decide when and whether they will be presented to the public. Therefore, this factor weighed against fair use.

3. **Amount and Substantiality of Use:** The defendant copied three hundred words from a 200,000-word manuscript, but the Court found that *The Nation* had taken the "heart of the book." In examining the amount of appropriated expression, the Court also measured that portion not only in relation to the copyrighted work as a whole, but also in relation to the totality of the defendant's work. This deeper inquiry weighed against the defendant, which had tied together quotes, paraphrases, and facts to construct an article of 2,200 words.

4. Effect on Potential Market or Value: In this case, this factor was the most important of the four factors. Where the purpose of the appropriation is linked to profit, as this was, the effect on the market for the work is likely to be negative. Although a critical review of a work will often harm the potential market for the object of criticism and still be a fair use, the *Nation* magazine article was not analytical or critical. It did not further the discussion of historical facts or political ideas, but rather substituted for the original, preempting its dissemination, without adding original expression to the facts contained therein. This factor also weighed against the defendant.

PARODY

Whether parody—copying parts of a work in order to make fun of it—is an infringement turns on whether the parody derives its value from what it took from the original work or whether its value comes from the added material that makes it a parody. If the parody's value derives mostly from the original work, application of the four factors is likely to result in infringement liability. The claimed parody must actually comment on the original work, not on a different topic. Three leading cases illustrate these points.

In *Campbell v. Acuff-Rose Music, Inc.,* 510 U.S. 569 (1994), the U.S. Supreme Court examined a rap group's version of Roy Orbison's "Oh, Pretty Woman." In this landmark decision, the band 2 Live Crew had been denied permission to use the song but had proceeded to release "Big Hairy Woman," based substantially on the Orbison work. The Court found that a parody of a copyrighted work could constitute fair use of that work. It defined parody as "the use of some elements of a prior author's composition to create a new one that, at least in part, comments on that author's work." In doing so, the Court refined the first fair use factor, the purpose and character of the defendants' work, to include the transformative nature of the second work as a key part of the fair use analysis. In fact, the Court decreed, "the more transformative the new work, the less will be the significance of the other factors, like commercialism, that weigh against fair use." It also distinguished a permissible parody from one that has "no critical bearing on the substance or style of the original composition, [but is merely used] to get attention or avoid the drudgery in working up something fresh." The Court also explained that in a true parody, the copyrighted work is the *object* of the parody, and not merely a vehicle with which to poke fun at a different target.

Following *Campbell*, the Second Circuit found fair use in the parody advertisement for the comedy film *Naked Gun 3*, which copied Annie Leibovitz's famous portrait of a pregnant and nude Demi Moore and superimposed actor Leslie Nielsen's head on the nude figure. *Leibovitz v. Paramount Pictures Corp.*, 137 F.3d 109 (2d Cir. 1998). The court pointed out that at least a major purpose of the parody was indeed to comment on the arguable "pretentiousness" of the original photo. By contrast, in *Dr. Seuss Enterprises, L.P. v. Penguin Books USA*, 109 F.3d 1394 (9th Cir. 1997), the influential Ninth Circuit Court of Appeals ruled that a book commenting on the O. J. Simpson murder trial using the style, characters, and rhyme scheme of Dr. Seuss's *The Cat in the Hat* was not a commentary on the first work but rather on a current event—the murder trial and the notoriety surrounding it. Therefore, it was ruled not a parody of the Geisel book, and it was not fair use, but infringement.

ARCHIVAL COPYING

Archival copying of articles might be fair use if the copying is neither systematic nor institutional. In *American Geophysical Union, et al. v. Texaco*, 60 F.3d 913 (2d Cir. 1994), eighty-three publishers of scientific and technical journals brought a class action suit against Texaco for unauthorized archival copying by its research employees. Although the researchers at Texaco numbered between four hundred and five hundred, by agreement of the parties, the court focused its fair use analysis on one employee who had photocopied eight articles for easy reference. Texaco appealed after it lost in the trial court. The Second Circuit affirmed the verdict but limited the application of the trial court's analysis.

   1. **Purpose and Character of the Use**: Although a commercial purpose weighs against fair use, the court did not find the fact that Texaco was a for-profit corporation dispositive,

noting that practically all research is at least partially commercially motivated. Here, the use itself was only indirectly commercial, but was nevertheless of great commercial benefit to the for-profit user. The court noted that the employee had copied the work for the same basic purpose for which one would normally purchase the original—to have it available on his shelf for reference. The court then looked at whether the use was transformative. While it found that photocopying is not transformative, it noted that the benefit of a more usable format might be transformative under different circumstances, such as the spontaneous copying of specific pages during a scientific experiment, where the original would be too bulky or might be exposed to hazardous chemicals. Because there was no transformative use to overcome the essentially commercial nature of the archival copying, the first factor favored the publisher.

2. **Nature of the Copyrighted Work**: This second factor favored Texaco, because of the factual, as opposed to creative, content of the articles. Copyright offers less protection to factual works in fair use analysis because of the greater public interest in their dissemination.

3. **Amount and Substantiality of the Portion Used**: Because the defendant copied the articles in their entirety, this factor weighed against fair use.

4. **Effect on the Potential Market or Value of the Copyrighted Work**: The court found the publishers had demonstrated substantial harm to the value of their copyrights and therefore weighed this factor against fair use.

Balancing the factors—and noting one additional factor—that Texaco could take advantage of available licensing schemes, the court ruled for the publishers and against a finding of fair use. In an amended version of its opinion, the court went to great pains to limit its holding to the specific facts of the case, emphasizing that the "systematic" nature of the copying done on an "institutional" basis was an important factor in the holding. The existence of the Copyright

Clearance Center, a corporation in the business of granting photocopy licenses for many academic and scientific journals to institutions (which helped fund the lawsuit), figured into the finding of infringement. Many observers take these additional factors as a signal from the court that occasional archival copying by individuals might be fair use.

EDUCATIONAL FAIR USE

After the 1976 Act passed, a group including authors, publishers, educators, and librarians prepared guidelines for classroom copying by nonprofit educational institutions. These guidelines, known as CONTU Guidelines *(www.cni.org/docs/infopols/CONTU.html)*, describe safe harbor conditions but do not purport to define the full extent of fair use.

Under these guidelines, brief portions of copyrighted works may be used for a class if the teacher individually decides to do so, the copyright notice in the owner's name appears on the class materials, and the use is not repeated systematically (for example, throughout a school system or a class semester). Educational use that is systematic, including unauthorized copying of excerpts from books to create coursepacks for students, is not fair use and has been punished by heavy damage awards. See *Princeton University Press v. Michigan Document Services,* 99 F.3d 1381 (6th Cir. 1996), *cert denied,* 520 U.S. 1156 (1997). For educators who do not know whether a contemplated use of a work falls within fair use, the University of Texas has created an excellent, clear, and comprehensive explanation and what it calls "Rules of Thumb" for all kinds of educational uses: library uses, performance and display in face-to-face and long-distance instruction, coursepacks, digitization, and multimedia uses. It is available at *www.utsystem.edu/intellectualproperty/copypol2.htm.*

OBTAINING PERMISSION TO COPY

You do not need anyone's permission to exploit public domain works to your heart's content. Unfortunately, it can be difficult or impossible to ascertain a work's public domain status simply by examining it. For works published after January 1, 1978, it is risky to rely on the lack of a notice as a basis for concluding a work is in the public domain because the 1976 Act protects some copyrights where notice was omitted, and notice is not required for works published since March 1, 1989.

Works published in the U.S. before January 1, 1923 are in the public domain. Works published in the United States between January 1, 1923 and December 31, 1977 are protected by copyright for ninety-five years from the date of publication. Legislation passed in 1994 restored copyright protection to virtually all foreign works that are less than seventy-five years old that entered the public domain in the United States, and which lost copyright here because of failure to comply with copyright formalities such as notice or renewal.

Unless you are sure a work is in the public domain, it is best to obtain legal permission to copy or quote from it. To obtain permission, you must determine who is the owner of the material you want to use, contact the owner, obtain permission (preferably written) to use the work in the territory and format you need, and sometimes pay a fee.

Some photocopying services will obtain copyright permission and add the price of license fees, if any, to the price of the copies. Permission may also be sought from the Copyright Clearance Center *(www.copyright.com),* which will quote a charge for works for which they are able to give permission. If you need to find out who owns the copyright, copyright registrations and all recorded assignments and licenses from January 1, 1978 to the present can be found and searched free of charge, twenty-four hours a day, at *www.loc.gov/copyright/.* However, many works have never been registered, making them protected by copyright but not in the records of the Copyright Office.

If you are seeking the author, contact the Authors Registry, a clearinghouse for payments to authors. This registry has a database containing the contact information of more than thirty thousand authors *(www.authorsregistry.org).* If the work is in print, the publisher, not the author, might well own the exclusive right to grant permission. The publisher should be able to give you ownership information or provide the permission. If you have trouble getting a response, your own publisher might be willing to help you track down the owner. To get permission to use song lyrics, you will need to contact the music publisher who owns the rights. You may search the Copyright Office searchable database to determine the claimant, or contact ASCAP, the American Society of Composers, Authors and Publishers, at (212) 595-3050 or BMI, Broadcast Music, Inc., at (212) 586-2000, the two major music performance rights associations. Either can tell you how to find the publisher or other claimant for songs in their repertoires, although they do not grant permission to quote lyrics.

Once you find the owner, you can secure permission with a brief letter describing your project, the material you want to use, the extent of the rights you need, the credit line and copyright notice that will be given, and the payment, if any, will be made. Permission fees are negotiable and will vary depending on the amount and nature of the material you intend to use. Some publishers provide permissions kits, which include forms and instructions. If your publisher does not have such a kit, you can use a version of the form included here. The sample permission form can be adapted to particular situations. The permitted use should be clearly delineated to protect the party granting the rights from giving up more than necessary to ensure that you are not buying and paying for more than you need, and to enable you to prove you have lawfully acquired the information you are using.

SAMPLE PERMISSION FORM

[Your name] (the "Licensee") is researching, writing and publishing a book [or an article] tentatively entitled [Title] (the "Work") to be published by [Publisher]

For valuable consideration [describe fee or free copies of the book, although sometimes neither is necessary], [Owner's name] (the "Licensor"] grants the Licensee the [non-]exclusive right to reproduce the following material (the "Material") in the Work in [specify medium or format, language(s), territory, time period, if any]:

Titles: _____

Author: _____

Publisher: _____

Pages and/or lines: _____

Licensee shall not alter the Material without the prior written permission of the Licensor, and the Licensee shall include proper copyright notice and the following credit line in all versions of the Work:

_____ .

Licensor warrants that [s]he has the sole and unrestricted right to make the grant contained in this agreement.

_____   _____

Licensor   Date

_____   _____

Licensee   Date

FIGHTING INFRINGEMENT ONLINE

Have you discovered your work featured on a stranger's Web site or e-mailed to a mysterious sender's favorite five hundred people, all without your knowledge, permission, or compensation? While it is relatively easy to find your work on the Web, stopping the infringement can prove more difficult. The copyright law normally considers anyone who contributes to another's copyright infringement, or who engages in unpermitted copying, fully liable to the copyright owner *whether or not they intend or even know they are infringing.* For online service providers—companies such as AT&T, America Online, and Yahoo—these doctrines of "contributory liability" and "vicarious liability" could result in legal responsibility for all their subscribers' actions. Merely by providing the means for a subscriber to copy, or by automatically transmitting the material online at a subscriber's command, service providers are technically copying or facilitating the copying of the material. At the same time, authors still feel helpless when their work is being copied and read countless times online. How does an author contact the service provider, or the infringer, to demand that the work be removed from a Web site?

After intense lobbying by online service providers, the 1998 amendments to the Copyright Act limited the liability of online service providers when they are passive and unknowing conduits of infringement. Under the law's safe-harbor provisions, service providers (including Internet service providers, Web site hosts, search engines, and portals) judged not to be directly at fault cannot be sued for money damages or injunction by injured copyright holders. But the quid pro quo for immunity is a requirement that the service provider make it easy for authors to address and eradicate online infringement. Service providers must also publish and enforce a policy of removing repeat infringers from the service. The new law attempts to address technologies that do not yet exist as well as those that currently do.

Many search engines can help you locate your works on the Web. Currently, one of the most thorough searches is on *www.altavista.com*. The author's name is not necessary—an advantage when the party posting the work doesn't credit the author. With Altavista, you can find your work practically anywhere on the Web by typing in a sentence or phrase unique to the work. Two other search engines, *http://google.com* and *www.directhit.com* are good URLs to try.

Do not assume automatically that an online posting of your work was done without permission. Your print publisher might have the right to license others to post your work online, and it may have acted on it. Check your contract. If the work is an excerpt from a book that is still in print and the contract was signed after 1994, it is likely (though not inevitable) that the publisher asked for and was granted electronic rights from you. A contract for a freelance article published in a periodical or newspaper might also have granted these rights to the publisher. If the contract does not explicitly set forth who owns electronic rights, the author owns the rights.

If you do find your work online, notify your publisher immediately and ask whether permission was granted. If the publisher has the rights but did not grant permission, ask them to have the work taken down, or removed, by taking the steps described in the following paragraphs. If the publisher has properly granted permission, you might be contractually entitled to a share of the license fee. If your print publisher is not involved, you can notify the service provider host to get your work removed from the offending site. First, be sure to download and print out everything that contains the infringed work.

Tracking down the service provider is fairly easy. If the infringement appears on a Web site, go to *www.internic.net,* the site of the organization that registers virtually every site on the Internet. Type in the infringer's URL (the site address). This should bring up contact information on the infringer's site and more important, the name of the service provider who has the power to shut down the infringing site and is obliged to comply with the new law to avoid liability. If the infringement occurs via e-mail, you must determine the e-mail service provider. Look for an icon appearing somewhere in the band across the top or bottom of the message. Click on it and you should find the service provider's e-mail address.

To qualify for immunity, a service provider generally must drop repeat infringers from its service, publish its policy of terminating repeat infringers, and accommodate "standard technical measures" used to protect copyrighted works. The only one of these you can easily check on yourself is whether the anti-infringement policy is published—but do check it. Most service providers must assign a specific party (called a "designated agent" in the law) to receive notice of infringement claims on their behalf. The identity and address of the agent must appear on the service provider's publicly accessible Web site and/or with the Copyright Office. The Copyright Office lists these agents on its Web site. If you do find your work on any site, check for a posting of the service provider's no infringement policy, and check the accessibility of its designated agent.

Once you have the correct agent's address, you or your representative must send written notification of the infringement and demand that it be removed. You may do this by e-mail, but be sure to keep hard copies of all correspondence. Many providers post their copyright policy prominently via their home pages specifying the information they need from you. No magic words are required in your notice, but you must identify the copyrighted work being infringed, identify the material that contains the infringement, provide sufficient information to allow the service provider to locate the material (for example, the Web site or e-mail address), and provide your contact information. You also must state that you have a belief that the appearance of your work in this forum is unauthorized and goes beyond fair use.

When its agent receives this notice, the service provider must "expeditiously" remove the infringed work or interrupt access to it. Make sure that it has done so by going online to confirm. If you want to go further and sue the infringer, the new law makes it fairly easy to subpoena the provider for the infringer's identity. After the service provider has removed or disabled the offending material, it must promptly inform the alleged infringer of the change. If the alleged pirate claims in writing that a mistake has been made, after informing you, the service provider must replace or permit renewed access to the material within ten days—unless you bring a lawsuit to prevent restoration of the material. However, a real pirate is unlikely to respond in this way because his counter-notice must include such bona fides— under criminal penalty for perjury—as full contact information and agreement to submit to the jurisdiction of a court if sued.

If an online service provider has met all these legal requirements, you cannot sue it regardless of how much damage you might have suffered from the infringement. If you can show that a service provider actually knew of a subscriber infringing your copyright, or that it supervised the content and received a specific benefit from its subscriber's infringement, you may still sue for contributory liability. (One exception to this scenario: Nonprofit institutions of higher education whose professors or graduate student teachers infringe on the institutions' Web sites carry a special immunity as long as they stop the piracy after learning of it.)

If a site actively encourages subscribers to upload others' published work, you should document that fact. Note any way in which the service provider might financially benefit from copying your work—charging a per-download fee or using it to help sell merchandise or advertising. If it does so, or it has failed to comply with any of the demands of the new law, it might lose its immunity, and you could file suit against this "deep pocket."

CHAPTER 6

COPYRIGHT:

PAST AND PRESENT

The following brief history of copyright reveals some of the underlying forces that have shaped the law in force today. A tension exists between the rights of the public and the rights of writers and other creators. Copyright is a monopoly and, like any monopoly, imposes limitations on the public. The writer reaps economic gains for the term of the copyright while the public is denied the fullest access to literary resources and culture. Justifying this monopoly by ancient concepts of property law, copyrights are called intellectual property.

INTELLECTUAL PROPERTY

The etymological derivation of "property" is from the Latin word *proprius*, which means private or peculiar to one. "Intellectual" comes from the Latin verb *intellegere*, which is to choose from among, hence to understand or to know. Contained within *intellegere* is the verb *legere*, which means to gather (especially fruit) and thus to collect, to choose and ultimately to assemble (the alphabetical characters) with the eyes and to read.

The private inspiration that finds fruition in written works is rewarded by monopoly rights that last for the writer's life plus seventy years. Yet new methods to create, store, and deliver information place pressure on the system of copyright. Arguments are made for rights of immediate public access to and use of all written works, perhaps on the model of a compulsory license in which copyright owners have no right to control usage but do receive a fee fixed either by voluntary arrangements or government fiat (albeit less than would be negotiated for by the writer). Would ending copyright as a monopoly and allowing the most widespread dissemination of literature, art, and other products of the mind better serve the public? Is the right of the public a paramount right, greater than any right that a creator might assert?

To place this debate in perspective, remember that copyright is neither ancient in origin nor a right enjoyed without controversy. The Roman legal system, for example, had no copyright. If a man could own slaves (who might carry fabulous creations in their minds), why should the ownership of words be separate from the ownership of the parchment containing the words? Trained slaves took dictation to create thousands of copies of popular works for sale at low prices. The poet Martial complained that he received nothing when his works were sold. Even if works could be sold, as were the plays written by Terence, no protection existed against piracy. The profits from any sales of the copied manuscripts went to the owner of the copy, not the author.

A MONOPOLY ON COPYING

This collective view of creativity held sway throughout the Middle Ages. Religious literature predominated; individual creativity was not rewarded. The reproduction of manuscripts rested in the dominion of the Church, and it was only with the rise of the great universities in the twelfth and thirteenth centuries that lay writers began producing works on secular subjects. Extensive copying by trained scribes again became the norm, with only the publishers, or *stationarii,* as they were called, gaining any profit. Even before the introduction of block printing into the West in the fifteenth century, the publishers had formed a Brotherhood of Manuscript Producers in 1357 and were soon given a charter by the Lord Mayor of London. Johannes Gutenberg's introduction of the printing press to the Western world in 1437 gave individual writers an ever-greater opportunity for self-expression. The printer's movable type foreshadowed the writer's copyright protection.

William Caxton introduced these printing techniques to England in 1476, which led to a growing demand for books. Seven years later, Richard III lifted legal restrictions against aliens, if those aliens happened to be printers. Within fifty years, however, the supply of books had far exceeded the demand, and Henry VIII passed a new law providing that no person in England could legally purchase a book bound in a foreign nation (this was the forerunner to the notorious manufacturing clause that finally expired in U.S. law in 1986).

At about this time, the Brotherhood of Manuscript Producers, now known as the Stationers' Company, was given a charter—a monopoly—over publishing in England. No writer could publish except with a publisher belonging to the Stationers' Company. This served the dual purpose of preventing both writings seditious to the Crown and those heretical to the Church. The right of ownership was not in the writer's creation, but rather in the right to make copies of that creation. Secret presses came into existence, but the Stationer's Company sought to maintain its monopoly with the aid of repressive decrees from the notorious Star Chamber.

Due largely to the monopoly of the Stationers' Company, a recognition arose of a right to copy, which might also be called a common-law copyright—that is, a right supposedly existing from usages and customs of the past as interpreted by the courts. With this concept of property distinct from the physical manuscript established, the Stationers' Company objected vehemently when their charter and powers expired in 1694 and Scotch printers began reprinting their titles. They pushed for a new law, and they got one—the Statute of Anne, enacted in 1710. Happily for authors, it was largely drafted by Joseph Addison and Jonathan Swift, and it was written to protect authors as well as publishers by creating a statutory copyright (copyright protected under statute) to encourage "learned men to compose and write useful books." Finally, authors had something of value that they could sell: a copyright.

COPYRIGHT IN THE UNITED STATES

The copyright laws of the United States are based on the Statute of Anne. The Confederation of States had no power to legislate with respect to copyright. Between 1783 and 1789, Noah Webster successfully lobbied twelve states to pass copyright laws. Finally, the U.S. Constitution that was ratified in 1789 provided that "The Congress shall have power . . . To promote the Progress of Science and useful Arts, by securing for limited Times to Authors and Inventors the exclusive Right to their respective Writings and Discoveries."

In 1790, Congress exercised its power by enacting our first federal copyright statute, providing protection for books, maps, and charts for an initial term of fourteen years plus a renewal term of fourteen years. In 1831, the initial term of copyright was lengthened to twenty-eight years. In 1865, the law was amended to include photographs and negatives. In 1870, it was revised to cover paintings, drawings, statuaries, and models or designs of works of the fine arts.

In 1909, the copyright law was thoroughly revised. The initial term of copyright remained twenty-eight years, but the renewal term was lengthened to twenty-eight years, giving protection for up to fifty-six years. The inventions of radio, television, motion pictures, satellites, and other technological innovations required revision of the 1909 Act. After a long gestation period, the complete revision of the law took effect on January 1, 1978. Subsequent amendments have addressed the inventions of new tools to make, store, and deliver creative works, including the Digital Millennium Copyright Act of 1998. Technology will undoubtedly continue to test copyright. A number of amendments to the U.S. law have resulted from responses to the global economy and the desire of the United States for greater international protection of copyrights.

INTERNATIONAL COPYRIGHT PROTECTION

Historically, copyright protection was almost exclusively limited to the nation of origin of a work, that is, the country in which the work was first published. More recently, protection has been extended through international conventions and bilateral treaties. Today, most developed countries and many developing countries offer a significant measure of international copyright protection.

Protection for American copyrights abroad is of increasing importance because the export of copyrightable works has become a thriving business, the fastest-growing sector of the United States economy and one that is continually threatened by widespread piracy abroad. Although the United States has often been referred to as a "copyright island," its accession to the Berne Convention in 1989, after refusing to join for more than a hundred years, shows a sincere effort to upgrade copyright protection internationally. The initial refusal of the United States to join Berne was the result of several factors: rivalries between American and British publishing houses; Berne's minimum standards requiring (at the time) at least a fifty-year term of protection and banning the formalities of notice, registration, recordation, and deposit; moral rights (the right to freedom from false attribution, improper editing or alterations, and mutilation, which has a long history in Europe and remains largely nonexistent in the United States); and national treatment (the rule that member nations must protect foreign works at least as stringently as they protect domestic works). Most important, international copyright protection was not a high priority here because until the late twentieth century the United States was a net importer of copyrighted works.

The reluctance of the United States to adhere to the Berne Convention, which was created in 1886 (and has been amended many times), can be understood as an aspect of the reliance of the United States on the cultural wealth of Europe. At the time there was no international market for American works. From 1790 until 1891, foreign writers had no copyright protection in the United States, even if their work was under copyright protection elsewhere. American publishers freely pirated the works of writers such as Charles Dickens, Anthony Trollope, and Victor Hugo out of sheer economic expediency. Dickens wrote of the "monstrous injustice" whereby writers were denied their rightful royalties from U.S. sales.

Before the United States joined the Berne Convention, American copyright owners of works could achieve international protection through the "back door" by simultaneously publishing a work in a

Berne country (e.g., Canada), making the "country of origin" a Berne signatory and thereby affording the owner full protection via that nation. This method often proved inadequate because of its complexity, uncertainty, expense, even embarrassment, apart from creating justifiable resentment internationally.

U.S. PROTECTION FOR FOREIGN WRITERS

Not until 1891, after years of controversy, did Congress finally pass the Chace Act and begin to allow foreign writers to copyright their published works in the United States (unpublished works of foreign origin being protected "in perpetuity" under common law). Under the Chace Act, foreigners whose nations provided reciprocal protection to American nationals could obtain copyright in the United States but the onerous "manufacturing clause," requiring foreign books to be printed from type set, negatives, or stone drawings made within the borders of the United States, made copyright for foreign works illusory.

Under the 1909 Act, foreign writers and publishers fared only slightly better. A foreign citizen could copyright a book in the United States as long as the writer actually lived in the United States when the book was first published and adhered to all necessary technical formalities. The 1909 Act was still fundamentally and irreconcilably at odds with both the specific tenets of the Berne Convention and the liberal copyright protection offered by most Western European nations.

Unwilling to join Berne, in 1952 the United States helped create the Universal Copyright Convention (UCC), which is still in force today. In most ways, the UCC merely codified existing American law. The only significant concession to foreign member countries was the abolishment of the manufacturing clause with respect to UCC member nations. Under the UCC, works created by American nationals, regardless of where they were published, are afforded the same protection that local works receive in any UCC member country. The United States still clung to its notice, registration, recordation, and deposit requirements although any major Western country that had such provisions (and few did) abolished them. Despite its shortfalls, the UCC opened copyright relations with over eighty countries and offered protection that, initially, seemed adequate.

In the mid-1980s, however, U.S. government research indicated that American corporations were suffering staggering losses from foreign piracy. As a result, we finally joined the Berne Convention on March 1, 1989, accepting its (at the time) life-plus-fifty years' duration of protection (which we had already adopted in the 1976 Act) and finally abolishing most of our formalities. (The life-plus-fifty years duration has since been extended by most Berne nations, including the United States, to life-plus-seventy years.)

When there were more books written abroad, especially in Great Britain, than in the United States, international copyright protection would have created an unfavorable balance of trade. But as economics change, political theories are usually not far behind. As cheap British knock-offs, published without advances or royalties, became competition for publishers and writers trying to market American literature, the first spark of interest in international copyright protection was kindled, although that spark took many years to ignite.

Today, more copyrightable works are produced in the United States than in any other country, and these works represent a substantial portion of U.S. exports. The industries involved—film and computer companies, book, newspaper, and magazine publishers—are large, profitable, and powerful. Because a substantial and growing portion of these profits come from foreign sales (creating a bright spot in an otherwise dismal balance of trade), there have been loud and indignant calls in the United States for stronger worldwide protection. All over the developing world, piracy of American computer and entertainment products is a booming business. Allowing American publishing companies the opportunity to publish foreign works without having to pay advances or royalties was one thing; allowing the worldwide misappropriation of American literary property is clearly another. In addition to joining most of the world in the Universal Copyright and Berne Conventions, the United States has begun to use other methods to protect its nationals' intellectual property.

TRADE SANCTIONS, GATT, AND BILATERAL AGREEMENTS
The United States has vowed to use trade sanctions and other economic weapons available under the General Agreement on Tariffs and

Trade (GATT) against nations that fail adequately to protect United States intellectual property rights. The issue of appropriate sanctions was initially addressed in a 1984 amendment to the Trade Act of 1974. This amendment, known as Section 301, authorized the president to impose trade sanctions against any country that fails to protect American copyrights adequately or engages in unreasonable or unjustifiable trade practices. Further legislation created the "special 301," under which the U.S. trade representative identifies and investigates pirate nations and then "must" recommend appropriate sanctions to the president, who in turn "must" institute retaliatory measures. Sanctions, or rewards, can also be meted out under the Generalized System of Preferences.

The United States' joining the Berne Convention helped the cause of stronger protection for intellectual property under GATT because it restored some of the credibility lost from our previous isolationism. The World Trade Organization (WTO), which evolved from the Uruguay round of GATT negotiations, came into force on January 1, 1995. One of its important aspects is the standard that dictates the minimum levels of protection member countries must incorporate into their national intellectual property laws. This part of the overall WTO agreement, which came into force on January 1, 1996, is called "Agreement on Trade-Related Aspects of Intellectual Property Rights" (TRIPs), and it impacts such areas as copyright, trademarks, industrial designs, patents, and trade secrets. On December 8, 1994, the United States enacted a law to approve and implement the Uruguay agreements. Included in the law were amendments to U.S. copyright law to conform to the obligations of the Uruguay requirements.

U.S. GOALS IN THE URUGUAY ROUND

The United States had a number of goals with respect to copyright in the trade negotiations. As a leading source of intellectual property and a net exporter of copyrighted works, it wanted to encourage strong protection and enforcement provisions, fight piracy, and increase the flow of revenues to U.S. entertainment and information producers. Therefore, it strove to incorporate the Berne Convention obligations as a requirement of membership in the WTO. It sought to require the protection of computer software (with respect to both copyrightability and rental rights) and databases for nations joining the WTO. The United States pushed for the Berne minimum term of copyright protection of life-plus-fifty years (now life-plus-seventy), and a minimum term of fifty years for works not granted the full Berne term (such as "sound recordings," CDs, and LPs).

In all of these respects, the United States succeeded in meeting its goals. The minimum protection and enforcement provisions that nations are obligated to meet are elaborated at length. Some basic requirements are that "Procedures concerning the enforcement of intellectual property rights shall be fair and equitable. . . . Decisions on the merits of a case shall preferably be in writing and reasoned. . . . Parties to a proceeding shall have an opportunity for review." The remedies are similar to those already existing under U.S. law—injunctions (to prevent or halt an infringement), damages (including the possible payment of expenses and attorneys' fees), and remedies such as disposal or destruction of infringing goods and materials used to create them. While other substantive and clarifying provisions sought by the United States were not adopted, the overall effect is considered very helpful in protecting the value of United States copyrights around the world.

RESTORATION OF U.S. COPYRIGHT FOR FOREIGN WORKS
Certain concessions by the United States encouraged adherence to its proposals in the Uruguay Round. The major one is the restoration of certain copyrights that entered the public domain in the United States but that are still protected in their nation of origin. Before joining Berne, United States law contained notice and deposit formalities that had to be followed in order to obtain or keep copyright. By degrees, starting in 1978 and especially in 1989, when the United States joined the Berne Convention, it softened these formalities and has now mostly eliminated them.

For citizens of nations that become members of the WTO who lost copyright in the United States, their copyright was restored on January 1, 1996, and they will exist for the term that they would have had if they had never entered the public domain. The restoration provision does not necessarily work in reverse, so United States works will not be restored to copyright in the rest of the world, but this is not a

THE WRITER'S LEGAL GUIDE **90**

significant loss—U.S. copyrights were more respected in most other nations than the reverse. Some of our important trading partners, such as China and Russia, offered little or no copyright protection for older U.S. or other foreign works until very recently, and have now agreed to reciprocate.

ENHANCED ENFORCEMENT

China offers a good example of the impact of the WTO. China had a brand-new copyright law, which appeared adequate on its face, but its provisions were not enforced. The result was extensive piracy in China of copyrights originating in the United States. China and the United States both belonged to the Berne Convention, but the only resort for the United States, with respect to China's failure to enforce, would have been a proceeding before the International Court of Justice. Because copyright is now an issue to be addressed pursuant to the WTO dispute settlement procedures, the United States can threaten trade retaliations against countries that fail to provide enforcement mechanisms for their copyright laws. China became a WTO member in late 2001, and its agreement to provide intellectual property protection was a prerequisite for membership. In the case of China, the United States threatened in the late 1990s to impose 100 percent tariffs on over $1 billion of imports of Chinese products if China continued its flagrant piracies. These threatened retaliations were under existing U.S. retaliatory trade provisions, which are strengthened under WTO procedures now that China has joined. To avoid this retaliation, China agreed to take both immediate and long-term steps to put an end to these piracies. Included among these steps were the creation of a copyright recordation system, the use of coded merchandise, the investigation of factories producing merchandise to make certain no infringements are taking place, regular consultations with the United States, and the provision of information and statistics about Chinese enforcement efforts. Similar successes have occurred in newly emerging markets in Russia and Eastern Europe. The increased international protection and enforcement resulting from United States membership in the WTO should work to the benefit of creators, producers, and distributors of works protected by copyright.

The threat of impending sanctions, or potential loss of concessions under GATT, can also be used to encourage bilateral treaties. Under the 1976 Copyright Act, the President has the right to extend copyright reciprocity where he determines that a foreign state is offering acceptable treatment to America copyrights. Bilateral agreements do not undermine Berne as long as they meet its minimum requirements without contradicting its provisions. A member country can set longer terms of protection than the minimum term Berne provides, and those terms will then be durational minimums for copyright holders seeking protection in that country. This bilateral approach is used to avail the United States of immediate copyright protection in countries that have not yet begun the often-cumbersome process of joining an international copyright convention, and it was used as a stopgap in some countries while the GATT/WTO was being negotiated. In addition, these agreements are used to obtain greater levels of protection than are possible under the UCC or even Berne. Effective treaties will tie protection of copyright to other trade or economic issues, including loan forgiveness and economic aid packages. The United States has entered into bilateral copyright agreements with more than seventy countries, most of which are already Berne members. Unfortunately, these agreements have so far proven difficult for local governments or the United States to enforce. Nevertheless, the GATT, trade sanctions, and bilateral agreements remain powerful weapons in the arsenal that can be brought to bear on those who pirate American copyrights abroad.

The United States has finally begun to shed its two-hundred-year-old notions of isolation in the area of copyright protection and is now moving toward a position at the forefront of the crusade for effective transnational copyright protection. This change is attributable to the fact that the United States has progressed from the piracy capital of the world to the foremost exporter of intellectual property. International protection of copyright requires us to reconcile contradictions—like the fact that we once practiced exactly what we now condemn. Details of the international copyright relations of the United States can be obtained from the Copyright Office in Circular 38a, *International Copyright Relations of the United States.*

PROTECTING ELECTRONIC RIGHTS

The Digital Millennium Copyright Act of 1998 was passed in response to the reality that the World Wide Web has made it simple and free to obtain, copy, and widely distribute to others copyrighted works of all kinds—books, periodicals, music, photos, motion pictures—anything that can be put into digital form. Copyright owners face a significant threat of having their valuable works copied and distributed freely to an enormous audience instantly and in violation of their rights. Entire books that have not been released in digital form by their authors or publishers have been freely available on "listservs" for at least a few years. At the same time, digital technology allows great advantages and opportunity for sharing information and entertainment, and it enriches society by providing benefits from long-distance education to telecommuting, while making the world smaller.

Some commentators, who posit that "information should be free," say that authors and societies benefit more if a large audience can enjoy copyrighted works at no charge. This is fine for those authors who choose this scale of distribution, even with all the loss of control it implies. It is not acceptable, however, if you need to choose how your work is distributed and to live from your writing income. As a result, copyright owners regard technological protections, such as encryption, "watermarking," and digital rights management systems, as critical to controlling online distribution of their work. Although these systems are not foolproof—tales of "hackers" defeating DVD and Adobe encryption are well known—they can significantly reduce infringement while giving individual authors greater control over how their works are marketed and distributed.

The DMCA made transmission of works through a digital network part of the copyright owner's exclusive distribution rights. By making the manufacturing and use of technologies that can circumvent encryption illegal, along with other protection technologies, critics charge that the DMCA inhibits permissible activity under the Copyright Act, including having "access" to works in order to decide whether to purchase them, and "fair use." A compromise provision of the Act made prohibition against the act of circumventing technological access controls go into effect two years after the date the DMCA became law. At the time, the Librarian of Congress had to determine whether any users of any particular classes of works are, or are likely to be, adversely affected in their ability to make noninfringing uses of those works because of the anti-circumvention provisions. In October 2000, the Librarian exempted two categories of works from the prohibition: (1) compilations of lists of Web sites blocked by filtering software applications, and (2) literary works protected by access control technologies that fail to permit access because of malfunction or damage. The Librarian must repeat this process every three years.

The Second Circuit Court of Appeals recently ruled that the anti-circumvention provisions of the DMCA are not unconstitutional restraints on free speech to the extent they prohibit publication of de-encrypting software code. *Universal City Studios Inc., et al. v. Corley, et al.,* 273 F.3d 429 (2d Cir. 2001).

THE LEGACY OF COPYRIGHT

At first blush, as copyright detractors have maintained for ages, the copyright law appears to limit the freedom of the public to benefit from artistic and literary works. Proponents of copyright maintain that the purpose of copyright is to benefit the public by providing a reward to authors for their labor and skill. As copyright expert Professor Jane C. Ginsburg points out, the words of the U.S. Constitution bear out this purpose: "to promote the progress of Science and Useful Arts by securing to Authors for limited Times the exclusive Right to their Writings . . ." Copyright laws are founded on the assumption that the stimulus to authorship provided by economic incentives ultimately bequests a richer cultural legacy to the public than would a system that allowed the public the liberty to copy at will. Societies renounce piracy in the belief that the cultural wealth engendered by this abstinence will enrich future generations. Viewed in this way, the conflict between authors and the public vanishes. After all, authors are part of society, and their creations reflect and record society's intellectual liberty and cultural legacy.

CHAPTER 7

OTHER RIGHTS

OF THE WRITER

B esides copyright and contract law, some other legal theories can remedy wrongful conduct against authors. Most of these fall under the doctrine of "unfair competition," which both federal and state law prohibit. The federal Lanham Act, the trademark protection law, also prohibits unfair competition, which it defines as "any false designation of origin, false or misleading description [or representation] of fact" that is "likely to cause confusion . . . or to deceive as to affiliation, connection or association." 15 U.S.C. Section 1125(a)(1)(A). The common law is similar: "The essence of an unfair competition claim is that the defendant assembled a product which bears so striking a resemblance to the plaintiff's product that the public will be confused as to the identity of the products. . . . The test is whether persons exercising 'reasonable intelligence and discrimination' would be taken in by the similarity," *Shaw v. Time-Life Records,* 38 N.Y. 2d 201 (N.Y. 1975).

Defined this way, "unfair competition" comprises many situations that could affect a professional author's interests. The general objective of the doctrine is to prevent others from confusing the public to benefit unfairly from the reputation for quality of another's work product. Thus, the doctrine can prevent an author from being called the creator of work that he did not create; prevent an author from being presented as the creator of a distorted version of his own work; prevent attribution to another person for a work in fact created by an author; and protect a title or a character that, although not copyrightable, is so well recognized that its reuse would create public confusion in distinguishing a new work from the original work.

This chapter groups unfair competition claims into two categories: protection against misappropriation of an author's idea, title, character, or name, and protection against the false designation of the origin of a work of authorship, including distortion of a work. Specific wrongs addressed by unfair competition law can fall into both groups and lawsuits often rely on a variety of them. The chapter will also explain the related doctrine of creators' "moral rights," recognized in France and a few other nations, but not in the United States. This chapter will end by describing other claims an author might make for damage caused to his or her reputation, including defamation and invasion of the rights of privacy and publicity.

PROTECTION OF IDEAS

As you know, ideas are not protected by copyright. Ideas can be freely and legally exploited by anyone who is privy to them. This freedom puts any author with a proposal, screenplay treatment, or even a detailed query letter for a work that has not yet been written at risk. A publisher, producer, or agent might like an idea conveyed in a proposal, but choose to retain a different author to express that idea in copyrightable form. Although no respectable publisher or agent ought to engage in this practice, it can and does happen. When disclosing your ideas to others, it is important to protect your interests with a proper contract, or at least a paper trail, whenever you can.

You are best served by a written contract that expressly provides for compensation if the purchaser uses your idea. This submission agreement need not be complex, but it should suit the individual circumstances. For example, you might use a brief letter:

Dear Sir/Madam,

I understand it is your practice to entertain or receive program materials, ideas, or suggestions for [specify the market]. I have developed such a [indicate what will be submitted] for submission and would like to disclose this to you. I understand that if you use it, you will pay reasonable compensation and give appropriate credit to me based on current industry standards. Please advise me if I should send this to you.

Yours, etc.

Although an express contract is the best way to protect your idea, it might be unrealistic to expect certain entities to agree to it. In fact, many purchasers of literary property require those submitting ideas (including unsolicited manuscripts) to sign releases before any consideration will be given to the submission. The typical release bars any claim by an author based upon the potential purchaser's subsequent use of similar material. It stipulates the maximum value of the material and the total recovery possible (limited to that maximum value) should the author sue and recover despite the release. These releases typically include a recital from the author, such as:

I recognize that there is always a likelihood that this material may be identical to, like, or competitive with material that has or may come to you from other sources. Identity or similarity of material in the past has given rise to claims and disputes between various parties and has caused misunderstandings. You have advised me that you will refuse to examine or consider material unless you obtain for yourself complete protection from me against the possibility of any such claims.

Obviously, you should exercise caution before signing such a release in order to submit an idea or manuscript. The risk might be worth taking, but evaluate it first. Research the organization to determine its reputation in the area of idea appropriation. Consider whether different companies would agree to your submission agreement.

If you cannot obtain an agreement to compensate you for your idea, consider writing some of the work before submitting it. This might seem counterintuitive, but the more complete the rendering of your idea when submitted, the more likely it is to be protected under the implied contract theory, the more copyright protection the work will have, and the less incentive a publisher will have to use a different author.

Another way to protect yourself is to place the proposal in one sealed envelope, and place that in a larger envelope with a cover letter. The cover letter can state that by opening the smaller envelope, the publisher implicitly agrees to hire and pay you if the idea is used. Another safeguard is to meet with a representative from the publishing house, bring along a third party, and verbally agree to these terms. The third party is a witness to the agreement, and you can also create a paper trail by reminding the publisher of the agreement in a follow-up letter.

The Writers Guild of America registers film and television scripts, synopses, outlines, ideas, treatments, and scenarios in order to document their completion date and identity. Writers Guild rules apply to the use of authors' work by producers that have collective bargaining agreements with the Writers Guild. You need not be a member of the Writers Guild to register your film- or television-related work with it.

MISAPPROPRIATION OF IDEAS

A "tort" is a civil wrong for which the law provides a remedy to the person wronged. The tort of misappropriation might protect the efforts of a writer who has invested a substantial amount of time in developing an idea. Recovery is possible under a variety of theories in a misappropriation lawsuit: express contract, implied contract (where the parties show by their conduct that an agreement to compensate and/or credit the author exists), and breach of fiduciary duty (in which an author invests her trust and confidence in another person such as her literary agent in disclosing the idea). In the common-law claim of quasi-contract, the law imposed an obligation on the exploiter of an idea to compensate the author of the idea. This claim is now largely preempted by the Copyright Act, which does not protect ideas. To avoid preemption by the Copyright Act, an idea misappropriation claim must involve breach of contract (express or implied), create a likelihood of public confusion, or allege some other "extra element" of conduct beyond one party's infringement of the idea. If the conduct complained of involves only unauthorized copying or other exploitation, the Copyright Act alone governs the case. *National Basketball Association v. Motorola,* 105 F.3d 841 (2d Cir. 1997).

Short of the publisher signing a written agreement to pay for an idea, when an author submits a concrete idea to a publisher (or other party), the parties' conduct might create an implied agreement to retain and pay the author if the publisher exploits her idea. Such an implied contract might arise when the publisher invites the author to submit the idea, or when the publisher agrees with the author's verbal request that the publisher not use the author's idea without compensating or retaining her.

If a party has requested that an author disclose his idea, most courts will find that the request or solicitation implies a promise to pay for the idea if used. When a person submits an unsolicited idea but also gives the recipient advance warning with the opportunity to decline the disclosure of the idea (such as by placing it in a sealed envelope with an explanatory cover letter), courts might regard the recipient's accepting the disclosure as implying a promise to pay in the event of use. On the other hand, many courts require solicitation of the idea as a prerequisite to implied contractual liability.

When the idea submission occurs without solicitation or advance warning, courts will generally not infer a promise to pay by the recipient. It can be argued that such a promise should be implied where the recipient is engaged in a trade or industry, such as the entertainment industry, which customarily purchases ideas of the type submitted. Although no court has expressly recognized this theory, some courts have implicitly adopted it by recognizing an implied agreement based on industry custom and practice where such a fact pattern can be established.

When an author claims an implied contract to compensate him for an idea, some courts require that the idea be "novel," that is, "not formerly known, of a new kind," *Downey v. General Foods Corp.,* 31 N.Y. 2d 56 (1972). Applying this principle in *Murray v. National Broadcasting Co.,* 844 F.2d 988 (2d Cir. 1988), the Second Circuit held that the plaintiff's idea, to portray a "strong" African American family in a nonstereotypical manner in a situation comedy, was not protected. The court reasoned that the idea was not novel because it merely comprised two concepts that had been circulating in the television industry for a number of years: (1) the standard family situation comedy, and (2) the casting of African American actors in nonstereotypical roles. The television networks had already cast African American actors in such roles, and the idea of combining the family situation comedy theme with an all-black cast had been publicly suggested by Bill Cosby twenty years earlier.

Today, the courts lean away from the novelty requirement so long as the idea disclosed was novel *as to the recipient* and the agreement was to pay for the disclosure, as well as when a fiduciary relationship, such as author-agent, led to the disclosure. See *Wrench LLC v. Taco Bell Corp.* (6th Cir. 2001); *Apfel v. Prudential-Bache Secs. Inc.,* 616 N.E.2d 1095 (N.Y. 1993).

The courts that follow the traditional view in implied promise cases are likely to require that the idea be "concrete." Concrete means sufficiently developed so as to constitute property. In *Ligget & Meyers v. Meyer,* 101 Ind. App. 420, 194 N.E. 206 (1935), an Indiana state court found concrete the idea of an advertisement in which one person extends a package of cigarettes to another who declines the offer by replying that he or she would prefer to smoke Chesterfield cigarettes. However, in *Plus Promotions, Inc. v. RCA Mfg. Co.,* 49 F. Supp. 116 (S.D.N.Y. 1943), the plaintiff was denied recovery on an implied contract theory because the following idea was held not to be concrete: World-famous concert artists would produce recordings for flat fees rather than royalties, and would not be entitled to name credit. The recordings would be sold, through newspapers, at a price affordable by low-income consumers.

MISAPPROPRIATION OF CHARACTERS, TITLES, AND AUTHORS' NAMES

A misappropriation is a wrongful taking or use of someone else's property. Some cases involving literary property do not fit easily under copyright infringement but might constitute misappropriation. For example, a character's name or a title can become so identified with a particular work or author that its use in a new work would create a likelihood of confusion as to the source or affiliation of the new work. In one case, a character's name that happened to be the same as the main character's in a well-known book series was used in a motion picture title. A court enjoined the use of the name in the film:

> The plaintiff's copyrights do not cover the titles to the stories. . . . But a name that has become descriptive, and is closely identified in the public mind with the work of a particular author, may not, during the life of the copyright, be used so as to mislead. . . . Nor may such a name be used even after the expiration of the copyright, unless adequate explanation is given to guard against mistake. . . . In the present case, the name has become associated in the public mind solely and exclusively with the plaintiff's authorship; it is a name which is highly descriptive of his work; and ordinary principles of unfair competition are peculiarly applicable. *Patten v. Superior Talking Pictures, Inc.*, 8 F. Supp. 197, 198 (1934).

Similarly, although the phrase "fifth column" was commonly used, Ernest Hemingway's play *The Fifth Column* acquired a sufficient secondary meaning associated with or suggesting his play to the public such that the title *Fifth Column Squad* could not be used for someone else's film. *Hemingway v. Film Alliance of the U.S.*, 174 Misc. 725, 21 N.Y.S.2d 827. The key to such a holding is proof that the public is likely to associate the use of a character's name or a title with a previous work. Therefore, if an adequate disclaimer is given with the second use, the plaintiff will have no claim. If the title or a name is not adequately well known, the doctrine of unfair competition does not apply, as in *Fishler v. Twentieth Century-Fox Film Corporation*, 159 F. Supp. 215 (1958). (Authors of an unpublished and unproduced play titled *Virgin Queen* about Queen Elizabeth could not prevent the use of the title *The Virgin Queen* for an independently conceived film based on her life.) The likelihood of public confusion can change as time passes and a title or name falls out of common use. *International Film Service Co., Inc. v. Associated Producers, Inc.*, 273 F. Supp. 585 (1921).

RETRIEVING INTERNET DOMAIN NAMES

Well-known people, including authors, can retrieve Internet domain names containing their names, titles, or characters from unrelated parties who do not have a legitimate right to the names. Unlike copyright, federal law recognizes and protects common-law trademarks. The Lanham Act makes registering another party's trademark as a domain name an infringement. The Internet Corporation for Assigned Names and Numbers (ICANN), a nonprofit organization that assigns and regulates the use of domain names, has established an arbitration procedure and rules for retrieving a name registered as a domain name. The arbitration panel has the authority to order a contested domain name to be transferred to the complainant, if the name is confusingly similar to a trademark, the respondent has no rights or legitimate interests in the contested name, and the respondent registered and used the name in bad faith.

A key precedent, set in a proceeding brought by the Authors Guild against an entity that had registered ".com" names using many famous authors' names, was the holding that bad faith, a necessary element of an ICANN case, was proved because the registrant was "not actually using any of the contested domain names to point to a Web site." The panel found that authors have common-law trademark rights in their names and that persons with no legitimate rights to those names who register domain names incorporating them and then warehouse those domain names or seek to sell them back to the author must be required, under the ICANN rules, to return those domain names to their rightful owners.

FALSE ATTRIBUTION

The false attribution tort is often called "passing off" or "palming off," which accurately describes the wrong done—attributing to an author a work that was not written by him by misappropriating his name. The doctrine has existed in common law for many years— representatives of Lord Byron successfully sued to enjoin publication of poems falsely attributed to him in 1816. As in all unfair competition cases, the wrongful use must be likely to cause public confusion as to the source of the wrongly designated product, so the claim's viability depends in part on how well known the author is. For example, a publisher reprinted a book that author Ken Follet had edited before he achieved commercial success. The publisher gave Follet top billing after he became famous, even though the other authors had written most of the book. The court held that the publisher could give equal but not greater billing to Follett because to do otherwise would violate the spirit of the Lanham

Act, which was designed to protect the public and creators from the harms of false attribution. *Follett v. New American Library, Inc.*, 497 F. Supp. 304 (1980).

False attribution might involve material that was partially written by the person claimed to be the writer. For example, a lawyer named Joseph Clevenger wrote and edited *Clevenger's Annual Practice of New York* from 1923 to 1956. In 1956, he terminated his editorship and revoked the publisher's right to use his name as editor of any subsequent editions. Nevertheless, a later edition stated that *Clevenger's Annual Practice* was "Annually Revised," without indicating that the revisions were done by the publisher's staff. Clevenger claimed the public would associate numerous mistakes in the text as his errors because his name was part of the title, thereby causing harm to his reputation as a competent lawyer and legal commentator. The court concluded that a jury might reasonably find that the wording and arrangement of the title page were libelous. *Clevenger v. Baker Voorhis & Co.*, 8 N.Y.2d 187 (N.Y. 1964). Under the likelihood of confusion test, Clevenger would probably have had no unfair competition claim if the book had correctly stated that others had revised it. Such was the case in *Geisel v. Poynter Products, Inc.*, 295 F. Supp. 331, 353 (1968), in which Theodore Geisel, also known as Dr. Seuss, failed to stop the defendant from accurately naming the source of its merchandise designs as his work.

Keep in mind that passing off claims cannot enlarge the scope of copyright protection. Samuel Clemens, as Mark Twain, published a number of literary sketches that he did not copyright and that therefore became part of the public domain. Years later, they were published without permission under the name Mark Twain. Although Clemens objected to use of his famous pen name, theorizing that it had become a trademark that could not be used without his permission, a federal court disagreed:

> Trademarks are the means by which the manufacturers of vendible merchandise designate or state to the public the quality of such goods, and the fact that they are the manufacturers of them. . . . A writer cannot, by the adoption of a *nom de plume*, be allowed to defeat the well-settled rules that the 'publication of a literary work without copyright

is a dedication to the public, after which any one may publish it.' No pseudonym, however ingenious, novel, or quaint, can give a writer any more rights than he would have under his own name. *Clemens v. Belford, Clark & Co.*, 14 F. 728.

NONATTRIBUTION OR "REVERSE PASSING OFF"

As you might have deduced, "reverse passing off" means attributing an author's work to somebody else. The unfair competition doctrine does not by itself entitle a writer to authorship credit if the publishing contract states otherwise. In the United States, a contract in which a writer agrees to work under a pseudonym or not to receive credit is enforceable. One romance publisher is notorious for "assigning" pseudonyms to authors, which it retains to assign to another author should the first author choose a different publisher for her subsequent novels. The first author may only publish under the pseudonym with the first publisher's permission. This practice has not been tested in the courts, though it seems intended to cause consumer confusion.

Several unfair competition cases have resulted in a Lanham Act violation founded on the theory of "reverse passing off" when an author did not receive appropriate credit for his or her contribution to a work. Some examples of this include *Marling, et al. v. Ellison,* 218 U.S.P.Q. (BNA) 702 (S.D. Fla. 1982), in which an infringer of copyright on travel guides was also liable for damages and injunction for Lanham Act violation for falsely attributing himself as author of infringing works; *R.H. Donnelly Corp. v. Illinois Bell Tel.,* 595 F. Supp. 1202 (N.D. Ill. 1984), where the failure to credit the copublisher of business directory in an advertising campaign violated Lanham Act and an injunction against continuing campaign was ordered; and *Dodd, et al. v. Ft. Smith Special School Dist., et al.,* 666 F. Supp. 1278 (W.D. Ark 1987), where, under the Lanham Act, the court enjoined defendants from distributing or advertising a biography that failed to credit a high school journalism class and the teacher and class's authorship.

Nonetheless, there is still some question whether a publishing contract that is silent on the question of credit requires attribution to the author. Although the customary trade practices in the relevant industry might require attribution in the absence of any specific contractual provision, it is also true that adequate disclaimers and/or acknowledgment of contributions to a work, even without author-ship credit, might eliminate the necessary element of likely consumer confusion. *Rosenfeld v. W.B. Saunders,* 728 F. Supp. 236 (S.D.N.Y 1990). If in doubt, expressly provide for authorship credit in your contracts, especially because attribution is likely to be a precondition to obtaining relief in an unfair competition case involving altered or distorted work.

DISTORTION

The hallmark of unfair competition is misrepresenting the source of a particular product, so it also includes attributing a work to an author that so distorts the original work that it cannot be fairly said to be cre-ated by the author. One of the more infamous examples of this con-duct was ABC's broadcast of several episodes of the *Monty Python's Flying Circus* series in the mid-1970s. In their original license agree-ments with the BBC, the members of Monty Python had approval rights over any changes in their scripts. When ABC licensed the right to broadcast the episodes from the BBC, it cut twenty-four minutes from each ninety-minute program to make time for commercials. The result was a gross distortion of the sketches, according to the Second Circuit Court of Appeals. When the horrified authors sued under the federal unfair competition act, the appellate court held:

> The Lanham Act . . . has been invoked to prevent misrepresentations that may injure plaintiff's business or personal reputation. . . . It is suf-ficient to violate the Act that a representation of a product, although technically true, creates a false impression of the product's origin. . . . [When] a television network broadcasts a program properly designat-ed as having been written and performed by a group, but which has been edited, without the writer's consent, into a form that departs sub-stantially from the original work . . . [it] present[s] him to the public as the creator of a work not his own and thus makes him subject to crit-icism for work he has not done. . . . In such a case, it is the writer . . . rather than the network, who suffers the consequences of the mutila-tion. . . . Thus, an allegation that a defendant has presented to the public a "garbled," distorted version of plaintiff's work seeks to redress the very rights sought to be protected by the Lanham Act . . . *Gilliam, et al. v. American Broadcasting Company,* 538 F.2d 14 (2d Cir. 1976).

Thus, a valid cause of action for distortion, based on an impairment of the authors' work and a misrepresentation of their talents, was recognized as unfair competition. The court further noted that even a pre-broadcast disclaimer of the writers' authorship of the edited work would not have protected them sufficiently because not all the viewers would have tuned in to the disclaimer.

Do not mistake ABC's distortion with a faulty editing job on your book or article. The plaintiffs here had to prove a high level of distortion of their programs. Story lines and even climactic moments in the episodes were eliminated. A book or article author has an equally difficult challenge if they disagree with editorial decisions. As always, you are much better off ensuring your rights in your publishing contract, especially the right to approve of editorial revisions of your work.

MORAL RIGHTS

"Moral rights" as such are not recognized in the United States, but they provide a good discussion point of comparison with the rights a writer does have in the United States. France has the most well-established system of moral rights.

Moral rights are not economic and are not based on the ownership of intellectual property. Instead, they derive from the belief that the creative person should have certain control over his or her work, regardless of who the owner of the property rights might be. The Berne Copyright Convention defines moral rights as follows:

> [T]he author shall have the right to claim authorship of the work and to object to any distortion, mutilation or other modification of, or other derogatory action in relation to said work, which would be prejudicial to his honor or reputation.

The United States has not adopted that optional provision of the Berne Convention, except with respect to some works of visual art under the Visual Artists Rights Act enacted in 1990. In France, *droit moral* are perpetual and inalienable, meaning they cannot be lost or given up by the author. The author alone may determine when a work is completed and ready to be communicated to the public. The author even has the right to reconsider or retract the work from public distribution after it has been published, although she must also pay in advance for any losses that such a withdrawal will cause the party owning the right of economic exploitation.

The right of paternity guarantees that the author's name and authorship will be acknowledged with respect to any of her works. Any agreement under which an author is required to use a pseudonym is invalid in France because it would violate the right of paternity. Also, the French law allows the author to prevent the use of her name in association with a work created by someone else. Finally, the right of integrity provides that there can be no alteration or distortion of a work without the author's consent. The author alone has the right to reshape a work—including rearranging, adapting, or translating it—and to prevent others from doing so.

HARM TO AN AUTHORS' REPUTATION

Defamation is an injurious attack on the reputation of another person by the publication of a falsehood about him. Both libel and slander are forms of defamation. Libel refers to print publication and slander to verbal publication. Most authors have more to fear from defaming others than from being defamed, so this tort is explained in greater detail in chapter 8.

Sometimes, the treatment of an author or his work can constitute defamation. In 1913, for example, Antonio d'Altomonte, an Italian of noble birth and a leading authority on criminology and African life and politics, was represented to be the writer of a sensational article about cannibals that appeared in the *New York Herald*. A New York court concluded that the false attribution of this article to d'Altomonte was libelous to someone of his reputation because "if false and a forgery, it [was] calculated to destroy his influence as a writer and a lecturer . . ." *D'Altomonte v. New York Herald Co.,* 154 App. Div. 453, 139 N.Y.S. 200, *mod.* 208 N.Y. 596, 102 N.E. 1101 (1913).

A critical review of a writer's work, no matter how vicious, does not in itself constitute defamation. Under the "fair comment" rule, a writer who places work before the public invites criticism of the work.

The criticism, no matter how hostile, fantastic, or extravagant, is not by itself defamatory. If untrue statements of fact are made that disparage the author, or if the author is attacked personally in a way unconnected with the work, the critic might have crossed the border into the area of defamation. Related to the fair comment rule is the possibility that an author might be a public figure. "Public figures" in the law of defamation are defined as those who, though not public officials, are "involved in issues in which the public has a justified and important interest," *Cepeda v. Cowles Magazines and Broadcasting Inc.,* 392 F.2d 417, 419, *cert. denied* 393 U.S. 840. In order to win a defamation suit, a public figure must show, by clear and convincing evidence, that a defamatory statement was made with "malice"—that is, with the knowledge that the statement was false or with a reckless disregard as to whether the statement was true or false.

It is possible to claim that publication of a distorted work defames the author, as in Attorney Clevenger's case, discussed previously. Work in the public domain can be freely copied by anyone, so no defamatory implication of the author's consent to exploit his work, as in a derivative work, is possible. For example, in *Shostakovich v. Twentieth Century-Fox Film Corp.,* 196 Misc. 67, 80 N.Y.S.2d 575, *aff'd* 275 App. Div. 692, 87 N.Y.S.2d 430 (1949), the use of Russian composers' public domain works in an anti-Russia film was found not defamatory.

RIGHT OF PRIVACY

The right of privacy is the right to be free from unwanted and unnecessary publicity or interference that could injure one's personal feelings or present a person in a false light before the public. This right is recognized in varying forms in almost every state.

An author might make out a case of invasion of privacy in some situations. For example, a professor's privacy was invaded when his name was used in the unauthorized publication of his course lecture notes, because the use of his name implied his consent. In fact, he reasonably believed the publication might jeopardize his professional standing. *Williams v. Weisser,* 78 Cal. Rptr. 542 (1969). False attribution might be ruled an invasion of privacy, but courts are not all in agreement on this. At least one old ruling indicated that no invasion of privacy occurs if a work in the public domain is published using the author's real name, even though the book originally appeared under a pen name. *Ellis v. Hurst,* 70 Misc. 122, 128 N.Y.S. 144 (1911). Courts have also ruled that the right of privacy does not protect pen names, only real names. *Geisel v. Poynter Products, Inc.,* 295 F. Supp. 331, 355 (1968). As described in more detail in chapter 8, the right of privacy diminishes when the author gains stature as a public figure, particularly with respect to those areas of her life in which the public has a legitimate interest.

RIGHT OF PUBLICITY

The right of publicity gives a person with a public reputation the sole right to benefit from the commercial value associated with his or her name, likeness, or persona. By definition, the right of publicity is of little value to a writer who is not well known. The right of publicity also does not overcome the First Amendment right to use a famous person's name and likeness in advertising, if those uses are incidental to a legitimate news article. *Hoffman v. Capital Cities/ABC, Inc., Namath v. Sports Illustrated,* 48 A.D.2d 487, *aff'd* 39 N.Y.2d 897 (1976). Ayn Rand's review of *Chaos Below Heaven* by Eugene Vale was accurately quoted on the book's jacket, without her permission. She sued over this "blatant commercial exploitation of her personality," but the court concluded the quotation was merely a comment by a public figure on a matter of current interest. *Rand v. Hearst Corp.,* 298 N.Y.S.2d 405, *aff'd* 26 N.Y.2d 806 (N.Y. 1970).

Most personal rights, such as the right to privacy and the right to redress for defamation, die with the injured party, but in 1984 California enacted a "celebrity rights" law to clarify the nature of publicity rights developed by California court decisions, and other states have followed suit. The basic approach of these laws is to protect the publicity rights of deceased people for up to fifty years after their death. The right applies to people whose names, voices, signatures, or likenesses had commercial value at the time of death, whether or not that commercial value had been exploited during life. Unlike defamation and invasion of privacy claims, the right of publicity can be assigned to or enforced by heirs. Prohibited uses cover commercial exploitation, including the sale of merchandise or services, and advertising. Typical exemptions include works in the public interest and material of political or newsworthy value. Given the effect these "dead celebrity" laws have on free expression, the New York legislature has repeatedly refused to enact them. However, creative works are usually distributed in more than one state, so the most restrictive celebrity rights law might apply to a nationally distributed work.

On the other hand, valuable as the right of publicity might be to well-known writers, it does not protect anyone from receiving accurate authorship credit for a work to which he contributed. *King v. Innovation Books,* 976 F.2d 824 (2d Cir. 1992). In this case, the author Stephen King objected to the use of his name in the credits and advertising of a film based on a short story he had written and optioned years earlier. The court agreed that calling the film "Stephen King's *The Lawnmower Man*" violated the Lanham Act because he had not written the screenplay or had any other involvement with the film. It also held, however it was appropriate to describe the film as "based on a story by Stephen King" because, in fact, it was, so there was no likelihood of consumer confusion.

CHAPTER 8

THE LIMITATIONS

ON FREE EXPRESSION

The First Amendment to the United States Constitution guarantees freedom from governmental constraints on expression, both spoken and written. It holds that "Congress shall make no law . . . abridging the freedom of speech, or of the press," and its reach extends to the fifty states by virtue of the Fourteenth Amendment. The word "press" includes not just newspapers, but books, magazines, broadcast media including the Internet, and motion pictures—virtually any means of conveying information. The simple theory on which the First Amendment is based was famously explained by Justice Oliver Wendell Holmes, Jr. in 1919: "The ultimate good desired is better reached by free trade in ideas . . . the best test of truth is the power of the thought to get itself accepted in the competition of the market . . ." *Abrams. v. United States,* 250 U.S. 616 (1919) (Holmes, J., dissenting).

This freedom is not absolute. You already know that copyright, trademark, and unfair competition laws punish published expression that infringes the rights of others. Civil remedies against the authors of defamation and for invasion of privacy are also available in every state. Laws punishing obscenity and allowing censorship of literature abound throughout the fifty states, and school and library censorship occurs daily.

The scope of any one of these topics can and does fill volumes of textbooks and treatises, as well as judicial decisions, and an in-depth study of any of them is not possible here. This chapter does attempt to explain the effects on professional authors—of both fiction and nonfiction—of defamation, invasion of privacy claims, obscenity laws, and censorship in schools and libraries. It assesses some of the legal risks facing writers and offers practical suggestions for self-protection. Keep in mind that state and federal courts have developed the law of defamation and privacy over the course of many years and that the legal standards vary, sometimes substantially, from state to state. It is not even clear which state's laws might apply to a work published nationwide. Happily, there is one set of standards that applies to all works—those set by the First Amendment as interpreted by the Supreme Court. This chapter also focuses on the important limits the Court has imposed on states' defamation and privacy laws.

DEFAMATION

Almost every state defines defamation as the publication of a false statement of fact about a person or organization, in writing, visually, or verbally, that is derogatory and that injures the subject's reputation. The statement must reach at least one person other than the subject because damage to a reputation is the essence of defamation. If the statement is spoken, the defamation is deemed *slander*. If the statement is expressed visually, through words or images (including motion pictures), it is *libel*. In many states, injury to a reputation is easier to prove when the claim is one of libel rather than slander.

Every party who actually participates in publishing or repeating the statement can be liable to the defamed person. A person who merely repeats a defamatory statement is equally liable to the subject, even if she names the original source, indicates that she does not believe the statement to be true, uses the customary news media phrase "it is alleged," or says that the story is based on rumors. A distributor of the statement, such as a bookseller, newsstand, or telephone service, is not liable unless it has notice of the defamation and continues to distribute the publication. Federal law makes Internet service providers immune from liability for defamation occurring through their services.

In almost every state, defamation liability requires that the statement be false. The truth or substantial truth of the statement is therefore an absolute defense. Unauthorized biographies are perfectly legal, as long as they do not make false and defamatory statements about their subjects. Once a plaintiff proves the other elements of her claim, that is, the publication of a derogatory statement that has actually injured her reputation, the burden of proving that the statement is true shifts to the defendant.

The kinds of statements that could injure a person's reputation vary as much as people do. Any assertion can injure a person's reputation if it reduces esteem or respect for him personally or professionally, casts him into an improper light, or generates negative feelings about him. Some kinds of statements, however, are considered so universally harmful that they are deemed defamatory *per se*. *Per se* defamation includes statements that impugn a person's honesty, ethics, mental health, that claim the subject has a dreaded disease, is an alcoholic or drug abuser, is sexually promiscuous or impotent, or is a criminal. Per se defamation, if false, is considered so obviously injurious that the plaintiff does not have to prove actual damage to his reputation. On the other hand, a person with a notoriously bad reputation is less likely to prove injury even when the statement is per se defamatory. *Brooks v. American Broadcasting Co.*, 737 F. Supp. 431 (1990).

STATEMENT OF FACT

Humor, ridicule, sarcasm, questions, alterations of quotes, and insinuations can all be defamatory if they are reasonably understood to injure a reputation, but a genuine statement of opinion is not defamatory. That distinction does not, however, give people license to state or imply a defamatory fact in the guise of an opinion. The Supreme Court has held that "expressions of opinion may often imply an assertion of objective fact," which, if false and defamatory, can lead to liability. *Milkovich v. Lorain Journal Co.*, 497 U.S. 1 (1991). If the author asserts facts on which he bases his opinion, the opinion might be defamatory if the facts are incorrect or incomplete. The key inquiry is whether the offending statement may be verified objectively.

In examining a statement's import for defamatory meaning, a court must interpret the words as they were reasonably understood in view of all the circumstances, including the entire context in which they were published. If the contested statement is "reasonably susceptible of a defamatory connotation," the case should survive a motion to dismiss. *Weiner v. Doubleday & Co.*, 74 N.Y.2d 586, 592 (1989). In making this determination, the court must give the disputed language a fair reading in the context of the publication as a whole. *James v. Gannett Co.*, 40 N.Y.2d 415, 419–420 (1976). For example, in *Moldea v. New York Times*, 22 F.3d 310 (D.C. Cir. 1994), Dan Moldea sued over a negative review of his book, claiming the statement that his work contained "too much sloppy journalism" injured his reputation as an investigative reporter. After first ruling that Moldea had stated a valid claim, a federal appellate court reversed itself, holding that in the context of a "book review, a genre in which readers expect to find spirited critiques of literary works that they understand to be the review's description and assessment of texts that are capable of a number of possible rational interpretations," the statement was a "supportable interpretation of" the book and thus the review was substantially true. Only where no reasonable person could conclude that a statement in a critical review is a "supportable interpretation" of a work may a statement be "verifiable" as a factual assertion and thus defamatory.

Defamation by implication is premised not on direct statements but on false suggestions, impressions, and implications arising from otherwise truthful statements. In *Memphis Publishing Co. v. Nichols*, 569 S.W.2d 412, 420 (Tenn. 1978), for example, the Tennessee Supreme Court held an article implicitly defamatory where it truthfully reported that a woman, upon finding her husband at the plaintiff's home, shot the plaintiff, but neglected to state that at the time they all were at a social gathering with several other people, including the plaintiff's husband. The concern that substantially truthful speech be adequately protected has led different courts to embrace different standards for measuring the sufficiency of claims of defamation by implication. In Connecticut, defamatory implication must arise from a material omission of information. *Strada v. Conn. Newspapers, Inc.*, 477 A.2d 1005 (Conn. 1984). A federal court ruled the defamatory implication must have been a reasonable reading, and the author must have intended to convey it. *Chapin v. Knight-Ridder, Inc.,* 993 F.2d 1087 (1993). A Minnesota court even rejected the concept of libel by implication altogether as contrary to free speech values. *Kortz v. Midwest Communications, Inc.,* 20 Media L. Rep 1890.

DEFAMATION IN FICTION

Defamation can occur in a work of fiction even if it does not refer to a real person by name. The vast majority of defamation lawsuits against writers are for nonfiction works, but the potential problems they can cause for fiction authors who use real events or people in their work are substantial. Decisions in the 1970s and 1980s suggested an alarmingly easy test for proving that the depiction of a fictional character was a defamatory statement of fact about a person. Two federal courts allowed the question of whether "the libel designates the plaintiff in such a way as to let those who knew him understand he was the person meant" to be decided by a jury. The Illinois Supreme Court held as recently as 1998 that, if it is reasonable for objective readers of a work who know both the author and the subject of the statement to have discerned the reference to the plaintiff, defamation liability is possible. In *Bryson v. News America Publication, Inc.,* 177 N.E.2d 77 (Ill. 1996), it was shown that the character's first name in short story matched plaintiff's last name and that there were twenty-five matching physical attributes, locations, and occurrences. New York courts have articulated a stricter test for plaintiffs. In 1991, a trial court acknowledged the "accepted fact" that writers base fictional characters on their own experiences and held that "identification alone is insufficient" to overcome a presumption that a character in a work of fiction is imaginary. Rather, the reader must be "totally convinced that the book in all its aspects as far as the plaintiff is concerned is not fiction at all." *Welch v. McMillan,* N.Y. Sup. 1992. Another court ruled "the description of the fictional character must be so closely akin to the real person . . . that a reader of the book, knowing the real person, would have no difficulty linking the two." *Randall v. DeMille,* N.Y. Sup. 1993.

If you are using some traits of people you know in your fictional characters, you can protect yourself by changing superficial features—their names, physical traits, professions, residences—as much as you can. The more you defame your character, the more distinct, at least superficially, you should make him or her from any person you know. The problem, of course, is whether your work will retain its artistic integrity after these alterations. Keeping in mind what prior courts have ruled, you and possibly your attorney can decide how much you must alter your characters.

Novels and motion pictures often include disclaimers, such as "This is a work of fiction. The people, events, and circumstances depicted in this novel are fictitious and the product of the author's imagination, and any resemblance of any character to any actual person, whether living or dead, is purely coincidental." Although a disclaimer means little if, in fact, a court rules your depiction of a character defames a real person, it can decrease the risk or amount of certain kinds of money damages.

FIRST AMENDMENT LIMITS TO DEFAMATION LIABILITY

Few would dispute the idea that unwarranted damage to a person's reputation should be avoided and remedied. If, however, writers and their publishers could be held financially liable to every person about whom an incorrect statement is published, news reporting and writing of all genres would be unacceptably constrained and delayed (or "chilled," in legal parlance). Cognizant of the importance of Justice Holmes's "marketplace of ideas" to a free society, in 1964 the Supreme Court began to interpret the First Amendment as severely limiting defamation claims, basing liability on the degree of the defendants' fault in publishing an untrue statement relative to the newsworthiness of the story.

In the 1964 landmark case of *New York Times v. Sullivan,* 376 U.S. 254 (1964), the Court held that the press may safely make inaccurate statements based on honest error. Public officials may not claim defamation for false statements relating to their official conduct unless the defendant published the false statement with actual malice—that is, with knowledge of its falsity or reckless disregard for its truth or falsity. The public official must prove actual malice "with convincing clarity," a higher level of proof than for most civil tort actions. In *St. Amant v. Thompson,* 390 U.S. 727 (1968), the Court explained that "reckless disregard" for a statement's truth or falsity means more than a failure to check the accuracy of a news story. Instead, there "must be sufficient evidence to permit the conclusion that the defendant in fact entertained serious doubts as to the truth of his publication," 390 U.S. at 731. Nevertheless, failure to verify the accuracy of information by the means and in the time available is risky. It can be a short step from that failing to "entertaining serious doubt about the truth," at least in a jury's opinion.

The Court has found that even a deliberate alteration of a plaintiff's quoted words does not amount to knowledge of falsity where the changes do not result "in a material change in the statement's meaning." *Masson v. New Yorker Magazine, Inc.,* 501 U.S. 496 (1991).

Since the *Sullivan* decision, the Court has refined the actual malice standard and extended its application to persons other than public officials. In *Curtis Publ. Co. v. Butts,* 388 U.S. 130 (1967), the actual malice standard was extended beyond public officials to "public figures." Public figures include individuals who, by their accomplishments or positions in life, give the public a legitimate interest in their affairs. They include politicians, sports figures, mass-media personalities, and other celebrities, but not necessarily family members of celebrities. Private individuals can become "limited purpose public figures," when they actively, voluntarily, or willfully seek the public eye, and are therefore required to meet the actual malice standard. See *Atlanta Journal-Constitution v. Jewell,* 251 Ga. App. 808 (2001), where a security guard who granted interviews following the bombing at the 2000 Olympic games injected himself into public debate about park safety and was held to be a limited purposed public figure. Where a person has no major role in society's affairs and has not voluntarily joined in a public debate with an intention to influence its outcome, she is much less likely to be deemed a "public figure" for libel purposes. *Time, Inc., v. Firestone* 424 U.S. 448 (1976).

States may, and most do, impose a much lower standard of fault, such as negligence, in a defamation claim brought by a private person. *Gertz v. Robert Welch, Inc.,* 418 U.S. 323 (1974). Statements made about private parties in reporting matters of public concern, however, are open to defamation suits only if the author conducted his fact finding in a "grossly irresponsible" matter, and no presumed or punitive damages are allowed without actual malice. Where a public official is defamed as to private aspects of his or her life, the official will be treated as a private person. *Crane v. The Arizona Republic,* 972 F.2d 1511 (1992). Gossip columnists take heed: Celebrity breakups are not matters of public concern, at least according to several New York courts. *Huggins v. Daily News, et al.,* 262 A.D. 2d 1087 (N.Y. App. 1st Dept 1999); *Krauss v. Globe International,* 251 A.D. 2d 191 (N.Y. App. 1st Dept 1998).

OTHER LIMITS TO LIABILITY

Judicial restraints on the publication of a work are presumptively unconstitutional. Illegal or not, no work of authorship should be judicially silenced prior to publication, according to the Supreme Court. Only exceptional circumstances justify a prior restraint on expression—in wartime, for instance, publication of the number, location, or sailing dates of troops might be legally prohibited. Therefore, although a work might cause damage to others and liability to its author, the courts will generally not prohibit it from being published and read.

In many states, damages for defamation against the news media are limited if a retraction of the defamatory statement is made or if the plaintiff fails to demand a retraction before suing. The relevant state laws generally hold that the retraction must be a complete and unequivocal attempt to repair the injury to reputation that has taken place. The retraction should be given the same prominence and publicity as the defamation and come as soon after the defamation as possible. Even where there is no statute addressing it, a retraction can help show that the plaintiff suffered less damage or that there was an absence of the malice necessary for punitive damages.

Only living people may sue for defamation because the dead cannot suffer personally from injury to their reputations. *Gugliuzza v. KCMC, Inc.,* 606 So. 2d 790 (1992). Some states make defamation of the dead a crime, but these statutes do not give surviving relatives a right to sue.

INVASION OF PRIVACY

While the truth of an offending statement is a defense to defamation actions, an author might nevertheless be liable for making an accurate statement under the doctrine of invasion of privacy. The right to privacy is defined as the right to be free from unwanted and unnecessary publicity or interference that could injure one's personal feelings or present a person in a false light. Recognized in varying forms by almost every state, invasion of privacy claims generally protect against four distinct types of injury:

- ☞ The appropriation of a person's name or likeness for advertising or commercial uses
- ☞ The disclosure to the public of embarrassing private facts
- ☞ The placing of a person in a false light before the public
- ☞ Intrusion into a person's seclusion or private life

Most states require that these invasions of privacy be "highly offensive to a reasonable person" to invoke liability. First Amendment concerns also limit the right of privacy, particularly if one's privacy right would interfere with the disclosure of a topic of legitimate public concern.

New York recognizes only the first of the privacy categories, also called invasion of the right of publicity. The New York statute provides:

> Any person whose name, portrait or picture is used within this state for advertising purposes or for the purposes of trade without . . . consent . . . may . . . sue and recover damages for any injuries sustained by reason of such use and if the defendant shall have knowingly used such person's name, portrait or picture in such manner as is forbidden or declared to be unlawful . . . the jury, in its discretion, may award [punitive] damages.

Most other states recognize similar rights, either by statute or in common law. The mere fact that by coincidence a name in a work of fiction is the same as a real person's name is not an infringement of the right of publicity. Magazines and newspapers may freely use names and photographs of people, famous or not, for newsworthy purposes and even for advertising the newsworthy qualities of the publication.

The public disclosure of embarrassing private facts is an invasion of privacy if the disclosure would be highly offensive to a reasonable person and is not of legitimate concern to the public. Courts use a liberal definition of newsworthiness or legitimate public interest. *Virgil v. Time, Inc.*, 527 F.2d 1122, *cert. denied*, 96 S. Ct. 2215 (1975). For example, courts have ruled that a statement that a person committed a crime is newsworthy, even if the statement is later shown to be false and defamatory. Where the disclosure is about a public figure, it also is less likely to be deemed an invasion of privacy, meaning again that unauthorized biographers can breathe easier.

Placing a person in a false light before the public is similar to defamation (except that a false light publication could be laudatory instead of defamatory). "False light" cases often involve a personality or event of public interest that is presented to the public in a fictionalized version. If substantially true, the account is protected by the First Amendment. If the statement is false, the actual malice standard applies: "[T]he constitutional protections for speech and press preclude the application of [state law] to redress false reports of matters of public interest in the absence of proof that the defendant published the report with knowledge of its falsity or in reckless disregard of the truth." *Time, Inc. v. Hill*, 385 U.S. 374 (1968).

The final category of invasion of privacy involves intrusion into another's seclusion or private life. "The First Amendment has never been construed to accord newsmen immunity from torts or crimes committed during the course of newsgathering." *Dietemann v. Time, Inc.*, 449 F.2d 245 (1971). The intrusion might be physical, such as trespass into someone's home, but it often relates to unauthorized electronic access or surveillance. Publication of the information obtained is not required to make a case for intrusion. On the other hand, the fact that it was obtained through intrusion is irrelevant to the newsworthiness of the information retrieved. "[W]here the claim is that private information concerning the plaintiff has been published, the question of whether that information is genuinely private or is of public interest should not turn on the manner in which it has been obtained." *Pearson v. Dodd*, 410 F.2d 701, 705, *cert. denied*, 395 U.S. 947 (1969). To make matters more complicated, damages for the intrusion itself might be larger because of subsequent publication of the information obtained.

The complexity of the doctrines relating to invasion of privacy makes resorting to a lawyer absolutely necessary if you anticipate difficulties. Your lawyer might advise obtaining a release from invasion of privacy claims from people who might bring suit.

AVOIDING DEFAMATION AND INVASION
OF PRIVACY CLAIMS

As explained in more detail in chapter 11, virtually all book publishers, and a fair number of periodical publishers, require their authors to indemnify them for all costs associated with defending defamation and privacy claims based on the content of the authors' work. If an aggrieved party sues your publisher, whether or not the claim is valid, you could be responsible for the publisher's costs, including its attorneys' fees. Most publishers have media liability insurance that should cover these costs, but these policies typically have very large—up to six figures—deductibles. If you have not been diligent enough, your publisher might require you to cover its out-of-pocket costs or at least will charge them against your work's earnings.

To protect yourself against libel claims, you need to document your fact-finding thoroughly and methodically to show you have not made a false statement about anyone. Be careful throughout the publication process—while researching, writing, working through the editing process, fact-checking, even approving jacket copy. You should be able to cite the specific source of the statements of fact in your manuscript. Keep copies of all documents you use, including printouts of online material, and make sure they clearly show their sources and identity. If a source has provided a confidential document, clearly indicate the conditions for its publication, if any, on all copies. Mark your notes and tapes to indicate the identity of their sources or interview subjects and the date, time, and place of the interview or research. When taking notes, identify the words that are direct quotes. Tape recordings or even handwritten contemporaneous notes carry more weight than word-processed versions.

When conducting an interview, consider tape-recording it (with the subject's permission, of course). Always begin each segment of a taped interview with a statement identifying the date, time, and subject. Within your time limits, you should always make the best possible effort to confirm sensitive statements. Consider the reliability of your sources, and try to evaluate whether your subject constitutes a public figure or the matter is newsworthy. In his book *Kirsch's Handbook of Publishing Law,* intellectual property attorney Jonathan Kirsch advises that while preparing your manuscript, you should cross-reference the manuscript to the source materials as much as possible. Word-processing programs allow you to easily create footnotes as you write and to create two versions of your work—one with and one without the footnotes. The version with footnotes will be much easier to fact-check and legally vet (that is, review).

If you are ever in doubt about your exposure to defamation or any other liability, consult an experienced publishing attorney. The larger publishers have attorneys on staff that can review your manuscript for risky content. If the publisher does not supply a legal vetting, and your work contains statements that could be considered defamatory, you should consult your own publishing lawyer. Defamation and privacy law, like all laws, are subject to constant change without warning, and only an attorney who knows the current law can vet a manuscript effectively. All the steps described previously will make the vetting job easier and faster, and therefore much less expensive.

PROTECTING CONFIDENTIAL SOURCES

Journalists need people to reveal information to them in order to investigate crimes and government activity. During the era of civil unrest caused by U.S. participation in the Vietnam War, it was not uncommon for prosecutors to subpoena journalists' notes or files and for government agents to make unannounced newsroom searches. Under those circumstances, sources would understandably fear revealing information to the media. Under the Privacy Protection Act of 1980, law enforcement officers seeking information about crime from the media must give reporters advance notice and an opportunity to contest a subpoena in court. Beyond the intangible loss to a journalist's ability to investigate, other harm can come from revealing the identity of a confidential source. A recent case illustrates the harm caused to journalists if they reveal the identity of a source when the source asks for confidentiality. In *Cohen v. Cowles Media,* 501 U.S. 663

(1991), the Supreme Court upheld a breach of contract claim against reporters who voluntarily revealed a confidential source's identity. The Court observed that the law of contracts applies just as much to confidentiality agreements with news sources as to other contracts because it does not interfere with the newsgathering process.

Occasionally, courts presiding over criminal cases have ordered journalists to disclose the sources of relevant information. Reporters have gone to jail, charged with contempt of court, for refusing to comply. Courts and legislatures have recognized the importance of allowing a reporter to keep his sources confidential because if reporters can regularly be compelled to reveal their sources, people will be less likely to talk to journalists. Many states have enacted so-called press shield laws giving journalists the right to refuse to disclose identities of confidential sources. Under both the First Amendment and state press shield laws, reporters can often, but not always, refuse demands by the government that they reveal their sources and notes.

This privilege, as are most others, is not absolute. Under many states' laws, journalists might in some circumstances be ordered to disclose this information. Some interests, predominantly a criminal defendant's right to a fair trial, can justify a court order of disclosure. The general rule is that a journalist cannot be forced to reveal sources of information or unpublished information unless the government can show that the reporter probably has information relevant to the commission of an unlawful act; the prosecution or defense has tried to get the information elsewhere; and the prosecution or defense needs the information to prepare its case.

OTHER CAUSES OF ACTIONS

Disgruntled subjects of media scrutiny have begun to rely on what media lawyers call "trash torts," such as trespass claims, to get around First Amendment accommodations for the press. Trespass is similar to intrusion and it has seen some success in the courts, which have proved unwilling to give journalists special treatment under trespass laws. In one New York case, a reporter went onto a person's property with criminal investigators who had a warrant to search the premises. The plaintiff objected to the reporter coming onto the property, and a court upheld his subsequent trespass suit against the reporter. Some courts award the plaintiff damages flowing from both the trespass itself and the resulting publication. Other courts, including those of New York, have allowed damages only for the trespass itself.

CENSORSHIP

The First Amendment limits the government's right to censor expression by punishing or restraining its dissemination. The only expression that may be censored absolutely is obscenity and speech that creates "a clear and present danger that it will bring about the substantive evils that Congress [or the state] has a right to prevent." *Schenck v. United States,* 249 U.S. 47 (1919). Objectionable material that does not fall into either category may, however, lawfully be kept from minors.

In 1971, the Supreme Court refused to issue a pre-publication injunction against publication of the Pentagon Papers. A classified report on U.S. policy in Vietnam came into the possession of Daniel Ellsberg, a former federal official, who turned them over to the press. The *New York Times* and the *Washington Post* jointly began publishing parts of the report. The Nixon administration moved to enjoin publication, but in what is considered a watershed victory for freedom of the press, the Supreme Court ruled six to three against the government. It held that any prior restraint on publication is heavily presumed to be unconstitutional, and that the government must prove that the restraint is justified. In this case, the government failed to prove its claim of harm to national security. *New York Times v. United States,* 403 U.S. 713 (1971).

CENSORSHIP OF OBSCENITY

Material containing sexual content has been persecuted since Victorian times. Prior to 1973, the test for banning erotic expression, as developed in Britain and substantially followed in the United States, was whether the material "tended . . . to deprave and corrupt those whose minds are open to such immoral influences." In the United States, this led to bans on such literary works as Giovanni Boccaccio's *Decameron,* John Cleland's *Fanny Hill,* Gustave Flaubert's *November,* Henry Miller's *Tropic of Cancer,* James Joyce's *Ulysses,* D. H. Lawrence's *Lady Chatterley's*

Lover, Eugene O'Neill's *Strange Interlude,* and Edmund Wilson's *Memoirs of Hecate County.* The law applied equally to works of clear literary merit and to hard-core pornography. Obscenity prosecutions became a common way to prevent people from having access to sexually explicit and violent works. Prosecution of authors, publishers, and distributors, as well as seizures of books by the post office, customs, and the police was commonplace until the mid-twentieth century.

The tide in favor of free expression began to turn in 1934, when the Second Circuit Court of Appeals held that Joyce's *Ulysses* was not obscene and could freely pass through U.S. customs. *United States v. One Book Entitled Ulysses,* 72 F.2d 705 (2d Cir. 1934). The court ruled that the use of "dirty words" in "a sincere and honest book" did not make the book as a whole "dirty." This distinction became a precursor to the most important part of the current legal definition of obscenity.

In 1957, the Supreme Court ruled that obscenity does not warrant the protection of the First Amendment, so obscenity prohibitions are constitutional. In *Roth v. United States,* 354 U.S. 476 (1957), it was decided that "implicit in the history of the First Amendment is the rejection of obscenity as utterly without social importance." Not until 1973, however, did the Court formulate a test for assessing whether a particular work is obscene. In *Miller v. California,* 413 U.S. 15, 34 (1973), the Supreme Court granted states and localities autonomous, though limited, authority to address obscenity in their communities. In assessing material, a jury must determine:

> (a) whether "the average person, applying contemporary community standards" would find that the work, taken as a whole, appeals to the prurient interest; (b) whether the work depicts or describes, in a patently offensive way, sexual conduct specifically defined by the applicable state law; and (c) whether the work, taken as a whole, lacks serious literary, artistic, political, or scientific value.

If the answer to all three questions is "yes," the work is obscene, and local authorities may remove it from circulation and prosecute the author, publisher, even the distributor. To what extent does this definition endanger sexually oriented works that might appeal only to a small minority of readers? Most pornographic work is not legally obscene because the Court subsequently has clarified that "contemporary community standards" may not be employed to assess a work's literary, artistic, political or scientific merit. That particular prong of the definition must be determined by a national "reasonable person" standard. Thus, if a work is intended to convey "serious literary, artistic, political or scientific value" to any material degree, it cannot be deemed obscene. Most pornography is considered to convey such value.

Henry Miller eloquently explained why this is so in his essay "Defense of the Freedom to Read," which he wrote in response to Sweden's attempt sought to suppress his book *Sexus:* "But it is not something evil, not something poisonous, which this book *Sexus* offers. . . . It is a dose of life which I administered to myself first, and which I not only survived but thrived on. Certainly I would not recommend it to infants, but then neither would I offer a child a bottle of *aqua vitae.* I can only say one thing for it unblushingly—compared to the atom bomb, it is full of life-giving qualities."

The First Amendment also offers procedural safeguards to the writer whose work is challenged as obscene. Law enforcement officials may not seize the work simply because they think it is obscene. Rather, they must serve notice of a judicial hearing to make the determination. A court must rule based on all relevant evidence. Only after observance of these procedural requirements may the would-be censors, if victorious, seize the work.

Obscenity is a complex legal area. If you fear that an obscenity issue could arise with your work, or you are facing such an issue, consult a lawyer, especially because most publishing contracts require the author to warrant to the publisher that the work is not obscene and to pay the publisher's costs if that promise is breached.

SCHOOL AND LIBRARY CENSORSHIP

The control of school boards over such matters as curriculum, textbooks, and library books can have a significant effect on students' access to books and the ideas contained in them. Most states give school boards the authority to dictate curricula, course books, and library holdings free from outside interference, but even those decisions have First Amendment limitations, especially regarding removal of books from school libraries. Book censorship in the schools expanded in the mid-1980s and throughout the 1990s. *The Color Purple* by

Pulitzer Prize winner Alice Walker was banned in Souderton, Pennsylvania after critics called the work "smut," "pornography," and "trash." Walker keeps good company with such authors as Toni Morrison, J. D. Salinger, James Baldwin, Mark Twain, and others whose books have been banned in public schools within the past few years. In censorship campaigns, the vast majority of which occur on the local level and which seldom receive attention beyond the communities in which they take place, targets range from works that some view as pornographic to works that others see as politically insensitive. For example, *The Autobiography of Miss Jane Pittman,* by Ernest Gaines, was removed from a seventh-grade class because it contained "slurs."

Censorship campaigns in the public schools and school libraries usually rely on book banning and removal to inhibit access to works found objectionable by parents, advocacy groups, school boards and community leaders. Their campaigns have led schools to refuse to purchase certain books, remove existing books from libraries, place them in restricted or infrequently used areas, and remove them from a teacher's curriculum. By far the majority of censorship attempts occur in response to the selection or placement of books in public school libraries.

In 1982, the Supreme Court analyzed the constitutionality of book removal from school libraries and curricula in *Board of Education, Island Trees School District v. Pico,* 457 U.S. 853 (1982). In this case, the school district's board of education removed nine books from school library shelves in response to a list of "questionable" books the board received from a conservative pro-censorship group named PONYU (Parents of New York United). Kurt Vonnegut's *Slaughterhouse-Five* and Richard Wright's *Black Boy* were two of the nine books the group listed; both were characterized as "anti-American, anti-Christian, anti-Semitic and just plain filthy."

The Supreme Court sought to find a balance between the First Amendment right of students to read freely and the right of school authorities to exercise discretion over student access to books within the public educational system. Although both groups have constitutional rights, these rights are not absolute, and clarification was needed in this area of law. The Court did not decide directly that the board of education's actions were unconstitutional, but it set a standard for

subsequent book removal issues. It held that a school board may maintain wide authority concerning removal of books, but that it may not
institute such actions because the works contain "partisan or political
views [the board] did not share." The decision was premised upon the
understanding of a student's right to access information when engaged
in "voluntary inquiry," coupled with the recognition of a library's role
as a place of inquiry essential to the student's understanding and mat-
uration. The Court distinguished an educator's selection of books for
the curriculum and a school administration's banning of certain books
in the library system. The Court gave greater discretion to school
boards in the matter of selection of books for the curriculum. This distinction was based on the view that educators—that is, the board—
should have the right to select what will be taught in their classes, as
long as they do not ban works based on partisan or political views.

Controversies over censorship continue in part because of the
ambiguity of the Court's opinion. The Court did not formulate guidelines articulating how school authorities may choose books for
libraries. In addition, the Court found that school authorities will have
acted within constitutional limits if books are removed because they
are deemed vulgar or of questionable "educational suitability." These
two exemptions carry great ambiguity and, depending on interpretation, can either broaden or narrow students' rights. In cases following
the *Island Trees* decision, lower courts gave greater protection to students' rights. In 1989, a California appellate court found book removal
to be an invalid use of a school board's authority in *Wexner v. Anderson
Union High School District Board of Trustees,* 209 Cal. App. 3d 1438
(1989). That court found that "[i]f school boards are granted such
authority, every library book bears the imprimatur of the present
board." When compared with students' First Amendment rights in
other areas (such as the curriculum), school libraries are afforded the
highest level of protection.

In a 1976 case, the Board of Education in Strongsville, Ohio,
refused to approve Joseph Heller's *Catch-22* and Kurt Vonnegut's *God
Bless You, Mr. Rosewater* as either textbooks or high-school library
books, despite favorable faculty recommendations. The board also
ordered *Catch-22* and Vonnegut's *Cat's Cradle* removed from the
library. The Sixth Circuit Court of Appeals decided that the board's

decisions not to use *Catch-22* and *God Bless You, Mr. Rosewater* as text-books was proper, but that the removal of library books curtailed free-dom of speech and thought, particularly since the board members apparently found the books personally distasteful. "Neither the State of Ohio nor the Strongsville School Board was under any federal consti-tutional compulsion to provide a library for the Strongsville High School or to choose any particular books. Once having created such a privilege for the benefit of its students, however, neither body could place conditions on the use of the library which were related solely to the social or political tastes of school board members." *Minarcini v. Strongsville City School District,* 541 F.2d 577, 582 (6th Cir. 1976).

School systems maintain formal procedures for the approval of books for libraries and curricula. Those who want to censor books in schools have learned these procedures and used them to their advan-tage. Opponents of censorship can obtain copies of this information through Government in the Sunshine and Freedom of Information Act requests (see chapter 9 for information on how to do this), in order to learn the administrators' policies and to determine whether they are following proper procedures in the particular case at hand. There is persuasive power in community involvement in the issue of censorship. Community views of what is offensive and what is appro-priate are central to the debate and directly determine outcomes, because, although the *Miller* obscenity decision discusses the use of juries to determine the constitutionality of a censorship attempt, many of these cases never reach a courtroom. In fact, the active participation of writers and anti-censorship groups in schools' administrative pro-ceedings has helped to defeat many attempts to censor what young people may read.

CHAPTER 9

THE FREEDOM OF

INFORMATION ACT

Research is, of course, the corner-
stone of most kinds of writing, including fiction. Under the federal
Government in the Sunshine Act and the Freedom of Information Act
(FOIA), writers can access a virtual treasure trove of information in the
possession of the federal government. The Sunshine Act requires that
most federal proceedings be accessible to the public. FOIA requires the
speedy disclosure of federal agencies' documents upon request.
Happily for researchers, every state has its own version of these laws.
For access to all the states' current open meetings and freedom of
information laws, visit the excellent Web site of the Reporters
Committee for Freedom of the Press *(www.rcfp.org)*.

FOIA applies to all federal agencies, including all executive-branch
departments (for example, the Office of Management and Budget),
military departments, government corporations (for example, the U.S.
Postal Service), government-controlled corporations like Amtrak, and
other establishments in the executive branch of the government,
including the Executive Office of the President, as well as to all independent regulatory agencies, such as the Federal Communications
Commission. Some entities are exempt from FOIA's requirements—
Congress, the federal courts, and the President's advisors. The

Government in the Sunshine Act gives anyone the right to attend meetings of the governing boards of dozens of federal agencies. A corollary law, the Federal Advisory Committee Act, allows people to attend federal advisory committee meetings. Criminal proceedings involving adults, and court records, are also generally open to the public unless a defendant's right to a fair trial is threatened by open access or another compelling interest favors a closed proceeding. Juvenile court proceedings and records are generally closed to the public.

The policy reasons behind passage of FOIA and the Sunshine Act were to ensure an informed citizenry in order to maintain a functioning democracy, and both were considered necessary as a check against corruption and as a way of holding the government accountable to the governed. As one court put it: "the basic purpose is to protect people's right to obtain information about their government, to know what their government is doing and to obtain information about government activities and policies and to remedy the mischief of arbitrary and self-serving withholding by agencies which are not directly responsible to the people." *Westinghouse Elec. Corp. v. Schlesinger,* 542 F.2d 1190 (1976). The amount of information that we may access from federal agencies is staggering. Borderline cases are usually adjudicated in favor of disclosure, and the laws stand as great tributes to the openness of our society. As another court observed, "Freedom of information is now the rule and secrecy is the exception." *Wellford v. Hardin,* 315 F. Supp. 768 (1970).

Congress intended for FOIA to open the door for disclosure of files relating to the structure, operation, and decision-making procedure of the various governmental agencies, including final opinions and orders, information and statistics compiled, indices, certain staff manuals and instructions, statements of policy, and interpretations thereof. Authors can use agency records to verify other sources, identify new leads or sources, and form new story ideas. Any member of the public who requests and "reasonably describes" the documents he or she seeks is entitled to them. The fact that the information requested has special importance for the person requesting it is irrelevant to the disclosure requirements, although it might affect the fees charged. In fact, the identity of the person requesting the information need not be revealed to the agency. The statute requires the agencies to respond to FOIA requests within ten days, and while many do, others have backlogs and could take much longer to respond. Denials of disclosure may be appealed to a specified official of the agency and then to a federal court. Each agency must publish its appeals process. Should a court reverse an agency's denial of a disclosure request, the government must pay the requester's attorneys' fees.

HOW TO MAKE A REQUEST

You can access the request and appeal procedures and contact officials for FOIA requests for every federal agency at its Web site, in the Federal Register (available online and at reference libraries), or by phoning the FOIA or public affairs department of the agency itself. If you are not sure which agency has the records you are seeking, those same sources or your local representative's office can help. Some agencies might accept an oral request, but most require that disclosure requests be made in writing. To obtain access to particular records, an individual must submit a written request that "reasonably describes" the records sought. Beyond that, each agency has its own, often highly detailed, procedures. You should address your request to a particular FOIA officer, in a specially marked envelope, and send it to a specific location. In most cases, describe what you are looking for as specifically as possible. You do not need to explain the reasons for your request, but doing so might help the agency find responsive documents more quickly. Depending on the scope and complexity of your request, you might need to spend substantial time and effort to obtain the desired documents. The following sample is merely instructive. Be sure to obtain specific instructions from the agency involved.

SAMPLE REQUEST FOR DISCLOSURE OF INFORMATION

Date:

FBI Headquarters [specify FOIA officer and address]

To: FBI Field Office [specify FOIA officer and address]

This is a noncommercial request under the Freedom of Information Act, 5 U.S.C. Sec. 552. I have attached a sheet setting forth my application for a waiver of any fees in excess of those that are provided free because I am a representative of the news media affiliated with [name organization if you wish].

I request a complete and thorough search of all filing systems and locations for all records maintained by your agency pertaining to and/or captioned:

[name of subject]

_____

_____

_____

including, without limitation, files and documents captioned, or whose captions include:

[describe records desired and/or insert full and formal name]

_____

_____

_____

This request specifically includes where appropriate "main files" and "see references," including but not limited to numbered and lettered subfiles and control files. I also request a search of the Electronic Surveillance (ELSUR) Index, or any similar technique for locating records of electronic surveillance and COINTELPRO Index. I request that all records be produced with administrative pages. I wish to be sent copies of "see reference" cards, abstracts, search slips, including search slips used to process this request, file covers, multiple copies of the same documents if they appear in a file, tapes of any electronic surveillance, photographs, and logs of physical surveillance (FISUR). Please place missing documents on "special locate" status.

I wish to make it clear that I want all records in your office "identifiable with my request," even though reports on those records have been sent to headquarters and even thoughthere may be duplication between the two sets of files. I do not want only "interim" documents. I want all documents as they appear in the "main" files and "see references" of all units of your agency.

If my request for disclosure of any of these documents is denied in whole or in part, please specify which exemption(s) is (are) claimed for each passage or whole document denied. Give the number of pages in each document and the total number of pages pertaining to this request and the dates of documents withheld. I request that excised materials be "blacked out" rather than "whited out" or cut out and that the remaining nonexempt portions of documents be released as provided under the Freedom of Information Act.

Please send a memo (with a copy or copies to me) to the appropriate unit(s) in your office to assure that no records related to this request are destroyed. Please advise of any destruction of records and include the date of and authority for such destruction. As I expect to appeal any denials, please specify the office and address to which an appeal should be directed.

I can be reached at the phone number listed below. Please call rather than write if there are any questions or if you need additional information from me. I expect a response to this request within ten (10) working days, as provided in the Freedom of Information Act.

Sincerely,

(Signed) _____

Name: (print or type) _____

Address: _____

Telephone: _____ Social Security number: [optional] _____

[for access to a person's files]

Date of Birth: _____

Place of Birth: _____

[for access to an organization's files]

Date of founding: _____

Place of founding: _____

Address of organization _____

To obtain documents pertaining to an individual, insert that individual's full name in the first blank space and include all other names used by that individual in the second blank space. To obtain documents about an organization, state the full name of the organization and any other name used to describe the organization. To obtain files about a specific subject or event, give the full name of the subject or event, including any relevant dates, locations, news coverage or other helpful identifying data. Be sure to keep a copy of any request letter you send, address it correctly, and clearly mark the envelope: "Attention: Freedom of Information/Privacy Act Unit." For FBI requests, you must send at least two letters—one to FBI headquarters, the other to each relevant field office. For the Immigration and Naturalization Service, send a request to each district office in the vicinity of the individual, organization, subject matter, or event in question. To save time and effort, always contact the agency involved and find out the specific procedures it mandates.

Once a request is properly filed, the government has an obligation to make records "promptly available" to the requesting party, whether or not he is a U.S. citizen. The agency has a statutory obligation to notify the writer within ten days that the request has been received and is being processed or that some required procedure was not followed. The exact amount of time that an agency may take to disclose requested documents varies from case to case. Whatever the proper period of time in a particular case, an agency may obtain an extension in unusual circumstances where it makes a good faith, diligent effort to comply. It is a good idea to contact the agency from time to time to monitor the progress of your request.

FEES

Agencies have discretion to charge the reasonable fees for searching, reviewing, and copying files. All agencies have fee schedules for producing documents under FOIA. Representatives of the news media, including book authors, pay only for duplication costs. Even so, fees can fluctuate wildly and in many cases, especially those involving computer searches by the agency, can be prohibitive. It is a good idea to request a fee schedule, to let the agency know in your request letter how much you are willing to spend, and to request an estimate of the costs to satisfy your request. If costs are too high, you might be able to obtain an exemption or reduction. Check the agency's Web site for information on how to go about doing so.

EXCEPTIONS TO THE DISCLOSURE REQUIREMENT

Legitimate government interests, such as national security, the right to privacy, and the requirements of law enforcement agencies to maintain secrecy in investigating crimes, override the strong disclosure policy of FOIA. In these cases, the agency involved might choose to disclose the information, but it cannot be compelled to do so. Neither the president himself, nor his staff, nor any of nine exempted categories of information, including information in the possession of most government-funded projects, are subject to FOIA.

CASE STUDY—*THE NATION MAGAZINE* *V. DEPARTMENT OF STATE*

Just prior to the presidential election of 1992, author Max Holland, a contributing editor to *The Nation,* attempted to obtain information concerning independent candidate H. Ross Perot from the Central Intelligence Agency (CIA) and other federal government sources. *The Nation* hoped to "contribute to the ongoing public debate about [Perot's] qualifications to become President of the United States" and noted that a similar request for information about candidate Bill Clinton, which had been filed after Holland's requests, had been expedited. In response to Holland's FOIA request, the CIA responded with a letter to the effect that, on privacy grounds, he must first obtain the formal, written consent of Mr. Perot. Holland replied that he was unable to obtain consent and was therefore requesting all the documents that were not protected by Perot's privacy right, as well as suggesting that his privacy right should be circumscribed due to Perot's national prominence. When he received no response, he hand-delivered a request for expedited processing to the CIA, claiming an urgent need for the documents on the grounds that the election was less than a month away. In denying his request, the CIA stated "that it granted requests for expedition only in the rare instances where health and humanitarian considerations create circumstances of exceptional urgency and extraordinary need and that his request did not satisfy those criteria." The other government sources involved, including the Department of Defense, the FBI, and the Department of State, also denied Holland's requests either explicitly on privacy grounds, or implicitly through silence.

Holland and *The Nation* sued the federal government for violation of the Freedom of Information Act, seeking a court order that would compel the government to disclose the requested documents. The court denied the motion because the plaintiffs had failed to show a "substantial likelihood of success on the merits" of their claim. The court found that as long as the agencies and departments were processing the requests with due diligence, even though they had exceeded the time periods outlined in FOIA, those periods were "not mandatory but directory" if the government could establish "exceptional circumstances," unless the party requesting documents could show "exceptional need or urgency." The defendants established to the satisfaction of the court that they were "deluged with FOIA requests" and the plaintiffs failed to show the requisite urgency. *The Nation v. Department of State,* 895 F. Supp. 68 (D.D.C. 1992).

A general request for documents, with the dual purposes of selling magazines and adding to the political debate, was held to be of questionable urgency. The court noted that if the information requested involved a deportation proceeding, a murder trial, or other felony criminal proceeding, the requisite urgency might have been shown. The court further noted that it had refused to expedite a FOIA request concerning "George Bush and his alleged connection to the Kennedy assassination even though the 1988 Presidential election was imminent." Responding to the plaintiffs' argument that the request for documents relating to Perot should be expedited because a similar request for documents about Bill Clinton was expedited, the court rejoined that no rule of administrative law requires an agency to extend erroneous treatment of one party to other parties, "thereby turning an isolated error into a uniform misapplication of the law." *Id.,* quoting *Sacred Heart Medical Center v. Sullivan,* 958 F.2d 537, 550 (3d Cir. 1992).

The court also pointed out that while the requests for the Clinton documents were expedited, the government had admitted its wrong-doing, curtailed the action mid-stream, and now attested to the fact that no documents had ever actually been released. The Clinton requests were now returned to their "proper places in the queue." Had the Clinton documents been released, the court said it would have required the Perot documents to be released as well.

Finally, the court noted that as it was deciding on a temporary restraining order it was obliged to balance the interests involved. While it recognized the public interest in knowing more about Perot, that interest was outweighed by the fact that at least some of the requested documents were protected by Perot's right to privacy, that the government had limited resources, and that the public interest would not be served by setting "an unworkable precedent [that] would severely jeopardize the . . . orderly, fair, and efficient adminis-tration of the FOIA." *The Nation v. Department of State,* 895 F. Supp. 68 (D.D.C. 1992).

CHAPTER 10

CONTRACTS:

AN INTRODUCTION

A *contract* is an agreement creating legally enforceable obligations between two or more parties. The author's business relationships with publishers, producers, and agents are all based on contracts. A contract provides the legal framework within which the rights and obligations of the author and the other party are specified. While verbal agreements are theoretically valid, the safer approach is to use written contracts. This chapter generally explains the law relating to contracts so that the subsequent chapters dealing with publishing and agency agreements can be more helpful. An excellent source of practical information about contracts is *Business and Legal Forms for Authors and Self-Publishers* by Tad Crawford (Allworth Press).

OFFER AND ACCEPTANCE

An *offer* invites entry into a contract. It is a promise that can be accepted by a return promise or, less frequently, by performance based on the terms of the offer. If a publisher says to a writer, "I am willing to pay you $1,000 for first North American serial rights in your story, 'The

Doves of Peace,'" an offer has been made. The publisher has promised to purchase in definite terms, which can be accepted by the author's return promise to sell the story on those terms. If the publisher says, "This story would be a gem in my upcoming anthology," or "This story should sell for a fortune," or "I'm going to keep this story for a few weeks," it has not made an offer. If the publisher says, "You write this story, and we'll agree later about the price," or "You write this story and I'll pay you as I see fit," no offer has been made because an essential term—the price—has been omitted. If the publisher says, "Write this article, and I will pay you $1,000 if I'm satisfied," it has made a valid offer. Beware of accepting such an offer, however, because as a rule, courts allow a dissatisfied commissioning party to reject a work, even if a reasonable person would have been satisfied. In other words, you would be working on speculation, an arrangement that you should always avoid.

Usually, the person making an offer can revoke it at any time before it is accepted. Another way to terminate an offer is by limiting the time for acceptance—"I will purchase your story for $1,000 if you will sell it to me within the next ten days." The offer would end if not accepted at the end of ten days. If no time limit is set, the assumption is made that the offer ends after a reasonable amount of time has passed. An offer is also terminated by a counteroffer. For example, if the publisher offers $1,000 for a story and the writer counters for $1,250, the original offer of $1,000 is no longer effective.

Acceptance is accomplished by agreeing to the offer. If the publisher offers to pay $1,000 to have a story written, the writer can accept by stating: "I agree to write this story for $1,000." The end result of the process of offer and acceptance is a meeting of the minds, a mutual understanding of the parties' intentions as manifested in the contract (written or verbal). In interpreting contracts about which the parties later disagree, courts must seek to determine the parties' intentions at the time of contracting. The language of the contract is the primary guide used. Only if the words of the contract do not clarify its meaning will a court examine industry custom, prior dealings between the parties, and the conduct of the parties with respect to the particular contract. Once either party has completed performance under an ambiguous contract, the court will try to resolve the ambiguities using a standard of reasonableness. For example, if an author prepares an article that a magazine publishes, the author should be paid reasonable compensation, even if no price was agreed upon. On the other hand, a publishing contract that has not been fully performed might be held unenforceable if it fails to specify royalty rates.

CONSIDERATION

To be valid, every contract requires the exchange of consideration, which is defined as the giving of something of value by each party to the other. The consideration each party to a contract receives is what induces entry into the contract. When the publisher promises to pay $1,000 for a story that the writer promises to write, each party has received consideration from the other in the form of a promise. The consideration must have been bargained for and agreed at the time of entering into the contract. If a publisher says, "Your story is so good that I'm going to pay you an extra $500, even though I don't have to," the publisher is not obligated to pay. The writer has already written the story and been paid in full, so the promise to pay an additional $500 is not supported by consideration. The one situation in which consideration is not required occurs when a person relies on a promise in such a way that the promise must be enforced to avoid injustice. If a patron makes a promise, such as offering money as a gift for the writer to buy a computer, and should reasonably know that the writer will rely upon it, he cannot refuse to pay the money after the writer has in fact relied on the promise by replacing her typewriter with a computer. This concept is known as "detrimental reliance."

COMPETENCY OF THE PARTIES AND LEGALITY OF PURPOSE

The law will not enforce a contract if the parties are not competent. The rationale is that there can be no meeting of the minds or mutual understanding in such a situation. Thus, a contract entered into by a person of unsound mind or a minor is generally not enforceable by the other party. A contract made for a purpose that is illegal or against public policy is void.

WRITTEN AND ORAL CONTRACTS

Most types of contracts need not be written to be enforceable, but it is always safer to get your agreements in writing. The terms of the contract could come into dispute after you have begun performance. Reliance on both parties' memories to provide the terms of the agreement can leave much to be desired, especially if no witnesses were present and the parties disagree about what was agreed. A written contract need not be a formal document. An exchange of letters constituting an offer and its acceptance creates a binding contract. Often one party proffers a signed letter agreement, and the other party completes the contract by also signing at the bottom of the letter beneath the words CONSENTED AND AGREED TO. A check can create or be evidence of a contract—for example, a check from a magazine to a writer stating: "This check for $1,000 is accepted as payment in full for first North American serial rights to publish the story 'Doves of Peace.'" If the check conflicts with a prior written or oral agreement, return it to the publisher so that the terms on the check accurately reflect the prior understanding. Where both parties have not signed an agreement, a memorandum signed by the party against whom enforcement is sought can be found to evidence a valid contract. Where the parties show from their conduct that a binding contract exists, an enforceable agreement might be inferred. But when a contract is written, courts will not allow oral evidence to vary the terms of the writing (except in the rare cases where the written contract is procured by fraud or under mistake or is too indefinite to be understood without the additional oral statements). Nor will courts accept evidence of promises made before the contract was signed if the promises do not appear in the final written document.

The copyright law requires that any transfer of a copyright or an exclusive right of copyright must be evidenced in writing. Nonexclusive licenses, on the other hand, may be entered verbally. In addition, an author might agree to render services, as opposed to licensing literary rights. In New York, oral contracts for services are usually enforceable if the services can be performed within one year. If the services cannot be completed in one year, the agreement must be made in a writing containing all essential terms of the contract.

WARRANTIES

Caveat emptor—"let the buyer beware"—expressed the traditional attitude of the courts toward the purchasers of property. Unless agreed otherwise, most property is sold "as is." Warranties, however, are express or implied facts or promises upon which the purchaser of property, including the publisher of your book or article, may rely. Warranties can be created orally, even if the contract must be in writing. They can be created during negotiations, at the time of making the contract, or, in certain transactions not usually relevant to writers, after entry into the contract.

An express warranty is created when the writer asserts facts or promises relating to the character or ownership of the work, upon which the purchaser relies in licensing or purchasing the work. In most book publishing contracts, the author must expressly warrant to the publisher that the work does not infringe any copyright, violate any personal or property rights, or contain any defamatory or unlawful matter. If any of these warranties prove untrue, the author is obligated to pay the publisher for any losses it suffers as a result. Sales talk or opinions by an author as to the value or merit of the work will not create warranties. If, for example, an author speculates aloud that the work will earn a fortune over the next few years, a publisher cannot rely upon such an opinion, and no warranty is created.

An implied warranty comes into existence by operation of law, rather than express representations of the parties, based on the circumstances of the transaction or the relationship of the parties. In some sales there is an implied warranty that the seller has title or the right to convey title in the goods being sold. It has been held that no warranty of marketable title is implied in the sale of literary property, *Loew's Inc. v. Wolff*, 101 F. Supp. 981, but an express warranty to that effect appears in virtually every publishing contract.

ASSIGNMENTS OF CONTRACTS

Sometimes one party to a contract may substitute another person to assume the obligations or rewards of the contract. This is not true for contracts that are based upon the special skills of one party to the contract. Where one's personal ability is crucial to the contract—for example, in a publishing contract—the author may not delegate her contractual duty to another author. However, she may assign to another person her right to receive the payment due under the contract. A well-drafted contract will state the intentions of the parties as to the right to delegate duties or assign rights under the contract.

NONPERFORMANCE EXCUSED

There are a few situations in which the author's failure to perform her contractual obligations will be excused. The death of the author is not a breach of the contract, so the publisher could not recover damages from the author's estate. Similarly, because the author's work is personal, a disabling physical or mental illness must excuse performance, although the contract might expressly extend the author's time for performance in the event of ill health. Grounds other than the unique nature of the author's work might excuse the failure to perform. If the publisher waives performance or if both parties agree to rescind the contract, no performance is necessary. If the publisher somehow prevents the author from performing, performance is excused and the author has a case for breach of contract. Similarly, impossibility might excuse performance, as in the case of the interviewer who cannot conduct an interview because of the subject's death. Also, performance is excused if it would be illegal under a law passed after the contract was made.

REMEDIES FOR BREACH OF CONTRACT

Unless performance is excused, a party who fails to perform its obligations under a contract can be liable for the money damages suffered by the other. Before damages can be awarded, however, the other party must suffer an actual loss or detriment because of the breach. The measure of damages is generally equal to the reasonably foreseeable losses, including out-of-pocket costs and lost profits, actually caused by the breach. The injured party must usually take steps to minimize (or "mitigate") the damages. Some contracts specify damages in advance to avoid the necessity of having to prove them at trial. The courts will enforce these provisions, known as "liquidated damages" provisions, if actual damages would be difficult to establish and the amount specified is not unreasonable or punitive. Many book contracts contain liquidated damages provisions for the publisher's breach of the obligation to publish.

SUBSTANTIAL PERFORMANCE

Unless the contract specifies that strict compliance with performance obligations is required, courts will accept substantial performance as complete performance. For example, in a case in which an artist created stained glass windows in compliance with the agreed design, but less light came through the windows than the parties had apparently intended, the court held:

> Where an artist is directed to produce a work of art in accordance with an approved design, the details of which are left to the artist, and the artist executes his commission in a substantial and satisfactory way, the mere fact that, when completed, it lacks some element of utility desired by the buyer and not specifically contracted for, constitutes no breach of the artist's contract. *Wagner-Larscheid Co. v. Fairview Mausoleum Co.*, 190 Wis. 357, 362, 208 N.W. 241, 242.

A similar rule should apply to an author who, for example, writes an article or book from an agreed-upon outline. On the other hand, partial performance of one's contractual obligations will not lead to recovery of the full consideration specified in the contract. In most states, partial performance will not require payment of the value thereof, unless the partial performance substantially benefits the other party who accepts and retains those benefits. This rule would not apply, of course, if one party prevented the other from substantially performing. Where the performance obligations in a contract can be separated from each other, as where a number of payments are specified for a number of different articles, recovery might be allowed for the partial contract price given for each partial performance.

SPECIFIC PERFORMANCE

In rare situations, money damages will not adequately compensate for the loss caused by a breach of contract. In those rare cases, courts might order the breaching party to perform its contractual obligations. Involuntary servitude is of course illegal, so contracts to provide personal services cannot be enforced by specific performance. Therefore, the obligation to create a written work cannot be forced on an author. Nor can a publisher be forced to publish a particular work. On the other hand, a court could enjoin the breaching party from rendering the promised performance to another party. Therefore, if a famous author is hired to write a story, her failure to honor the contract might be difficult to value in dollars. If, however, the work she has prepared already exists, a court might order specific performance of the author's promise to license the copyright to the work.

STATUTES OF LIMITATION

Statutes of limitation set forth the time within which an injured party must bring suit to have the injury remedied. In contract cases, the limitations period runs from the time of the breach, and after it has expired, no lawsuit may be initiated. The limitations period for actions based on contracts varies from state to state. In New York it is six years, and in California it is four years (two years, if the contract is not in writing). Many states recognize a longer limitations period for written contracts than for oral or implied contracts. The limitations period may be changed in a contract, and in book publishing contracts they are frequently decreased for claims of royalty underpayment. If you are contemplating legal action you should initiate it promptly to avoid limitations problems.

BAILMENTS

A *bailment* is a situation in which one person gives his property to be held by another person. For example, an author or illustrator might leave a manuscript with unique art at the office of her agent, publisher, or printer. In all these relationships, in which both parties benefit from the bailment, the person who takes possession of the property must exercise reasonable care in safeguarding it. If that person is negligent and the work is damaged or lost, the other party may recover damages. Even if the work has no easily ascertainable market value, damages might still be awarded based on the intrinsic value of the work.

CONTRACTS FOR READINGS AND LECTURES

Many authors are invited to lecture or read to groups interested in their work. Fees for lectures and school visits can amount to a significant part of an author's income, so it is important to insure that you receive the agreed upon fee. A good way to do this is to present your host with a written contract, detailing not only the amount of the fee and any reimbursements for expenses but also when payment is due. Request that your travel expenses be paid in advance, but you might agree to take the fee and other expenses upon completion of your first day of the engagement. The time that you will spend with the group and the nature of the services should be specified. In addition to giving a reading of poetry, for example, you might be asked to read students' work or to participate in creative-writing seminars. If you will be lecturing or reading, reserve the copyright in any recordings made. A contract for a lecture or reading must meet the needs of each occasion, but a simple model is shown on the following page as a starting point.

Dear Sir/Madam:

I am pleased by your invitation to address your group and would like this letter to serve as our agreement with respect thereto. I agree to travel to [specify the location] on [specify the date or dates] and to perform the following services: [specify what is to be done]. In return, you promise to pay my round-trip travel expenses in the amount of [specify amount] fourteen days prior to the date of said engagement, and pay me at the end of my first day of services a fee of [specify amount] and additional expenses in the amount of [specify amount and detail the reasons for the expenses, such as lodging and meals]. No recordings of my appearance shall be made without my express written consent. Recordings shall include any electrical transcription, tape recording, wire recording, film, videotape, or any other method of recording voice or image, whether now known or hereinafter developed. In the event permission to record my appearance is given, all copyrights to material contained therein shall be reserved to me, and no use of said material shall be made without my written consent thereto and an appropriate placement of copyright notice in my name. If these terms are agreeable to you, please sign this letter beneath the words CONSENTED AND AGREED TO to make this a binding agreement between us. Kindly return one signed copy of the letter to me for my records.

Sincerely, etc.

Consented and Agreed to:

_____

CHAPTER 11

NEGOTIATING A

BOOK CONTRACT

If you have received an offer from a book publisher, congratulations! For most authors, it is a mark of great distinction (unless the publisher is a subsidy, or vanity, publisher—see chapter 18). It means that editorial and publishing professionals have reviewed your submission, prepared a statement of projected profit and loss from publishing your work, and have concluded either that the publisher can make a profit from investing in your book, or that it is so remarkably good that it demands to be published, even at a loss. To publish a book is to make a large investment, so the receipt of an offer to publish proves that the publisher has a lot of faith in your work.

Do not panic when you receive the publisher's form contract in the mail. It will be very long and appear to be written in a foreign language—known to some as "legalese." You will see some provisions you recognize—the proposed title of the book, the advance payment you might have previously agreed to—but you will be very tempted to sign on the bottom line without trying to decipher the rest of the document. To protect your interests and your work, you *must* resist that urge.

It is a rookie mistake to believe that your negotiation with the publisher ends when you receive the form contract in the mail, with the major financial terms previously negotiated filled in. In fact, the negotiation is just beginning. Many other critical terms governing your publishing relationship appear in the contract, and your agreement on the advance and royalties has not obligated you to accept these other terms. No matter how many or how few books you have previously published, many of these provisions can be negotiated successfully. If you sign the form contract as you received it, you might well regret it later because the terms you ultimately accept will govern your relationship with the publisher for years after the contract is signed.

At the same time, there is always tension between the ideal publishing contract (for authors) and the attainable one. You will undoubtedly find that some of the recommendations here differ significantly from what your publisher is offering. Select those issues most important to your particular needs and concentrate on negotiating the corresponding contract clauses in order of priority. Consider a successful negotiation of your high-priority clauses a significant accomplishment in today's publishing environment. If you have an agent, he or she should be knowledgeable about and practiced in successful negotiations, although you owe it to yourself to discuss the negotiation with your agent while it is ongoing.

Members of the Authors Guild receive a Recommended Tradebook Contract and Guide and may have attorneys review and advise them about their contracts at no charge. If you need help understanding or negotiating provisions and you do not have a literary agent, you should join the Guild and take advantage of these valuable products and services. Any author who has received an offer to publish his or her book in exchange for an advance and royalties is eligible to join.

Most publishing contracts appear on printed forms called "boilerplate," prepared by the publishers and supplied to authors. The terms of the boilerplate can be changed in each individual agreement simply by deleting, adding, and revising the language according to the result of negotiations. *Make sure both parties initial all revisions, additions to, and deletions from the printed form contract,* or the legal effectiveness of those changes might be at risk.

This chapter discusses the typical provisions of book publishing contracts in the order in which they usually appear, not necessarily in the order of importance (to you), and it suggests some helpful changes.

PREAMBLE

If a contract is offered at an early stage of the project, the publisher might identify the work by describing the proposed content, format, length, and/or market. If the publisher has not seen a draft of the complete work, make sure the description is consistent with your proposal and what you plan to deliver. You might also want to leave yourself some room to maneuver, by not characterizing the point of view of the book, and with descriptions of length in terms of the number of book pages (which can be adjusted by a typesetter) rather than words or manuscript pages.

GRANT OF RIGHTS

In any publishing contract, the main transaction involves the author's grant of parts of her copyright to the publisher to exploit in exchange for compensation. The grant of rights clause details those rights granted. The rights you grant can be limited as to the media or formats the publisher intends to exploit (e.g., the right to publish and sell paperback editions), territory (e.g., the right to sell in North America), language(s), and duration (e.g. length of the copyright). Because these rights are so valuable, the basic dynamic in the negotiation is that the author seeks to limit the scope of the grant to those rights the publisher can effectively exploit and reserve other rights to herself, while the publisher seeks control of (and a share of the income earned from) the broadest rights possible. The final allocations of control and income will depend on the parties' bargaining strength and ability.

It is certainly necessary to grant the right to print, publish, and sell the work in book formats. Other formats related to print publishing, including abridgments, book clubs, reprints by another publisher, first and second serial rights (magazine excerpts before and after book publication), and sometimes audio books, are usually appropriate to grant, even though the publisher will probably license the right to exploit those formats to a third party. Rights that are not directly exploited by your publisher, but are instead licensed to third parties to use, are known as subsidiary rights, or "sub rights." The grant of rights clause or a separate "Subsidiary Rights" clause will address the allocation of these rights. By definition, it costs your publisher very little to allow another licensee (called the "sublicensee") to exploit a subsidiary right. For that reason, the publishing contract typically gives the author a large share of the publisher's proceeds from sublicenses. Nonetheless, retaining certain sub rights is useful if you can sell those rights yourself or through your literary agent. Subsidiary rights can include syndication, merchandising uses, films, television, multimedia, and e-books. Foreign territory and translation rights might also be subsidiary rights, unless included in the main grant of rights or reserved entirely to the writer.

The duration of the grant set forth in most publishers' contracts is "the whole term of copyright and any renewals and extensions thereof." A publisher is likely to oppose a shorter term of grant, but the Copyright Act's inalienable right to terminate a grant after thirty-five years makes changing this clause somewhat less important.

FOREIGN RIGHTS

With publishing conglomerates increasingly going international, many publishers routinely demand exclusive English-language rights in non–English-speaking countries, or "world" rights. Before you grant these rights, scrutinize the royalties the publisher offers for sales in foreign countries. If you grant your U.S. publisher the right to license British Commonwealth or foreign-language editions, consider requiring the publisher first to obtain and match or top the best offer available on the open market, or to allow you to bring in a better offer for these licenses. For all foreign rights, consider requesting a provision that reverts the rights if they are not exploited within a year or two after U.S. publication.

If you have an agent, he or she ought to reserve the rights to sell the work in any language in foreign nations, including Canada, the United Kingdom, Ireland, South Africa, New Zealand, and Australia. If you do not have an agent, then it is acceptable to grant these rights to the U.S. publisher, with the division of income usually approximating 75 to 85 percent to the author and 15 to 25 percent to the U.S. publisher. Be aware that the publisher will typically subtract its expenses, including a foreign agent's commission, from this income before splitting it with the author. Keep in mind that having your agent market these rights allows you to receive the income without having it applied against your advance. Agents will usually take a 15 to 20 percent commission on foreign rights income to cover both their commission and the foreign agent's commission.

SUBSIDIARY RIGHTS

Your agent usually places first serial (prepublication magazine excerpt) rights, so reserving them is appropriate. If the publisher takes and places first serial rights, it customarily takes the equivalent of an agent's 10 to 15 percent commission of the income from their sale. Other subsidiary rights publishers can reasonably expect to exploit, whether or not you have an agent, are second serial, book club, reprint, and audio book rights. The division of income for these rights is usually one-half to the author, one-half to the publisher. It is unreasonable for the publisher to take more than a one-half share for *any* subsidiary right.

Most publishers' contracts permit publishers to license publication of selections from the work in anthologies or other publications without your consent. Many authors want to be informed about and to retain approval over where their work will be reprinted, how much will be used, and the reprint fee charged. If this is the case, try to add this provision to your contract.

NON–PRINT-RELATED SUBSIDIARY RIGHTS

Because of the large amounts that can be earned, established authors and those with agents typically reserve motion picture, stage, television, merchandising, and related rights and receive all the income from them. If you have an agent, he or she will hold on to these rights on your behalf. If you have no agent, the publisher might insist on these rights and it is reasonable to grant them, at least on a nonexclusive basis, but the publisher will probably not ask for (and should not receive) more than 10 to 15 percent (or 25 percent for foreign sales of these rights) of generated income as its share. Some children's book publishers seek up to 50 percent of the income for these rights. Any attempt to take more than that is unusual and unreasonable.

If you authorize the publisher to license these rights, try to retain the right to prior approval of all licenses (especially of those for dramatic and merchandising rights; without approval, you might not be happy about who gets these rights and what is done with them), a limit to the number of years the publisher has authority to license the rights, and the royalty accounting provisions of the appendix at the end of this chapter on any licenses granted.

ELECTRONIC RIGHTS

Because of the rapid development of new media technologies, electronic rights are a potentially valuable source of current and future income for publishers and for those authors who are able to retain and exploit them. The Authors Guild recommends that you negotiate the disposition of electronic rights at the time you negotiate your advance. A furious struggle over electronic rights has been waged the past several years, and most publishers routinely ask for very broad grants of electronic rights. If yours requires you to grant these rights, at least negotiate for some safeguards. Retain the right of approval of any abridgment or anthologizing of the work and over any illustrations, sound, text, or computerized effects added to the work. Because of the ease with which pirates can digitally copy and distribute huge numbers of the work, obtain assurance from the publisher that the work will be protected from unauthorized copying. Licensees should be required to display copyright warnings prominently and to use the best available means to prevent unauthorized copying. Insert a reversion of rights clause for unexploited electronic rights so that if the publisher fails to exploit the rights in electronic formats for a specified period of time, they will revert to you.

Many publishers' contracts provide that royalties for electronic exploitations will mirror hardcover royalties (that is, 10 percent of the retail price, up to 15 percent); this amount does not take into account prevailing market conditions and could damage the economic value to you of the work in other formats. The sale price of e-books is low and the unit costs of production and distribution are dramatically lower than the costs for printed copies. For these reasons, most publishers can be persuaded to follow the lead of Random House, the largest English-language publisher in the world, and pay 50 percent of its net income from sales of e-books.

RESERVATION OF RIGHTS TO AUTHOR

A reservation of rights clause states that any right not specifically granted in the contract will belong to you and not to the publisher. In connection with this possibility, make sure that any noncompetition clause in the contract does not defeat the purpose of the reservation of rights by limiting your use of a new, or newly popular, method of exploiting the work.

DELIVERY OF MANUSCRIPT

Be sure to give yourself enough time to deliver the finished manuscript. If your book depends on future events, availability of information, or similar contingencies, it is prudent to add a clause permitting you to extend the delivery date by written notice where circumstances prevent completion within the specified time period. Above all else, remove any words to the effect that the time of delivery "is of the essence." Most courts allow a reasonable grace period for contract performance, unless the deadline is stated in the contract to be "of the essence." In that case, if you fail to deliver by the due date, you have breached. After the contract is signed, if you agree to extend the delivery deadline for any reason, make sure that you get the extension in writing and signed by the publisher.

Beware of clauses requiring the author to provide "all" additional materials deemed necessary "in the publisher's discretion." This leaves you vulnerable to demands for work—an index, illustrations, appendices, for example—that you did not consider when you agreed to the advance. It is much safer to specify in the contract as precisely as possible the materials you have agreed to provide. If you are providing illustrations, consider inserting a clause requiring the publisher to provide insurance against loss or damage to the original artwork and to return it to you when no longer needed. The publisher might require that illustrations be delivered at the same time as the manuscript for art books, children's books, and similar works. Otherwise, allow yourself a reasonable time and grace period to prepare the other materials you have agreed to provide.

Most contracts make the author responsible for obtaining—and paying for—permissions to use others' work in your book. You might argue that the publisher is better able to pay for permissions, but consider that this might lead to a smaller advance. For anthologies, textbooks, and similar works, publishers often pay part or all the cost of permissions. For more information about obtaining permissions, see chapter 5.

SATISFACTORY MANUSCRIPT

Almost all publishers' boilerplates contain "satisfactory manuscript" clauses that allow them to reject a delivered manuscript and terminate the contract, despite the work's actual fitness for publication and professional competence. Should this occur, the author will be obliged to repay the advance received. The Authors Guild opposes "satisfactory manuscript" clauses that give publishers complete discretion to reject an objectively competent work after submission. When the publisher agrees to publish a book, it is accepting at least some risk along with the writer. The advance should not be turned into a repayable loan, and the contract should not be treated as an option, by allowing the publisher complete discretion to reject manuscript creates. If the clause requires that the manuscript be "satisfactory to the publisher," the publisher's subjective judgment that the manuscript is not "satisfactory" will not be set aside, unless it can be proven that the publisher acted in bad faith. Publishers know that proving "bad faith" is difficult. Thus, your editor's departure from the publisher, a competing work by another author, a decrease in the general interest in the subject, or a change in the publisher's financial plans could lead the publisher to reject a publishable manuscript. As a realistic compromise, state that the manuscript must be "acceptable to the publisher in form and content" or "satisfactory in the publisher's editorial discretion" as opposed to "sole discretion." You can also protect yourself against the specter of contract termination under the "satisfactory manuscript" clause with provisions such as limitations on your advance repayment obligation, a requirement that the publisher must give you written editorial assistance and the opportunity to submit revisions before rejecting, and an accurate, specific description of the work envisioned in the preamble and delivery clauses.

If the publisher made you an offer on the basis of an entire manuscript draft rather than a proposal, indicate that the satisfactory manuscript "has been delivered," or that it will be deemed satisfactory after minor editorial changes have been made. Consider stipulating that you may submit portions of the work in progress, and the publisher shall indicate whether each portion is satisfactory within a reasonable time after receipt. Stipulate that if any portion of the advance must be repaid upon rejection, it will be paid only from proceeds of a subsequent publishing contract with another publisher for the same book (a "first proceeds" clause). Some contracts provide that repayment shall be made from proceeds of subsequent contracts or by a specified date, whichever occurs first, but that does not limit the author's obligation to repay if no new contract has been obtained by the deadline, or if the proceeds received from a new contact do not equal the advance to be repaid. At least try to delete the requirement to repay by a specified date.

Some contracts have been terminated by publishers in recent years because of the financial prospects of a manuscript; changes in a publisher's management, business policies, or financial condition; or because the publisher feared that intervening events had diminished the appeal of the work. None of these circumstances justify termination under a clause requiring that the manuscript be "in form and content satisfactory to the publisher." Nevertheless, if you can keep the entire advance and quickly end the contract, thus freeing you to negotiate with another publisher for the work, you might be better off allowing termination instead of having the book remain "in limbo."

Finally, provide that if the contract is terminated despite your delivery of a satisfactory manuscript, you will be entitled to receive and retain the entire advance, as well as automatic reversion of all rights.

WARRANTIES AND INDEMNITIES

This provision is your promise to the publisher that you own the work and that the work does not infringe on anyone else's rights or cause harm to anyone. If you fear any such accusation arising out of publication of the work, you should discuss it with your publisher and try to work together to eliminate the risks of suit. Many publishers' contracts require the author to indemnify them not only against judgments resulting from the author's breach of warranties, but also against any "claims and demands." Try to limit your obligation to damages recovered in a suit against the publisher resulting only from an actual breach of your warranties. Be advised, however, that most publishers are stubborn about changing their warranty and indemnity clauses. You must evaluate the legal risks of your project when weighing the importance of this clause. If you are writing on a controversial subject or person, you have good reason to ask the publisher to eliminate the indemnity clause completely with respect to libel and invasion of privacy suits. If the book contains material written by others, for example, if it includes an introduction or substantial quotations, consider adding language that excludes this material from your representations and warranties. Indemnity clauses should never apply to parts of the book that were added as a result of suggestions, corrections, or additions made by an editor or other employee of the publisher.

Most publishers extend insurance coverage to their authors under their own media liability policies. Particularly if your work might offend a potential plaintiff, be sure to raise this issue during contract negotiations. If the publisher agrees to add you as an insured to its policy, make sure that promise appears in your contract and try to limit your share of the deductible to a portion of the first $3,000 in damages, or a percentage of the advance, whichever is lower. If the publisher will not provide libel insurance, or if it requires you to pay the entire deductible, which is usually quite high, consider obtaining your own liability insurance. In practice, publishers often pay for legal expenses, settlements, and judgments resulting from suits, especially meritless suits. Publishers might choose to collect some of their expenses when the author is highly successful. In close cases, some publishers might seek to recoup their costs from royalties earned.

COPYEDITING, PROOFREADING, AND CORRECTION OF PROOFS

Copyediting changes can range from punctuation, grammar, spelling, and capitalization to correcting errors of fact or manuscript inconsistencies. Because changes might be substantial, copyediting should be subject to your review. You should have the right to approve any substantive changes to the manuscript, although the publisher might insist that approval not be "unreasonably withheld." Most publishers will ask you to pay the cost of "author's alterations" to page proofs that exceed 10 percent of the cost of composition of the proofs.

PUBLICATION

Most contracts require the publisher to *publish* (that is, print and distribute) the work within twelve to eighteen months of acceptance of the manuscript, or up to twenty-four months for smaller publishers or children's picture books. Any period longer than that is unreasonable. If you can, provide that if the publisher fails to publish the trade edition within the applicable time period, you may terminate the contract, recover all rights granted, and keep the advance without prejudice to your right to sue for additional damages. Art books and children's picture books are especially vulnerable to open-ended publication clauses that depend on the selection of the artist and completion of the artwork, two details that fall outside the author's control. Negotiate deadlines for these events; otherwise you could wait many years for publication.

Most contracts allow the publisher to publish the work "in a style, manner, and price" that they determine unilaterally. The author's right to consult on retail price and print runs is likely out of the question for all but the most powerful authors. However, title, design, and artwork can be crucial elements of the book, making your right to consult over or even approve of these elements important, and publishers will often agree to change the title only with the author's consent, and to consult with the author about the format and style of the text, graphic material, and cover.

Marketing and promotion are the areas in which most publishers almost universally frustrate their authors. If your contract contains no specific provisions for promotion, author's travel and tour, and publicity, you can expect very little from the publisher beyond a listing in its catalog, and perhaps the mailing of promotional copies. If the advance offered is more than $25,000, it is worth discussing an advertising budget and promotional plans. The Guild recommends that you add as much about publicity as possible into the contract and that you plan on making your own publicity efforts. If a tour is promised, insert it into the contract, including the number and names of cities and the proposed travel budget and timetable.

COPYRIGHT REGISTRATION

The contract should require the publisher to register the copyright with the Copyright Office in your name within three months of publication. This requirement is very important for full copyright protection. Registration filed later than three months after publication (unless you previously registered the manuscript) would bar the recovery of statutory damages and attorneys' fees in cases of copyright infringement. Do not allow the publisher to take your copyright or to publish the copyright notice in any name other than yours. Except in very unusual circumstances, this practice is not standard in the industry and harms your economic interests. No reputable publisher should expect you to agree.

PAYMENT

ADVANCE

The *advance* is a sum of money paid to the author before the book is published that is then deducted from the book's earnings. No royalties are paid until the publisher recoups the full amount of the advance. Advances vary considerably, depending on such factors as your reputation as an author, the success of your last book, the subject matter, the audience, the illustrator's reputation (for children's books), and the likelihood of book club and paperback licenses. Try to learn from your editor the publisher's projected first year's sales and expected retail list price, both of which the publisher calculates before making you an offer. The advance normally reflects royalties on projected first year sales, at least. Sometimes the author's share of projected first year subsidiary rights income is included in the advance. Frequently, the publisher determines the amount of the advance after assessing whether licenses can be sold, or even after completing deals for them. Again, it is worth your while to try to find that out from your editor before you agree to the advance.

Negotiate for as large an advance as possible. The advance is your only hedge against the risk that your years of work might produce a commercial failure. Through the advance, the publisher shares this risk. The higher the advance, the greater the publisher's incentive to increase the size of the first printing and the advertising and promotion budgets. Generally, publishers promise to pay one-half of the advance on signing and the balance on acceptance of the manuscript. To avoid long payment delays, it is important to limit the publisher's time to accept the manuscript or respond with specific comments after delivery. Avoid agreeing to wait for publication to receive any payment (if the advance is large, however, the publisher might insist on this). Never agree to return an unearned advance except for failure to deliver a satisfactory manuscript.

ROYALTIES—HARDCOVER TRADE BOOKS

For adult trade hardcover books, publishers typically offer 10 percent of the retail price for the first 5,000 copies sold, 12.5 percent on the next 5,000 copies, and 15 percent on all copies sold in excess of 10,000. Established authors can often obtain better terms, such as 10 percent on the first 5,000 copies and 15 percent thereafter. The primary royalty rates in most trade book contracts are based on suggested retail (or "list") price of each book sold. Avoid royalties that are based on "net" (or wholesale) price, or increase the rate accordingly over those recommended here. "Net receipts" means the amount the bookseller or wholesaler actually pays to the publisher, so net-based royalties usually are 40 to 50 percent lower than list-based royalties computed on the same percentage rate. For example, when a book is sold at a 43 percent discount, a 15 percent royalty on the list price is equivalent to a 26.3 percent royalty on the net price.

ROYALTIES—CHILDREN'S BOOKS

Royalty rates for children's books are often the same as those for adult trade books. The author of young-adult books should negotiate for the same royalties as for adult trade hardcover, trade paperbacks, and mass-market paperbacks. The royalty escalations for books for younger children (up to about eight years old) are sometimes set at higher numbers sold, for example 10 percent on the first 10,000 copies, 12.5 percent on the next 10,000 copies, and 15 percent on all copies in excess of 20,000. When illustrations represent a significant portion of the work (in which case the book is referred to as a "picture book"), the illustrator usually receives half the advance and half the royalties and has a separate contract with the publisher comparable to the text author's. Some children's book contracts provide that the royalty for library editions is based on "net receipts" (the wholesale price), rather than on retail list price. Authors should try to delete such a provision and match the royalty for the library-bound edition with that of the trade edition, because a substantial part of the book's total sales could easily be in this category.

ROYALTIES—TEXT AND EDUCATIONAL BOOKS

Royalties for professional, scientific, and technical books are customarily based on the net price instead of retail price. The publisher's discount to distributors and retailers for textbooks is in the range of 25 to 33⅓ percent, so the effect of a net-based royalty is not as bad as it would be for trade books. A typical royalty rate might be 15 percent, but keep in mind that a substantial part of the sales are likely to be mail order, library, or export, so try to increase the rates for such sales. For college textbooks, the royalties are also based on net price, and the standard discount to bookstores is 20 percent (although some publishers offer as much as 33 percent). On a hardcover textbook, try for 15 percent of net on sales up to a specified number of copies (perhaps between 7,500 and 15,000), and 18 percent thereafter. Textbooks often have their best sales in the first few years after publication, so escalations for sales over a given number of copies in each calendar year are another possibility. An original paperback textbook might have royalties in the range of 10 percent to 15 percent of the net price.

TRADE PAPERBACK ROYALTIES

The typical initial royalty rate for "quality" trade paperback editions (as distinct from "mass market" paperbacks) is at least 6 percent, with an escalation to at least 7.5 percent at 10,000 copies (or fewer, if the first printing is less than 10,000 copies). Sometimes, a flat rate of 8 percent is offered. Some authors are able to do better. For example, one might receive 7.5 percent up to 20,000 copies and 10 percent thereafter, or a three-tiered escalation. The advantage of permitting the hardcover publisher to issue its own paperback edition, as opposed to sublicensing it, is that you do not share the royalties received from the paperback publisher; the disadvantage is that you are not paid a separate advance for the paperback edition. In negotiating the grant of rights provision, request an addition to your advance if the publisher prints the paperback edition.

MASS-MARKET ROYALTIES

Mass-market books are the cheaper paperbacks you find for sale at newsstands, airports, and grocery stores. So-called genre fiction titles, such as category romances, westerns, and science fiction, are often published in this format only, while bestsellers are often published in this format after hardcover publication. Most publishers agree to pay an initial royalty of at least 6 to 8 percent on sales of up to 150,000 copies and 10 percent thereafter. Established authors sometimes negotiate rates of 8 or 10 percent up to 10 or 12 percent, or more, or receive a three-tiered escalation.

"DEEP DISCOUNT" ROYALTY RATES

Most contracts provide that when a discount of more than 50 percent or so is given to a distributor or retailer, royalties on those copies are reduced to 10 percent of the publisher's *net* receipts. This "deep discount" provision could sharply decrease your royalties and puts far too much control over your royalties in the publisher's hands. An unscrupulous publisher could actually increase its profit, and give the bookstore a better deal, by selling at just enough of a discount to cut your royalties by more than half.

Larger bookstore chains now demand discounts of up to 55 percent or higher. Try to specify that the decreased royalty rate applies only when the deep discount is given "to a purchaser not ordinarily engaged in the business of bookselling" (this is known in the industry as a "special sale"). This might not be easy to accomplish, since publishers want to slash royalties for both special and deep discount sales. If the publisher resists, find out the publisher's standard discount to the big chains for books like yours and push to increase the triggering discount percentage beyond that standard by at least a few percentage points. Another important—and realistic—change you could make is to reduce your royalty rate by one-half of 1 percent for each 1 percent that the publisher increases the discount over the triggering percentage. Many authors have successfully negotiated this kind of "shared-loss" royalty provision. See the Authors Guild Recommended Tradebook Contract and Guide for the appropriate wording if your publisher cannot provide it. Publishers' contracts vary in their provisions for royalties on mail order, book club, export, and other sales outside normal trade channels. The publisher's standard rates could be increased through negotiation, and it is certainly worth attempting, especially if your book is likely to sell many copies through these channels. Finally, if you grant the publisher world rights, strive to avoid reductions in royalties for exports.

REMAINDERS

Remaindered books are overstock copies that are sold to special remainder houses and resold to consumers for one-tenth to one-half the retail list price. Most contracts offer to pay the author 10 percent of the gross price received for the sale of remainders, a scant amount. An alternative would be to require the remainder purchaser to pay you the hardcover royalty on the "new" retail price it sets on the book, or to renegotiate percentages with the publisher prior to overstock sales. Because income from such sales is usually minuscule, you might prefer to purchase the copies to be remaindered and arrange for their distribution via the Authors Guild's Backinprint.com *(www.backinprint.com)* online bookstore, or on your own. If so, require the publisher to notify you before it remainders the work and to allow you to purchase the remaining copies at cost or at the remainder price. If you grant the publisher the right to publish mass market or trade paperback editions, make sure any favorable revision of the remainder clause covers each edition.

ACCOUNTING AND STATEMENTS

Most trade publishers send semiannual statements and payments accounting for your book's sales and royalties and license fees owed to you. Some smaller presses offer quarterly accounting and payment, and this is a good goal to work toward. In no event should you accept accountings and payment less frequently than twice a year. Otherwise, it is the publisher—not you—that is earning interest on your money. Accounting periods might depend on your publisher's fiscal year. It is not uncommon for publishers to send statements and payments two or even three months after the end of the accounting period. Some publishers will agree to disclose the number of copies of the work that were printed, bound, and given away, as well as the number of copies on hand at the end of the accounting period, either in the statements themselves, or upon your request. Indeed, that information will certainly have to be revealed if you exercise your right to audit the publishers' records. In any event, review your royalty statements carefully and do not hesitate to ask your publisher for any information needed to verify the statement's accuracy. Royalty statements should include the subsidiary rights income received in each rights category as well as the name of the licensee.

Virtually every publisher's contract permits it to withhold a reserve against returns, that is, to retain some of the money otherwise owed the author in order to avoid overpayment for returned books. Royalties are not due on returns, because almost every publisher refunds retailers and distributors in full for returned books. If the reserve is too high, or if it is held for too long, authors lose the use of money actually owed to them for an unacceptable period of time. Amounts withheld often far exceed any reasonable estimate of future returns or the amount of copies actually returned. The Guild's recommended reserve against returns for hardcover books is no more than 15 percent of reported sales in a given accounting period. This percentage reflects the general industry reserve for hardcover trade editions, and you should try to negotiate this ceiling into the clause. The reserve percentage is higher—30 percent or more—for paperback editions. You might find that the publisher will argue for a higher or even unlimited percentage. If the publisher's boilerplate states merely "reasonable reserve," you are somewhat protected, though not as well as if you negotiate a specific percentage limit. The Guild's recommendation also limits reserves to the first three accounting periods or eighteen months after initial publication, whichever is shorter. After that, publishers have no reason to be receiving significant returns.

JOINT ACCOUNTING

Some publishers' form contracts provide that amounts the author owes the publisher under contracts for other books may be deducted from payments due the author under the current agreement. Some publishers might even claim this clause entitles them to deduct unearned advances on other books (though this is not a reasonable claim if the advances were deemed "nonrefundable"). Even reasonable readings of such "cross-collateralization" or "joint accounting" clauses would allow the publisher to deduct from this book's earnings amounts owed by you for page-proof alterations, permissions payments, copies of books purchased, or other obligations associated with different books.

Joint accounting provisions are unfair and should be stricken from contracts wherever they appear. If a publisher refuses to delete the clause, modify it to exclude withholding of any portion of the current advance, or any portion of the advances or royalties paid by paperback or book club publishers for rights in the current book. Finally, specify that unearned advances from other contracts will not constitute indebtedness to be repaid out of earnings from the current contract.

SUBSIDIARY RIGHTS PAYMENTS AND ACCOUNTS

The complexities of subsidiary rights accounting have plagued publishers for years. The result has been grossly inadequate and undocumented payments to authors for their income share for licenses such as book clubs, foreign publishing, and audiotapes. Publishers have revealed—under pressure—that their licensees routinely issue inadequate and inconsistent reports with their payments to the publisher.

In response to this problem, a committee of the Book Industry Study Group, which included publishers, royalty accountants, authors, and authors groups representatives, drafted the Subsidiary Rights Payment Form that appears as the appendix at the end of this chapter. Try to provide that the publisher will require sublicensees of your work to include this form with their payments. Publishers endorse this system because while simple, it allows them to collect previously unpaid dollars in subsidiary rights income, and to keep accurate accounts of what they owe to their authors.

EXAMINATION OF THE PUBLISHER'S RECORDS

Most publishers' contracts give the author the right to audit its records regarding the book's financial performance; if yours does not, it is very important to add a right to audit to the agreement. Take care to ensure that the audit clause allows either you or your representative to conduct the examination and that it does not limit whom your representative may be. The obligation of the publisher to pay your examiner's fee if the audit reveals that it erred to your detriment by more than 5 percent is typical. Insist on it. Finally, do not let the publisher limit the time you have to examine the records for a given period. You should be able to detect and object to a discrepancy on your statements for as long as the discrepancy exists.

FREE COPIES AND AUTHOR'S DISCOUNT

At least twenty-five free copies and a 40 percent discount rate is common for hardcover trade editions. This clause in publishers' boilerplates often requires that copies purchased must be for the author's "own use, and not for resale." If you anticipate situations in which you will want to have copies on hand for resale, negotiate that use into the contract.

REVISED EDITIONS

Publishers' contracts for textbooks, technical books, and some children's books often contain a provision requiring the author to make revisions for a new edition at the publisher's request, sometimes without further payment (beyond continued payment of royalties, of course). They do not belong in contracts for novels and the like, so strike a revised editions clause, unless it is appropriate for the kind of book you are publishing. The typical boilerplate version states that if the author will not or cannot make the revisions, the publisher can retain the services of another author and charge that person's payment (on a flat fee or royalty basis) against your royalties. To protect yourself from losing control of your work and the money owed you, try to ensure that the publisher's requests for revisions shall be subject to your approval; that if revisions are made by another author, the selection of the second author shall be subject to your approval; that in no event shall your compensation be reduced below a specified minimum; that the credit to be given to you and to the subsequent author in connection with the revised edition shall be subject to your approval; and that you shall have the right to remove your name from the later edition if you wish.

OUT-OF-PRINT PROVISION

Any reasonable publisher will include in its boilerplate an *out-of-print clause* (also called a "reversion of rights" clause). The out-of-print clause is designed to encourage your publisher to keep the work selling for as long as it is profitable—for both parties—by providing for reversion to you of the rights granted when the work is no longer in print. When the publisher no longer chooses to invest in printing, distributing, and marketing the work, then it should no longer have the right to profit from it (except the right to profit from third-party licenses already made). Your book should therefore be deemed "in print" only while copies of an English-language hardcover or paperback edition are readily available and offered for sale in the United States through regular trade channels and are listed in the publisher's catalog. It is important to make the definition of "in print" as close to this description as possible. Many publishers' contracts do not define "in print" at all, and the publisher could use that obscurity to argue that the existence of a foreign edition or nonprint version makes the work "in print" and prevents you from reclaiming U. S. rights. If digital formats (including "print-on-demand") can make your book "in print," then stipulate that the author must earn at least a certain amount in royalty payments (say, $300 to $500) each accounting period from these formats to prevent reversion of rights.

Try to provide that rights will revert automatically if the publisher fails to place the work back into print upon request. This is better than having to rely on the publisher to prepare and mail a confirmation of reversion.

BANKRUPTCY

Once a bankruptcy petition is filed, control over the publisher and its assets are in the hands of the bankruptcy court. All rights in the work held by the bankrupt publisher are considered assets, and no bankruptcy clause in a contract can override the court's control over those assets. For that reason, do not expend too much capital over negotiating a bankruptcy clause. Other kinds of financial calamity for a publisher do not lead to court control, however, so it is worthwhile to provide that your rights will revert upon the publisher's insolvency or failure to remit royalties due for a specified period of time.

TERMINATION

Unless you provide for this right in the contract, you may not terminate the contract, even if the publisher breaches important obligations—such as the duty to pay you. Your remedy under the law for a breach is limited to money damages, and you might need to sue or threaten suit to receive them. Therefore, it is a good idea to get a right to terminate if the publisher fails to provide statements of account, make required payments, or publish within its deadline.

AGENCY CLAUSE

If an agent represents you, he or she will likely make sure that an agency clause is added to the publishing contract. The usual clause authorizes the publisher to make all payments to the agent for the author's account and allows the agent to keep his or her commission from the payment for the author. You should negotiate the material terms of this clause with your agent *before* the agent negotiates the publishing contract for you. The publisher will probably not argue the terms of a typical agency clause. The clause must confirm any separate agency agreement you have, so read it carefully before signing the contract.

ADJUDICATION OF DISPUTES

The Authors Guild recommends that a publishing contract provide that disputes arising out of the publishing agreement be determined by arbitration instead of litigation. Arbitration is cheaper, simpler, and quicker than litigation; for simple cases, lawyers are not needed. For that reason, large publishers will often strenuously resist arbitration clauses, because they can afford the cost and delays of litigation better than authors. Smaller publishers, however, might agree more readily.

OPTION CLAUSE

Do not be fooled by the glamorous sound of the word. Options favor publishers only, not authors. An option clause gives the publisher the privilege of publishing your next book or books—but only if it chooses to do so. No option clause obligates the publisher to do anything in your favor—not even to read your next book. Options bind you to the publisher for your subsequent works, even if the current publishing relationship proves unsatisfactory to you, or the publisher's performance is inadequate, or your editor leaves, or better terms can be obtained elsewhere, or the publisher falls into a perilous financial position. Options prevent you from considering other publishing opportunities for a period of time that is often wholly dependent on the first publisher. This could impede or injure the progress of your career. From the publisher's perspective, investing in the first book of an unknown writer is very risky, but if it stands to gain from publishing future works of the writer, the investment is less risky. Even so, many publishers are willing to delete the entire option clause upon request. If your publisher refuses to strike it entirely, it is very important that you negotiate some revisions to the boilerplate option provision to eliminate the more damaging features of these arrangements.

You might encounter different kinds of option clauses: same terms and conditions, terms to be mutually agreed upon, right of first refusal, no less favorable terms, or right of last refusal. Options to publish your next work on the "same terms" as the previous contract and "last refusal rights" (allowing the publisher to acquire the work by matching other offers the author has received) eliminate your ability to negotiate terms of your next publishing contract. Change such terms to permit the publisher a limited-time "right of first refusal," on terms "to be mutually agreed upon" at the time the second contract is negotiated. Provide that the author must submit only a summary or proposal of the optioned work, not a complete manuscript. The latter requirement would require you to write an entire manuscript without an advance or a guarantee of publication. You should be allowed to submit the proposal or summary of the next work, and the publisher should have to decide whether or not to make an offer for the work, within a short time after submission or acceptance, not publication, of the current manuscript. Try to limit the option to cover only books specifically similar to the current work (e.g. "biography for children" or "computer industry study").

NONCOMPETE CLAUSES

Publishers' boilerplate contracts often contain clauses restricting the author from publishing another book based on the material in the current work, or from publishing material competing with the sale of the current work. A broadly worded noncompetition clause can cause considerable harm. Depending on the scope of the subject matter forbidden to you, the publisher might claim that the characters in a novel or children's story may not be used in sequels and prequels, or that the author of a textbook may not write other works on the same subject, or that one cookbook or other specialized work is all that an author may write without the publisher's release from the noncompetition clause. Though such claims might be held unenforceable in court because judges require that these terms be reasonable in scope and not unduly restrictive, it is obviously better to limit the publisher's ability to make such a claim.

The type of work to which the clause applies should be described as specifically as possible as to subject matter, market, and format. Do not give the publisher the discretion to decide whether a work will compete with the contracted book—limit the restriction to works that will actually compete with the primary work. In addition, adding the following sentence to the noncompetition clause may provide helpful qualification:

> It is understood that the author will continue to write and publish _____ books in the field of _____. This provision is in no way intended to prohibit or limit such publications.

APPENDIX

(To be sent by Publisher to licensees)

SUBSIDIARY RIGHTS PAYMENT ADVICE FORM

This form must be completed and attached to your check or faxed to this number: _____ when you send payment pursuant to licenses granted by us to you.

Failure to do so may result in our inability to record your payments and prevent us from determining that you are in compliance with the terms of your license(s).

- ◆ Amount remitted: _____

- ◆ Check or wire transfer number: _____

- ◆ Check or wire transfer date: _____

- ◆ (for wire transfers) Bank and account number for which moneys were deposited: _____

- ◆ Publisher/agent payor's name _____

- ◆ Title of the work for which payment is being made: _____

- ◆ Author(s) of the work: _____

- ◆ Our Unique Identifying Number for the work as it appears in the Appendix to the relevant contract. If none, the original publisher's ISBN number of the work: _____

- ◆ The period covered by the payment: _____

The following information will be very helpful, so we ask that you also provide it:

- ◆ Reason for payment (guarantee earned royalty, fee, etc.): _____

    _____

- ◆ Payment's currency: _____

◆ Type of right (book club, reprint, translation, etc.): _____

_____

_____

◆ Summary justification of your payment:

Gross amount due: _____

Taxes: _____

Commissions: _____

Bank charges: _____

Net amount paid: _____

CHAPTER 12

PERIODICAL AND

SYNDICATION CONTRACTS

Licensing rights to periodical (that is, newspaper and magazine) publishers involves many of the same issues as book-publishing contracts, except that the contracts are simpler. In fact, freelance articles are frequently sold without a written contract. If an editor calls with a rush job, you might be more immediately concerned with meeting the deadline than with acquiring the appropriate paperwork. If you and the publisher do not have a written agreement, then the copyright law governs the extent of the publisher's rights in your work. In such a case, the law presumes that a collective work publisher acquires only the right to copy and distribute a freelance contribution in that particular issue, any revision of that issue, and any subsequent issue of that periodical. Without a contract, the publisher has no right to make any other use of your contribution. The rights granted are nonexclusive, so you are free to license the contribution to other periodicals, even for simultaneous publication.

The Supreme Court recently ruled that the publisher's rights in this scenario do not include the right to reproduce your contribution in electronic databases. *New York Times, et al. v. Tasini, et al.*, 121 S. Ct. 238 (2001). When it comes to rights granted, the lack of a formal, documented meeting of the minds is therefore more favorable to the author than it is to the publisher. Unfortunately, following the *Tasini* decision, you will doubtlessly be pressured to give up your electronic rights to your article by signing a standard contract. When it comes to other basic issues, you are better off with a written agreement. For example, you will probably want to clarify the nature of the project, the due date, the fee to be paid, whether or not expenses will be covered, how and when payment will be made, the effect of cancellation, and how revisions will be handled. You might begin your negotiations with a telephone conversation with your editor, in which the assignment, length, and fee are set. Usually, the editor will follow that with a formal contract. Keep in mind that it is merely an offer, and the terms should be open to negotiation. If the editor does not send a contract, consider sending your own confirmation of the assignment. It need not be long or formal. A sample is included at the end of this chapter. Following is a discussion of typical terms and favorable changes.

GRANT OF RIGHTS

The grant of rights is the writer's main concern when dealing with periodicals. This is due in part to the publisher's tendency to overreach due to its perceived superior bargaining strength and in part to misunderstandings about the meaning of some commonly used terms. Some publishers purchase "first serial rights," the right to be the first periodical to publish the work. After such publication, the writer is free to sell the work elsewhere. "First North American serial rights," the right to be the first publisher of the work in North America, is another typical grant. "Second serial rights," more generally referred to as reprint rights, grant the right to publish work that has previously appeared elsewhere as, for example, in a book. "One-time rights" are the rights to use the work once but not necessarily first.

Depending on your plans for reusing your article, you should try to limit the grant of rights with regard to exclusivity (whether you may sell the article to another periodical simultaneously), number of uses (the number of times the periodical may run the article), types of uses (the formats in which the article may be published), languages, duration (the length of time after which the article may no longer be run), and territory (the countries in which the article can be published). You might also want to provide that no rights will be transferred until you are paid in full, and you should reserve all rights not specifically granted.

THE ASSIGNMENT AND DUE DATE

The contract should describe the assignment in enough detail, including content and word count, to ensure that there is no misunderstanding. You should not agree to language containing the words "satisfactory manuscript" or giving the publisher discretion to reject the work outside mutually agreed upon and objective standards. Acceptability of the work should be based on objective criteria such as length, topic of article, professional competence, and fitness for publication. A due date, expressed as a specific date or a number of days from the date that the client periodical signs the confirmation contract, is also necessary. In cases in which the periodical will provide reference materials of any kind, the due date might be expressed as a number of days from the receipt of any such materials. The contract should not make the time of delivery "of the essence." It should also provide for an extension if delays beyond the writer's control occur, such as illness, but not beyond a specified period of time.

Include a clause stating (1) that the publisher shall inform the author whether or not the work is acceptable for publication within a specific period of time and (2) that the publisher agrees to publish the work by a certain date. Because the grant of rights clause is often linked to the publication date of the work, the publisher should inform you of the planned publication date; if the work is not published by this date, then all rights in the work should revert back to the author. You should also seek the right to revise the work if the publisher deems it unacceptable for publication. The publisher might agree to this second chance if it is of limited duration—and, perhaps, if it incurs no additional expenses.

FEES, EXPENSES, AND PAYMENT

The fee should be specified along with whether the publisher will pay your expenses. If the expenses are going to be high, as when there is travel or extensive research involved, the writer should provide a list of the expenses which will be covered and should seek a nonreturnable advance against such costs. You might consider asking for a provision that unforeseen or extraordinary, but nevertheless necessary, expenses will be covered, subject to the publisher's approval. Such costs might include situations where you must make extensive and costly revisions due to a situation beyond your control. If the publisher fails to advise you about necessary permissions or privacy releases, require the publisher to bear these extra costs.

Payment should be made within thirty days of delivery of the article. If the publisher requests an expense budget, provide for a variance percentage, perhaps 10 percent, to allow for flexibility in the event of unforeseen costs. For extensive projects, a schedule of payments is especially important. Provide also that if the publisher decides not to publish the work, your expenses shall still be reimbursed and that if they already have been reimbursed, you need not return them to the publisher. If the publisher promises to pay on acceptance, try to provide in the contract that no part of the payment need be returned, and rights will revert to you if the periodical fails to use the work. If the publisher cancels the assignment before you have completed it, the amount of the kill fee might be tied to the stage of the work at the point of cancellation and the reason for the cancellation. You deserve to be paid in full if the project is completed and the publisher's reason for canceling the contract is the fact that an article on the same subject appeared in another periodical the day before. If you are to be paid upon acceptance of the article, try to obtain a provision that states that no part of the payment need be returned if the periodical never publishes the article. Less desirable but more likely is an agreement to pay you a "kill fee" of 50 percent or more if the publisher fails to publish. Make sure, in that case, that all rights granted will revert to you immediately, and accept no less than 50 percent.

OTHER CONTRACT ISSUES

Make sure to establish that you own the copyright in the work. Periodicals fall under the category of "collective works" as defined by Section 101 of the Copyright Act. Contributions to collective works might be considered works made for hire—thus divesting the author of copyright ownership—if there is an express written agreement to that effect. If you are a freelance writer, as opposed to an employee or staff writer at a periodical, provide in the contract that you are an independent contractor. This definition is highly preferable to defining the relationship as one of work-for-hire. The contract should specify what credit you will receive. In the usual case, you should expect to receive credit for the article under your name, unless you do not want it.

Magazines and newspapers often edit articles extensively for length and style, but it is reasonable to request the right to review and discuss modifications made to your work. Due to time constraints, the publisher might refuse to give you a right of approval—or even review—over changes, so keep the time you request to a minimum. If the revisions that are required are extensive, seek the right to make the changes yourself. If you strongly disapprove of extensive revisions made, you should be able to request that your name be removed from the work.

A publisher might try to hold you responsible if a claim is made against it, based on your article. If your contract contains a warranty and indemnity clause, make clear that you shall be liable only where there has been a final judgment based on an actual breach of a warranty. Also seek to limit your liability. If you have published works similar to the one covered by the contract, specify in the warranty that "the work has not been published before." If you foresee that the publisher will be using your name, photograph, or biographical information in advertising and promoting your work, try to require the publisher to consult with you before making use of your name and likeness.

ELECTRONIC RIGHTS

Following the filing of suit by the writers in *New York Times et al. v. Tasini et al.*, periodical publishers, many of which had been licensing the rights to archive their entire publications to large electronic databases without asking permission of their freelance contributors, began to require that their contributors grant extensive rights to their articles. The result has been a furious struggle between freelancers and publishers. As these rights have proven extremely lucrative, the uses have harmed the secondary use market, in which freelancers used to earn significant income from reprints of their articles. The value of the copyright in works will likely increase as technology makes delivery of them faster and more efficient. For these reasons, and to avoid additional infringement liability, publishers have begun to insist upon clear language granting the publisher rights in "all media now known or hereafter invented" or "by any and all means, methods, processes, whether now known or hereafter invented." The more aggressive publishers are demanding that the works be designated "works made for hire," which, as you know, would make the publisher, not the author, the legal "author" of the work.

Keep in mind that some periodicals and newspapers might be better situated to license electronic rights in articles than you or your agent. The optimal decision might not always be to retain rights. Often it will be to negotiate adequate compensation for them, including a share in all electronic reuse fees.

SYNDICATION

A syndicate is, in a sense, another publisher, one that gathers written materials and distributes them to a broad periodical market. Once an article is picked up for syndication, it can be published by many newspapers and periodicals. Regardless of who grants the license for syndication—the author or the original publisher—there are some things to keep in mind. Just as you try to limit the grant of rights to a publisher, so too should you limit the grant of rights to the syndicate. Retain the copyright in your works. Subsidiary rights granted to a syndicate should be determined on a case-by-case basis, but should always be limited in scope and amount. For example, a syndicate should only be given a license for works it can directly exploit.

The most important term to obtain from the syndicate—either directly or through your publisher—is a guaranteed minimum payment for your syndicated work that is not based upon the success (or lack thereof) of the syndication. Payment for syndication will vary depending on the nature and success of the syndication relationship. For example, are you selling one feature or column, or a continuing series? Which newspapers or periodicals are picking up the work? How much above the guaranteed minimum in the license are they paying? The syndicate can be expected to keep 40 to 60 percent of the gross receipts, with the remaining percentage to be given to you—or, if the publisher has licensed the work, to be shared between you and the publisher, at an ideal ratio of 85 percent author, 15 percent publisher.

Try to avoid inclusion of your work into packages of features and columns to be sold by the syndicate at a special price, thereby possibly obscuring the value of the author's individual work. Entering into contracts of limited duration will ensure your ability to renegotiate a successful syndication relationship or to get out of an unsuccessful one. Since any kind of automatic renewal option would defeat the purpose of a short term, only agree to one if it is accompanied by increased compensation. Just as in book publishing contracts, noncompete and option clauses can seriously hamper your ability to place your work elsewhere and should not be lightly given. Finally, consider the amount of control you wish to retain over the organizations that will place your work, the markets in which they want your work to be placed, and any changes to the final form of their material.

SAMPLE LETTER TO A PERIODICAL PUBLISHER

Dear Mr. Editor:

I am honored by Happy Publishing Company's offer to publish my article, The Great American Article. I would like us to come to a more specific agreement over a few important issues:

1. Happy Periodical Publisher's exclusive right to publish the article will be limited to first serial rights in the English language to be sold in the United States, its territories and Canada, for a term of 90 days beyond the U.S. sale date of the issue in which my article is first published. The right to publish the article in other countries and in other languages shall be nonexclusive.

2. I agree not to publish the work elsewhere, in whole or in part, until Happy Periodical Publisher has published the work in [Periodical] and for [X] months after.

3. Happy Periodical Publisher agrees that, after acceptance, if it decides not to publish the article, I shall be entitled to the entire payment agreed upon.

4. Happy Periodical Publisher agrees to reimburse me for the following reasonable expenses: _____,
for which I agree to submit receipts, within thirty (30) days of the delivery of my article.

5. I agree to allow Happy Periodical Publisher to use my name, biography, and likeness for promotional purposes, subject to my right of approval, not to be unreasonably withheld.

I appreciate your attention to these concerns, and look forward to working together on my article. Please contact me if you wish to discuss any of these issues. If these terms are acceptable, please sign this letter where indicated below and return it to me.

Sincerely,

Accepted by: _____

CHAPTER 13

FILM AND TELEVISION

CONTRACTS AND

DRAMATIC PRODUCTIONS

F ilm and television producers must draw together many financial and creative elements that are necessary to put together a finished product. This process is generally known as the "development stage." The first thing the producers must do in this stage is to obtain control of the rights to the project's storyline, before any project can be presented to potential financiers or creative talent. As with theater, it is common for film or television producers to obtain an *option* to buy a particular book or script from the author(s). An option allows the producer the exclusive right to shop the work, to see if there is sufficient financial and creative interest before deciding whether or not to actually purchase the work outright from the author. Thus, the author will be required to negotiate at least two fees: one (or more) for the length of the option period, including extensions, and the other for the purchase of the work in the event the option is exercised. Film and television options and the purchase agreements that accompany them are quite complex. This chapter is meant only to serve as a starting point from which you can begin to understand the basic terms and structure of such a transaction. There are several excellent books for authors by experts in this field that explain all components of these deals in great detail, including *Dealmaking in the Film and Television Industry* by Mark Litwak and *Hollywood Dealmaking: Negotiating Talent Agreements* by Dina Appleton and Daniel Yankelevits. If you contemplate writing for these industries or having a book or story optioned, you should read more about these transactions. Be advised: Any author contemplating a film or television offer needs to retain an agent or an attorney who specializes in this field.

FILM AND TELEVISION OPTIONS—BOOK AND FREELANCE AUTHORS

The process of turning your book into a motion picture involves two contracts: (1) the "option," which places the rights on hold and gives the purchaser the right to purchase them in the future, and (2) the related "purchase agreement," through which the rights themselves are actually transferred. The prospective purchaser of the movie rights usually presents the two contracts to the author in tandem.

As the holder of copyright in a book or article, only you may legally create—or authorize the creation of—a movie or other work based on your work. The option does not entail the actual purchase of the rights to make a movie; rather, it secures the exclusive right to purchase those rights at some later time. Payment for an option is smaller than the payment to be made upon exercise of the option and actual purchase of the property. Often, an option agreement will have attached a completed purchase agreement to be used if the option is exercised. Both contracts are negotiated at the same time. This might appear to be an unnecessary extra step, or evidence of a lack of commitment on the part of the purchaser; in fact, it is common practice in the industry, and it makes sense. Even the initial planning stages of a film or television project can be very expensive, so a would-be purchaser usually needs the opportunity to analyze a project's potential before he decides to buy. The option serves this practical purpose for the buyer. It should also serve to protect you, the author.

A valid option is irrevocable for as long as it lasts. Once you give someone a valid option on your work, you can neither take it back nor interfere with the optioning party's ability exercise his right to purchase the property while the option period lasts. It is also important to keep in mind that a letter or a simple memo memorializing a deal (often called a "deal memo") can be binding as a "short-form" option contract. Any such memo, therefore, should be negotiated with care, even if you and the other party plan to enter into a more formal contract later. The good news is, if an established producer options your unpublished book for the movies, it is almost assured a publishing deal, because if the film is made, the book will usually have strong sales. This is what happened with *The Horse Whisperer* by Nicholas Evans, which was first sold to the movies, but also quickly reached the bestseller list for books.

The following sections provide a general explanation of terms and clauses you will encounter in option and purchase agreements.

GRANT OF RIGHTS

Be aware of the potential breadth of what might appear at first glance to be a very simple grant of rights. The phrases "all allied" or "ancillary" rights, for example, can be stretched to include just about anything—not just the right to make a film based on your work, but the right to make sequels, television movies and series, the right to publish a special "movie version" of your book, and even merchandising and advertising rights. The seemingly narrower phrase "motion picture and television rights" is in reality similarly broad, potentially including a conflict with rights you have already granted in a publishing contract.

Most option purchasers will try to get all of these rights for one price, but sellers with leverage and good representation can often retain some of these rights, thereby negotiating additional royalties for the reserved rights. Authors should be able to retain the rights to print publication, novelizations, author-written sequels, audio rights, live TV and radio, and dramatic stage rights. For any of these reserved rights, the option purchaser might impose a so-called hold back, which would preclude you from exploiting any of the rights reserved for a period of three to five years (it is possible to vary these numbers) from the motion-picture release date, or from writing more than one sequel in a particular time period.

In addition to understanding and limiting the scope of your grant, take express care to reserve all rights you are not granting. Consider the following sample language: "All rights not specifically granted in this agreement, including but not limited to [the rights you wish to reserve], are reserved to the author."

TERM

The length of an option can vary, but a typical range might be any-where from six to eighteen months. To make sure there is no confu-sion over the exact end date, provide expressly that "the term shall expire at midnight, [X] months after the date of the execution of the agreement." Option terms can be, and frequently are, extended or renewed automatically. That is, all the purchaser will have to do is pro-vide you with notice and payment for the renewal period. Often, the payment for the second term is higher than the original amount. Try not to agree to more than one automatic renewal—the purchaser can always offer you another option payment for a new term. If the exer-cise of the option is your main goal, you might want to provide that the option can be extended or renewed only if the purchaser can prove to you that he has taken steps toward actually exercising the option. These might include the purchaser having searched out and secured the participation of one or more of the necessary players in making a film: director, screenwriter, or actors. You might also try to do the following:

- Limit the number of times, and terms under which, the purchaser can renew the option
- Provide for renewal periods that are shorter than the original option period
- Get paid more for the renewal period(s) than for the original option

Sometimes, an optioning party purchases an option (and several renewals) without any intention of actually exercising it. Purchasers might do this for any number of reasons, including eliminating poten-tially competitive rights or similar ideas. That might be fine with you; there are more than a few writers out there making a very nice living selling options they expect will never be exercised. Whatever your real expectations, you should try to negotiate your option as if it is all you expect to realize from Hollywood.

While most book-based movies follow publication of the book, it is possible for a valuable option opportunity to arise before a book's publication—for example, if a producer gets hold of an unpublished manuscript. If faced with this situation, try to negotiate the deal so that your option expires, without possibility of renewal, before your book's planned publication date. The excitement of seeing a property before it has been published may drive up its value. If the book is a success, you will have a second chance to market it to Hollywood.

OPTION PRICE

While the price of an option will always be negotiable and will vary according to a number of common-sense factors—such as your reputation, bargaining power, and the scope of the rights you are granting—you might reasonably expect an option payment to be approximately 10 percent of the full purchase price. The average option fee probably falls somewhere around $10,000 (closer to $50,000 for authors with powerful representation), but the price of an option can vary enormously, from hundreds of thousands of dollars to almost nothing.

Unless you perceive no chance of selling your rights elsewhere or the situation otherwise dictates (for example, you are dealing in the arena of independent films, where there is less money to be had up front, or you have extreme confidence that the movie will ultimately be made), you should probably push for the largest option price you can get. Always remember that the odds are against the possibility that your option will ever be exercised, so the option price is likely to be all that you realize in the end. It pays to negotiate accordingly. If the purchaser claims not to be able to pay a large option fee, one way to grant the option but still protect your interests is to ask for what is known as a "lay off" or "set up" bonus. For example, if your purchaser offers $1,000 instead of the $10,000 you want for your option, you might grant it for $1,000, but include a statement providing that if that purchaser is able to transfer the option to a major party, such as a motion picture studio, that $1,000 becomes $10,000 (or more) when the purchaser transfers the option. The following language provides another important precaution: "Whether or not notice is ever provided, any commencement of principal photography by the purchaser or its assignees will constitute exercise of the option, and will trigger the obligation to make immediate payment of the specified purchase price." Much like an advance against future book royalties, the initial option payment is usually applied against the purchase price should the buyer exercise the option. However, extension or renewal fees are commonly not credited against the purchase price.

If the purchaser fails to exercise the option during the specified time period, the option should call for the agreement to terminate automatically, with all rights reverting to you (and of course, all option money retained by you). Authors with considerable clout are also sometimes able to stipulate that, if after the exercise of the option, there has still been no production of the work for a specified number of years, all rights will revert to the author, albeit with a lien against the project for the amount invested in production, to be satisfied by any future purchaser. By reclaiming your rights in this way, you improve the odds that a picture will ultimately get made by someone, if not the original purchaser.

PURCHASE PRICE

The ideal situation would be for an author to postpone negotiation of the purchase price until the purchaser is ready to exercise the option. By then, he will have invested considerable time and money in the project, placing you in a far better negotiating position than when the movie is just a distant possibility. Knowing this, your purchaser is sure to insist on settling both the option and the purchase price up front.

If you believe that the film being planned is the type that might lend itself to a big budget, you might want to push for a percentage of the budget (3.5 percent is considered favorable), with a fixed floor and ceiling, in lieu of a fixed purchase price. However, when negotiating, you might begin by asking for something like 3.5 percent of the budget, with a floor of perhaps $125,000 and no ceiling (floor and ceiling figures will vary, depending upon a number of factors). When the budget is uncertain and a fair purchase price is difficult to ascertain, the purchaser may be equally interested in a percentage-based purchase price (but will surely insist on a ceiling).

Beware of offers of a share of the film's "net profits." No matter how thrilling it sounds to be offered a percentage of the profits on a film (ideally 5 percent, although 2 or 3 percent is common), for various reasons, not least of which is the movie industry's fantastic method of calculating "net" profits, you should view a percentage of the profits as a highly unlikely bonus. Instead, weigh the option and purchase payments as if they constituted total payment, and negotiate accordingly. Authors with genuine clout can, of course, try—as the producer, director, and stars of the film will have—to negotiate for a percentage of the *gross* profits, which do mean something. For all but the most powerful authors, this is rare. If a share in gross profits is out of reach, try asking for a percentage of something called "adjusted gross." It is not "true" gross, but it is better than "net profits." Working closely with an experienced agent or lawyer, your goal will be to negotiate some portion and/or combination of initial option price, renewal price(s), purchase price, bonuses, and a percentage of something that works for you.

WARRANTIES AND REPRESENTATIONS

As in a standard publishing contract, you will probably be asked to promise that your work does not infringe any third-party rights, including copyright, defamation, and privacy. The same general principles apply here as are applied for books—seek both to qualify your promises realistically and to limit your financial responsibility should someone bring suit.

FILM AND TELEVISION OPTIONS—SCREENPLAYS

Before submitting a script or treatment to anyone for purposes of optioning it, you would do well to register the work with the Writers Guild of America (WGA). Upon entering into any agreement, either with an agent or directly with a production company, refer to the

WGA's Theatrical and Television Film Basic Agreement, which provides minimum compensation levels to consider before you begin negotiations. If the production company interested in your work is a signatory to the WGA Agreement, then these minimum compensation levels, in addition to the other terms and conditions set forth by the WGA, must govern your contract. Even if the WGA Agreement is not applicable, its terms and conditions are still considered important guidelines for writers in non-Guild arrangements.

Writers employed in the creation of television and film scripts are usually required to join the WGA. The WGA periodically negotiates revisions of its collective-bargaining agreement with numerous production companies. You may obtain a copy of the agreement from the Writers Guild.

In a screenplay author's contract for film rights, the grant of rights will usually be quite extensive, although distinctions have to be made between television and film, which reach completely different markets. The practice with respect to artistic control is exactly the opposite as it is with dramatic plays and musicals. You can expect to have little control over changes in the property and the final form it takes. You should seek the right to perform the first and/or subsequent revisions of the script. Also, you will invariably have to give the production company the power to assign the contract (although the production company may remain liable if the assignee fails to fulfill its obligations), because financing arrangements require this. If you negotiate a share of receipts from the film's distribution, the contract must specify whose receipts, the producer's or the production company's, and how receipts are defined. A well-known writer who sells a novel to a film company can negotiate up to 5 percent of the film company's income from the film. Billing credit also requires specification because of the number of people and companies involved in creating the end product. The WGA will arbitrate disputes over billing credits. This aspect, along with many other benefits, makes membership in the WGA worthwhile, if not essential, for screenwriters.

One increasingly common scenario is the simultaneous sale of a novel to a publishing company and a film studio. The writer, who has recently sold a novel to a publishing company, will have his or her agent negotiate screenplay rights with a production company. If the novelist is a first-time screenwriter, he or she will usually be paid WGA scale (anywhere from $35,000 to $50,000) to produce a first draft, and receive equal amounts for second, third, and final ("polish") drafts. The terms of these agreements give the producer or production company the option to reassign the material to another writer if they deem the first or subsequent drafts unsatisfactory. The WGA has a current list of scale rates for all theatrical and film deals.

DRAMATIC PRODUCTIONS

Before negotiating any agreement for the use of your work in a dramatic production, investigate the theater market in which the producer intends to stage the production. By talking with writers and others who work in the industry, you can obtain important information about realistic terms and clauses. The Dramatists Guild is a valuable resource for those seeking information about certain theater markets. The Guild has developed many contracts for use by its members, which in some instances are considered standard in the industry and in others are good references. The Guild's minimum basic production contract for an Off-Broadway production was never completely negotiated between the Guild and the League of Off-Broadway Theater Owners, so it is not the true industry "standard" for that market, but it is helpful as a model. Any writer marketing a dramatic play or musical can benefit significantly by joining the Dramatists Guild for both advice and information from which to start negotiations.

Generally, theaters are classified as one of three market standards: Broadway, Off-Broadway, and Off-Off-Broadway. These classifications reflect the overall theater market in New York City and are based on a theater's size and geographic location. Broadway theaters, also known as first-class theaters, are located in Manhattan between Fifth and Ninth Avenues from 34th Street to 56th Street and between Fifth Avenue and the Hudson River from 56th Street to 72nd Street. These theaters have a seating capacity of five hundred or more. For the Broadway market, the Dramatists Guild and the League of American Theaters and Producers negotiated what is now known as the Approved Production Contract. This contract contains a range of minimum and maximum terms to be negotiated between writer and producer.

Off-Broadway theaters include all other theaters located in Manhattan that seat fewer than five hundred people and are located outside the area defined for Broadway theaters. As mentioned previously, there are no standard contracts that present guidelines for writers negotiating with producers in this market. Off-Off-Broadway theaters are generally all theaters that do not fall into the previous two classifications. These theaters include profit and nonprofit theater organizations. Negotiating with such theaters typically comes down to what terms the theater can afford to give, versus what the author will accept. There are no "standard" terms in this class of theater. These three classes of theaters do not cover every type of theater willing to produce plays, but understanding the differences between the classes and the terms governing their production contracts can help you formulate a reasonable strategy to negotiate any production agreement.

In most circumstances, producers initially take an option to produce a dramatic play or musical. The option agreement addresses issues such as terms of payment, billing credit, script changes, usage rights for the script, creative approval rights, travel and other expenses, and reserved seating for productions of the play. An advance against future royalties is paid for the option, which typically lasts for anywhere between a six-month and one-year term, and is usually renewable for additional terms if certain conditions are met.

If the producer successfully previews and opens the play before the expiration of a time period specified in the option or extensions of the option, the writer's compensation is then based on a percentage of the box office's weekly receipts ("receipts" are carefully defined in the Dramatists Guild's standard contracts). A production that runs beyond a stipulated number of performances gains additional rights for the producer, such as the right to do first-class tours, to do a British production, to move from Off-Broadway to Broadway, to reopen the show after it has closed, to have a share in motion picture rights, and to have a monetary interest in other subsidiary rights. Typically, the producer acquires no control over the subsidiary rights; he merely receives a right to share in proceeds, if the original play or musical has a long enough run. The author retains control over the disposition of subsidiary rights, which can include worldwide motion picture rights and the following rights in the continental United States and Canada: radio, television, second-class touring performances, foreign-language performances, concert tour versions, condensed and tabloid versions, commercial uses, play albums or records, stock and amateur performances, and musicals based on the play. The producer's right to a percentage of subsidiaries (that is, income from subsidiary rights) applies only to contracts executed within a specified number of years after the close of the production.

CHAPTER 14

ELECTRONIC RIGHTS, E-BOOKS, AND AUDIO LICENSES

The extraordinary power of digital technology and computer networks, obviously including the World Wide Web, has in the last decade revolutionized the way information reaches the public. This transformation raises complicated issues regarding ownership and control of the information (the "content"). Technology has often pushed the boundaries of the copyright law, but since the passage of the 1976 Act, the courts have generally interpreted the law favorably for creators (the "content providers"). The Digital Millennium Copyright Act of 1998, discussed in chapter 6, demonstrates the government's commitment to continuing to reward creativity in the Information Age. This chapter will discuss publishers' attempts to take more than their appropriate share of the proceeds that new technologies make possible and the courts' rejection of those attempts. It will also discuss the current market for e-books and other new media in which literature can be distributed, and explain how to protect your interests in contracting with new media publishers and producers (including audio book licenses).

Today, a writer's work can be disseminated through media not imagined by most even ten years ago, including CD-ROM (which can store tens of thousands of pages of text and images), CD-Interactive, electronic databases (which might be accessed through the Internet or other online services), and, of course, the Internet. There is now the capacity to produce printed books "on demand," eliminating the necessity of a print run of thousands of copies of a title. E-books (digitized books distributed through and appearing on computer screens), could revolutionize the economics of publishing by virtually eliminating the costs of production, storage, shipping, and returns, and they are currently receiving much attention from traditional print publishers and new companies. The market for all of these new media uses of books has grown slowly, and there have been failures along the way. In the mid-1990s, CD-ROMs proved prohibitively expensive to produce and generally unattractive to consumers, so they quickly fell out of favor with most producers and publishers. The earliest "dedicated" e-book readers were cumbersome, expensive, and did not supply the screen resolution needed to make the reading experience comfortable. Few of the start-ups that marketed them in the late 1990s now remain. Nonetheless, advances in technology will relieve all those problems in time, and the range of works published, disseminated, and read via new technologies will most likely increase dramatically in the coming years.

The World Wide Web and the proliferation of private electronic databases and intranets have already created opportunities and threats to the interests of both publishers and writers. On the one hand, publishers have the opportunity to cut out suppliers, manufacturers, and wholesalers, and sell directly to consumers. The danger for publishers is that they will be unable to control access to the content they are selling and so will suffer losses through unauthorized dissemination. The lower cost of entry into the field of publishing might increase competition among publishers, not just for readers, but for the writers who learn they no longer need traditional publishers and traditional publishing contracts to reach their readers. The reading public, inundated with content and benefiting from pirates' efforts to make information "free" on the Web, will become less willing to pay for books and articles, hurting publishers and authors. On the other hand, for writers, information technologies promise new opportunities to earn compensation from reuses of their previously published work. Many authors have seen the placement of their work online build, rather than cannibalize, their traditional markets.

Predictably, traditional publishers have reacted to the promise and the threats of new technologies by trying, through hardball tactics (including litigation), to obtain as many rights from authors for as little money as possible. Fortunately, courts have recognized that creators must be fairly compensated if they are to continue to create "content"—the lifeblood of the industry. This chapter will also examine the struggle between producers and creators over ownership of literary work in the Digital Age.

DIGITAL REUSES OF FREELANCE CONTRIBUTIONS

In June 2001 the Supreme Court ruled that the *New York Times, New York Newsday,* and *Sports Illustrated* (a publication of Time, Inc.) had infringed the copyrights of six freelance writers by selling their articles for inclusion in the LEXIS/NEXIS electronic database and University Microfilms International's CD-ROM products without the authors' permission. *New York Times, et al. v. Tasini, et al.,* 121 S. Ct. 238 (2001). The decision could have far-reaching economic ramifications for thousands of freelance journalists and authors as well as for the hundreds of print publishers and electronic databases that make freelance articles available to subscribers.

The Supreme Court decision finally determined, after more than eight years of litigation, that the plaintiffs, all freelance contributors of articles to the print publishers, have the exclusive right to authorize the reproduction and distribution of their articles through electronic databases. Their print publishers do not have this right. The defendants, which included the three print publishers and the two electronic publishers, had argued that the Copyright Act automatically allowed them to reuse freelance contributions in the lucrative electronic databases, without permission from the authors. The publishers also turned a familiar argument made by anticopyright activists against the authors, namely that electronic databases have become so necessary to modern-day research that a requirement to obtain the freelancers' permission would lead to the wide-scale removal of freelance articles from the databases, with "devastating" effects on scholarship. The Supreme Court rejected both arguments. First, the publishers claimed that a privilege afforded to publishers of collective works under the Copyright Act justified their actions. The privilege appears in Section 201(c) of the Act:

> In the absence of an express transfer of the copyright or of any rights under it, the owner of copyright in the collective work [here, the print publisher] is presumed to have acquired only the privilege of reproducing and distributing the [freelance] contribution as part of that particular collective work, any revision of that collective work, and any later collective work in the same series.

The defendants argued unsuccessfully that the databases' reproduction and distribution of the contributions along with the staff-written content of the periodicals was simply the exercise of this "privilege of reproducing and distributing the contributions as part of [a] revision of that collective work." For this argument to make sense, the Court would have had to accept either that an immense electronic database such as NEXIS is a "revision" of each of its constituent publications, or that when a freelance article is found and read by a user of the database it is at that point still a "part of" the original periodical.

The opinion looked at the freelance articles "as presented to and perceptible by" the users of the databases—that is, disconnected from the original periodical. When users search an electronic database for articles, the results are not presented in the context provided by the original edition or a revision thereof, as they might be in microfilm or microfiche. The articles found in the search are copied and distributed to the user separately, without any visible link to the other stories originally published within the periodical. Therefore, in the majority's view, the articles in the databases are not copied and distributed "as part of" the original publication or a revision of it. Furthermore, to deem the databases a "revision" of each constituent edition would be akin to calling a four-hundred-page novel that quotes a sonnet in passing a "revision" of the sonnet. Thus, the opinion concluded, the publishers' uses of the freelance articles "invade the core of the Authors' exclusive rights under [Copyright law.]"

To the second argument, that a ruling for the writers would decimate the "nation's historical archives" by requiring the databases to remove freelance materials, the majority pointed out that such a result is not required by the recognition of freelancers' electronic rights. "The parties . . . may enter into an agreement allowing continued electronic reproduction of the Authors' works; they . . . may draw on numerous models for distributing copyrighted works and remunerating authors for their distribution. . . . In any event, speculation about future harms is no basis for this Court to shrink authorial rights Congress established in 201(c)." *New York Times et al. v. Tasini et al.,* 121 S. Ct. at 243.

Important as the Supreme Court's ruling was for establishing the principle of freelancers' electronic rights in their articles, the task of obtaining an effective financial remedy for these lucrative reuses is still just beginning. Shortly after the lower court ruled in favor of the authors in *Tasini,* several other freelancers brought a copyright infringement action against nine electronic databases, on behalf of themselves and all others who wrote articles for publication since January 1, 1978 that then appeared in any of the databases without the authors' permission. The Authors Guild is a plaintiff in that putative class action. *The Authors Guild, Inc., et al. v. Dialog, et al.* Two similar suits were filed at around the same time, in one of which the National Writers Union is a plaintiff. All three cases have been consolidated into a Multi-District Litigation ("MDL action") in the Southern District of New York under the name *In re Literary Works in Electronic Databases Copyright Litigation.* The *Tasini* ruling removes a tremendous hurdle for the freelancers, because liability for the databases' past actions has been irrefutably established, but *Tasini* only established the principle for its six plaintiffs. It was not a class action, so the other suits are necessary to effectuate the Supreme Court decision for all affected writers. The MDL court has ordered mediation, which was slated to begin shortly as of this writing.

Publishers and databases have said publicly that the consolidated suits against them precipitated some purging of freelance material from online databases following the Supreme Court decision. They point to the decision as heralding the demise of a complete historical record of published news. This argument is nonsensical. The removal of freelance articles from electronic databases has nothing to do with the class action lawsuits against those databases. When the Supreme Court decided *Tasini,* the liability of the databases for copyright infringement was confirmed. Databases and some publishers have chosen to respond to the decision by deleting articles, rather than negotiating with writers for the use of their works. Taking the freelance articles down does not change the databases' liability for past infringement (which is the bulk of the MDL lawsuits' claim), although if they had left the articles up without negotiating a license, their liability, regardless of the existing suits, would have been substantial. Therefore, the class actions provide a mechanism for either a blanket release from the claims against all the defendants via a negotiated settlement, or a mass judgment regarding the claims. If you published a freelance work in one of thousands of newspapers and magazines any time after January 1, 1978, chances are high that it appears in one of the defendant databases. If you did not expressly grant to your publisher the right to relicense your work to a database, then you might well be a member of the class. A settlement of all the claims together is the best opportunity for authors and publishers to restore the works to electronic databases while fairly compensating the authors. Ironically, use of these databases is very expensive, leaving most freelance authors unable to afford access to their own articles, unless they work for educational institutions or corporations.

THE AUTHORS REGISTRY

Bookkeeping demands have been a major stumbling block to getting publishers to negotiate licenses for electronic reuses with their contributors, because they argue that they cannot make many payments of small sums of money for electronic reuses. The Authors Registry was created in 1995 by fifteen writers' organizations, including the Authors Guild, the American Society of Journalists and Authors, Association of Authors Representatives, and the Dramatists Guild, together with eighty literary agents, specifically to alleviate that problem. The Authors Registry is a nonprofit organization formed to help expedite the flow of royalty payments and small reuse fees to authors, particularly for new-media uses. It has been called the ASCAP (the American Society of Composers, Authors and Publishers, the licensing society for songwriters and performers) for writers. Virtually every important writers' organization and more than a hundred literary agencies currently work with the Registry. It has approximately thirty thousand writers registered in its database. The Registry's services are ideal for helping authors control the rights to their works and can help ensure income due for those rights that might otherwise be lost.

As payment clearinghouse for certain categories of royalties and fees, the Registry lifts the burden from publishers and delivers checks to freelancers. Such publications as *Cooking Light, Food & Wine, Harper's* and *Travel & Leisure* have worked with the Registry to share database royalties from third parties or pay fees for articles reused on the Internet. The Registry also distributes to U.S. authors fees paid for photocopying of their work in the United Kingdom. To date, the Registry has distributed more than $1,500,000 to authors. The Registry retains a 5 percent commission to offset some of its costs in distributing these payments. You might already belong, if you are affiliated with one of the Registry's cooperating writers' organizations or literary agencies. Contact your agency or writers group for confirmation. Individual authors not covered may join for $10.

Protecting copyright is a paramount concern for authors and their advocates, despite the tension that exists at times between the goals of widespread dissemination of works and fair compensation for the creators of that work. Publishers are certainly steadfast in arguing to courts and Congress that others should not disseminate or profit from copyright owners' property without permission and compensation. The electronic-database lawsuits actions could serve to extend that basic principle to publishers and databases, and the Registry could be the mechanism "for distributing copyrighted works and remunerating authors for their distribution . . ." that the Supreme Court in *Tasini* suggested the publishers find.

E-BOOKS

"E-books" are what the publishing industry has come to call digital works that can be read on a computer screen or an electronic device such as a personal digital assistant or a dedicated reading device. Typically, e-books can only be read after they are purchased and downloaded into a computer that contains Microsoft Reader, Adobe Acrobat Reader, or Adobe Acrobat eBook Reader software. Those software formats are available for downloading for free through the Internet.

Although the text of an e-book might be exactly the same as the text of a printed version of a work, the e-book contains functions that its digital format makes possible beyond those of a printed book. For example, e-book users can search the work electronically to find specific words and phrases. They can electronically "highlight" and "bookmark" certain text, which can then be automatically indexed and accessed through hyperlinks. They can use hyperlinks in the table of contents to jump to specific chapters. They can type electronic notes that are stored with related text, and the notes can be automatically indexed, sorted, and filed. Users can also change the font size and style of the text to accommodate personal preferences and can find a definition of any word in the text. Most e-book publishers provide certain security features to prevent customers from printing, e-mailing, or otherwise distributing the text to others.

RANDOM HOUSE V. ROSETTA BOOKS

In February 2001, Random House, the largest English-language book publisher in the world, sued Rosetta Books, a startup e-book publisher, claiming copyright infringement of its exclusive book publishing rights. Rosetta had licensed the e-book rights to eight classic novels from William Styron, Kurt Vonnegut, Jr., and Robert Parker, all of who had signed standard book-publishing contracts with a Random House predecessor in the 1960s, 1970s, or 1980s. No mention of electronic rights or e-books was made in these contracts. Instead, Random House argued that the traditional right to "print, publish and sell the Work in book form," which appears in approximately twenty thousand of its "backlist" book contracts still in force, necessarily includes the exclusive right to exploit the works in e-book form.

In July 2001, Judge Sidney Stein of the federal court for the Southern District of New York denied Random House's motion for a preliminary injunction that would have barred Rosetta from publishing the e-book editions. *Random House, Inc. v. Rosetta Books, et al.,* 150 F. Supp. 2d 613 (S.D.N.Y. 2001). Judge Stein decisively rejected Random House's argument that such a grant should be construed to include electronic books. "Relying on the language of the contracts and basic principles of contract interpretation," wrote Judge Stein, "this Court finds that the right to 'print, publish and sell the work[s] in book form' in the contracts at issue does not include the right to publish the works in the format that has come to be known as the 'eBook.'" This preliminary ruling was affirmed on appeal to the Second Circuit Court of Appeals, and the litigation continues.

For authors, at stake in this case is the fundamental interpretation of book contracts, documents that carefully and explicitly define the rights and formats that are being licensed to a publisher and clearly spell out the royalties to be paid for the exploitation of these rights. Should Random House prevail on appeal, the traditional interpretation of other specifically enumerated rights, including the traditional "reservation of rights" clause, could be thrown into question. This could prevent authors from fairly sharing in the rewards of the electronic publishing industry by allowing only publishers to exploit these rights and preventing entrepreneurial companies such as Rosetta Books from acquiring the rights to tens of thousands of works. For these reasons, the Authors Guild has been actively involved in the case, advising Rosetta's attorneys on book industry practice and filing joint amicus briefs with the Association of Authors' Representatives, the organization of literary agents. The Guild/AAR briefs urged the court, among other things, to consult Random House's own dictionary for definitions of "book" and "form."

E-BOOK CONTRACTS

If Rosetta wins on appeal, published authors will have the opportunity to license the e-book rights to their works to anyone. Even if Random House wins, all authors will have the opportunity to negotiate e-book contracts for works that are not currently licensed to print publishers. This section will discuss important terms of e-book contracts that all authors ought to consider.

First and foremost, authors who are interested in digital publishing should find a publisher who respects their work and a publishing agreement that reflects fundamental standards of fair industry practice. Do not grant broad rights. Beware of the contract that defines digital rights unnecessarily broadly to include audio book rights and rights to digitally printed books, such as print-on-demand books. It is not appropriate to ask for rights that the publisher does not have the means or intent to exploit to your advantage. Only grant what the publisher needs to serve both parties' purposes here—to create and sell e-books.

Royalties for e-books should be generous, because they can be produced at practically no cost. Although Random House is attempting to overreach in suing Rosetta and claiming the e-book rights to its entire backlist, it does offer a competitive royalty for e-books—50 percent of its net income from sales. How it defines "net income" might be flexible, unfortunately, but Random House and three other large publishers recently signed to distribute e-books through Yahoo.com, an online service provider, in exchange for 15 percent of the sale. If the author receives 50 percent of 85 percent of the retail price for e-books, that is a good deal. Even at a low retail price of $5, the author would enjoy a fairly generous royalty—more than $2 per sale. Other publishers are selling through Amazon.com and BarnesandNoble.com at higher discounts, which makes less economic sense. Still others offer 25 percent of net, or 10 to 15 percent of the retail price. Those offers are unreasonably low. Remember, there is little cost in manufacturing an e-book compared to a print book. If the e-book publisher selects works to publish electronically, it should pay an advance, just as it pays the author an advance when it selectively acquires rights to publish a work in traditional form. Only then might the publisher be justified in tying up other literary rights as well.

Some e-book publishers will publish anything they receive, charging the authors the up-front costs and paying them the lion's share of sales income. The best way to assess these publishers and these deals is to do some research:

- ➭ What other authors, and what caliber of title, is the company publishing? If you do not object to your book appearing in their company in the eyes of the world, great. If not, then stay away.
- ➭ Are the costs reasonable, in light of the technological services the publisher is providing?

✏ What is the cost of converting your work to e-book form and making it available for distribution through Internet retailers? If you are sending your work in digital form and no editing is to be done, this should not be a large expense.

✏ Does the company's business model rely on authors' participation payments, or on sales? Obviously, the latter is preferable.

✏ What rights is the publisher interested in? If you decide to go with a pay-for-service company, you should not have to grant exclusive rights. Only grant the rights that the publisher needs to copy and distribute the work in the chosen formats, for example, "a nonexclusive, transferable, worldwide right and license to copy, promote, transmit and distribute the Work in the following digital formats and channels of distribution . . ." Do not grant any subsidiary rights, unless your up-front payment is low.

✏ Does the company offer state-of-the-art piracy protection? Always satisfy yourself that your work will be protected from online piracy.

In all cases, the publisher should promise to collect and remit all monies due to you from sales of the e-book and issue a report of earnings at least once per quarter. If royalties are based on "net proceeds," define "net" explicitly. Most contracts, if they define net, call it the retail price of the work sold, less third-party discounts, fees, and less the cost of conversion and encryption. Make sure pay-per-service e-book publishers will consult with you as to the price, appearance, format, production, copyediting, style, and promotion of your work. Perhaps most important, retain a right to cancel the contract on reasonable notice—at most, sixty days—to the publisher. If another publisher wants to publish the work in print form and requires an e-book license as well, you should be free to accept the offer. It is fair to provide that in the event you terminate, the e-book publisher will have the right to sell the work for a reasonable period of time after termination. This should not hurt your dealings with your new publisher, as it takes many months to make the work ready for print publication. The important consideration is that you retain the freedom to exploit your work fully, if it succeeds as an e-book.

AUDIO LICENSES

Interest in audio rights has grown dramatically over the past fifteen years. In the past, audio rights were nearly always granted to the publisher as a subsidiary right, but with the recent popularity of audio books on tape, established authors are now reserving the rights. Consider whether or not your publisher will be able to sell audio rights better than you or your agent. In addition, consider whether the publisher can produce its own audiocassettes. If so, you might want to grant an option or a right of first refusal to the publisher of the printed book.

There are a number of issues that arise in all audio rights contracts, which you should bear in mind in order to avoid common and costly errors or omissions. Limit the grant of rights with respect to duration, territory, language, and exclusivity. The duration of audio rights is often shorter than the duration of book rights, which are usually tied to the term of copyright (provided, of course, that the book remains in print). The reason for this is simple: As with digitized books, audiocassettes need never go out of print because it is relatively inexpensive to make single copies. On the other hand, even though new technology has increased the viability of small printings, books usually must be printed in lots of at least 1,500 to 2,000 copies. The money laid out by the publisher in reprinting the book justifies the longer duration of book rights. If the publisher's grant was limited to a specific number of years, the company would be likely to let the book go out of print sooner than it otherwise would, in order to prevent a forced remainder sale when its rights in the book expire. As a result, it is not at all uncommon for the grant of audio rights to be limited to a term of between seven and ten years after initial publication. The publisher will usually demand an option, which you might be able to limit to a period of time not to exceed ninety days after the initial term expires, in which to negotiate in good faith for an extension or renewal of the audio rights grant.

Publishers generally want the widest possible territory, such as worldwide rights and all languages, but might settle for English-language rights, although they will likely insist upon the right to distribute such English-language tapes throughout the world. Again, make certain that the publisher has access to all the markets included in the grant of rights. One way to do this is to ask the publisher for a breakdown of gross sales by country.

The question of whether to grant exclusive or nonexclusive audio rights turns on similar factors as the grant of territory and language. Is the publisher better situated than the author or agent to sell audio rights? If you believe that the book will have strong sales, consider retaining at least a nonexclusive right to make audiocassettes because the value of the rights, and the potential players in any sale, will change dramatically if the book is successful. On the other hand, a grant of nonexclusive rights might eliminate the publisher's incentive to market them at all because of the lower value and the greater difficulty in selling them. Specify that the audio version of the book will be stored on "magnetic tape in the form of an audiocassette." This is important to ensure that there is no confusion as to rights in other possible forms of audio or audiovisual works, such as multimedia productions, the soundtrack to a movie, or even the movie itself. Indicating that the reading contained on the tape is non-dramatic will further ensure that future film rights are not jeopardized.

If you enter into a separate contract for audio rights, you should receive an advance against royalties. Because the standard royalty rates in audio-rights contracts are generally low, often escalating from 5 to 10 percent (sometimes with 1 percent added per 10,000 units sold), and are based on net receipts rather than retail price, you should negotiate for a substantial advance on the theory that there might not be much more money forthcoming.

Some of the issues involved in the sale of audio rights are similar to those encountered when negotiating printed book contracts. For an overview and analysis of the contractual issues that arise between writers and publishers, see chapter 11. For a checklist of negotiation points for audio rights contracts, see *Business and Legal Forms for Authors and Self-Publishers* by Tad Crawford (Allworth Press).

CHAPTER 15

LITERARY AGENTS AND

AGENCY AGREEMENTS

Having a literary agent can mean the difference between success and disappointment in your writing career. A good literary agent gives you the best chance to counter the disadvantages most authors face on the business side of their craft. Finding a publisher, especially the right publisher, can be a monumental challenge. Even if authors succeed in this search, they often lack the experience, business knowledge, contacts, and ability to negotiate effectively with would-be licensees of their work. Experienced agents have a superior ability to locate the right publisher, negotiate the best possible contract, and collect and police the fees, advances, and royalties due. As a liaison between writers and editors, an agent simplifies the search for a publisher. A good agent can often tell quickly whether a book will sell in its present form within the channels to which he or she has access. Knowledge of the market for different categories and genres of literature helps agents decide where to shop particular works or authors. Good agents have developed relationships with publishers and editors over time, and they should know which publishers are buying which kinds of books.

For their part, editors rely on agents to screen manuscripts. Many editors, especially those with the major houses, rarely consider unsolicited manuscripts that were not brought to them by agents. It has been reported that major trade publishers license more than 80 percent of the titles they publish through literary agents, and they often return unsolicited submissions with a form letter explaining that the house does not consider unsolicited materials. Smaller houses read through the "slush pile" more often, but are apt to make quick and superficial decisions because they lack the manpower of the larger houses. Often an agent will have to make twenty to thirty submissions before a book will find an appropriate publisher; independently, any author might have given up hope long before then.

Once a publishing company expresses interest, agents are better situated than authors to negotiate good deals without jeopardizing the author-publisher relationship. They can conduct auctions for specific rights that an author could never set up alone. With their experience and clout, agents are at least theoretically able to negotiate the narrowest grant of rights, the most generous royalties and subsidiary rights splits, and the most liberal delivery and satisfaction terms possible with a given publisher. The unwary author, negotiating for herself, is more likely to grant unduly broad rights, accept lower pay, and retain less control over her book's fate. Although authors of poetry, magazine articles, and short fiction might find they are quite capable of placing their work with a publisher, and textbook authors and other non–trade-book authors commonly sell their own work to publishers, many trade book authors believe that finding a good agent means the difference between a manuscript's publication and its stagnation.

FINDING AN AGENT

Given the close relationship that often develops between author and agent, and an author's need to trust in the agent's loyalty and business acumen, the process of selecting an agent is much like that of selecting a doctor or a lawyer. First, talk to other authors whose work and judgment you respect and ask them for referrals. To add to your target list of agents to contact, there are a number of other resources with valuable information. Foremost among these is the Association of Authors' Representatives (AAR) *(www.aar-online.org)*. Membership in the AAR is restricted to agents whose primary professional activity for the two years preceding their application for membership has been as an authors' representative or a playwrights' representative. To qualify for membership, literary agents must have been principally responsible for executed agreements concerning the grant of publication, translation or performance rights in ten different literary properties during the eighteen-month period preceding application. To qualify as a playwrights' agent in the AAR, the agent must have been principally responsible for executed agreements for the grant of rights for at least five stage productions before live audiences during the preceding two-year period. No license is required to call oneself a literary agent, but membership in the AAR is as close to a professional seal of approval as one can find. AAR members must conduct their business in compliance with an agent's legal and fiduciary duties to his clients, and each member agent must agree, in writing, to adhere to the AAR's Canon of Ethics, which you can find at AAR's Web site.

The AAR Web site also offers a list of its members, with contact information, but they urge authors before contacting any agents to review the latest edition of the *Literary Market Place* or the *Writer's Digest Guide to Literary Agents* for the agents' specific submission guidelines and marketing areas. A self-addressed, stamped envelope (SASE) *must* be enclosed with all queries and submissions. AAR members are proven experienced and ethical, but they are not necessarily the only agencies worthy of your business. Many good agents simply choose not to be members of the AAR.

The Literary Market Place (R. R. Bowker) is an annual directory that geographically lists literary agents and includes their areas of specialty. It is available in any library that has reference holdings. Although the *LMP* states that it requires agents to submit client references prior to being listed, it also accepts advertising, and some of the entities that advertise as agents are not listed in the agents' directory. As in any situation in which valuable property is to be entrusted to strangers, use caution and common sense before signing a contract or giving money or your manuscript to any person you do not know.

While the attainment of instant wealth need not be the sole focus in your search, knowing which agents and agencies consistently place manuscripts is valuable information. One great way to stay effortlessly plugged into the industry, its players, its deals, and the books that are making news is by subscribing to "Publishers' Lunch," an insightful and entertaining daily e-mail column by Michael Cader of Cader Books *(www.caderbooks.com)*, an experienced distributor and publishing industry entrepreneur. For good measure, Cader Books also sends out special "Deal Lunch" columns that list the major deals that literary agents have recently closed. *Publishers Weekly*, the leading industry publication, also has two daily subscription-based email columns that provide comprehensive industry news *(www.pwdaily.com)*.

Two classic books, *How to Get Happily Published* by Judith Appelbaum (HarperCollins) and *How To Be Your Own Literary Agent* by Richard Curtis (Houghton Mifflin), contain many helpful suggestions for finding an agent, preparing an initial query letter to an agency, negotiating the author-agent agreement, and severing the author-agent relationship. Another enterprising way to find agent candidates is to study the acknowledgments pages in your favorite books. If an author (preferably writing in the same field as yourself) has such fond sentiments for his agent that they are worthy of publication, that is a good sign that the agent is worth at least a query. Finally, you have to network, at least to some degree. Attend writers' conferences and conventions. These forums can give you excellent opportunities to meet agents looking for writers to represent, as well as other writers and editors who might be able to provide additional referrals.

Now that you have a list of potential literary agents, the next logical step is to send a query letter as opposed to blindly sending an entire manuscript to an agent. A query letter should be professional in tone, no longer than one 8.5" × 11" page, and should describe your publishing track record (if any) as well as your areas of expertise. List any completed manuscripts that are ready to be shopped. If you have never been published before, do not waste an agent's time by describing the great idea you have for a novel. A respectable agent will most likely ignore first-time authors with great ideas but nothing tangible to market to editors. By the same token, never send an entire manuscript. If someone referred you to the agent, mention that person's name—it might get an agent's attention if someone they know and respect has referred you to them. As an accommodation to an agent's busy calendar and to hasten a favorable reply, enclose a self-addressed stamped envelope.

Once you have received an agent's statement of interest, then you may send a manuscript or sample chapter(s) (policies vary from agency to agency). Agents do not like to consider simultaneous submissions, so the best approach is to submit to one agent at a time and withdraw the submission if the agent does not respond within a reasonable time (such as three or four weeks). You might also inquire up front how long an agent is likely to take to read submissions from potential new clients. If you are thinking of sending work (not just a simple query) to more than one agent, you should clarify that fact to each agent with whom you deal. The industry is very small, and the agents could learn about your multiple submissions even if you do not mention it. Agents are unlikely to take on as clients anyone they think has not been honest with them.

Be very wary of anyone who asks for money from you in exchange for reading your manuscript ("reading fees") or who gives your manuscript to a third party (who then asks you for money for "editorial services"), or who suggests a publishing deal is imminent, if only you will pay for some "insider's" way to break into the business or to "fix" your manuscript. Aspiring authors have been victimized many times by schemes set up to exploit their hopes by people who are not legitimate agents, editors, or publishers, with the sole object of separating the authors from their money. In 1996, the AAR rejected the practice of charging reading fees by its member agents. That was done because while some respected agencies do charge reading fees—which can cost upwards of several hundred dollars—many self-styled "agencies" charge reading fees but do little more than cash the author's check. An agency's income should be overwhelmingly comprised of commission fees for placing their client's intellectual property rights with licensees. Be sure to research thoroughly any agency that charges a fee and ask for a list of recent titles placed. If you are unsure about a practice you observe or any statement you are told, ask an experienced author, another agent, trusted editor, or a writers' group or forum to which you belong.

CHOOSING AN AGENT

If an agent expresses interest in representing you, arrange a personal meeting if possible, or at least a telephone conference. One of the best ways to find out about an agent is to talk with her current clients and professional colleagues. Interested agencies should be happy to put you in touch with some of them. Be diligent about doing so. Prior to signing on with a new agent, do not be afraid to ask questions:

- How long has the agent been in the business? What is her track record in placing works similar to yours? What size is the agency?
- Are there specialists in the agency that handle specific subsidiary rights?
- How are clients informed of the agent's activities in their behalf?
- Are all offers brought to the client? If not, which ones aren't?
- What is the agency commission for placing primary and subsidiary rights?
- How and when are client funds distributed?
- What expenses are charged to clients?
- Does the agent have a standard author-agent agreement, or will a simple handshake cement your business relationship?
- How may the agency agreement be terminated, and on what terms?
- Specifically what services will the agent perform for you?
- How many other clients will this agent represent in addition to representing you? If there are too many, you might not get the individualized attention that your career deserves; if too few, your prospective agent might lack the contacts needed to place your book expeditiously with a publisher.

Another question to consider is whether you want to work with a large agency such as ICM or William Morris or one of the numerous smaller agencies. The differences are comparable to attending a small college versus a large university. At a small agency, you should receive more personal attention, calls could be returned faster, and there should be more overall access to agency staff. Representation by a large agency lends clout when dealing with a publisher or subsidiary rights licensee, both in the placement stage and in the negotiating stage. The downside is that you are one of many authors represented, so your concerns will not always be foremost on your agent's mind. He or she might be trying to place more than just your work to the same market.

Whoever you end up choosing, call your agent only as often as you call your doctor or lawyer. If a writer takes too much of an agent's time, the agent might quickly conclude that the relationship is not economically worthwhile.

AGENCY AGREEMENTS

As your literary representative, the agent has a fiduciary duty to you, meaning that she is legally forbidden from harming your interests, disclosing confidential information about you, or even acting in conflict with your interests. She has some legal control over your rights. She can sometimes bind you to agreements made on your behalf even if you did not know about them. For these reasons, once you have made a good match and you are ready to work with an agent, consider putting the author-agent agreement in writing. Virtually any publishing contract your agent negotiates for you will include a clause that makes the agent a third-party beneficiary of the publishing contract, and it generally confirms that the agent represented the book and is entitled to collect her commission. Still, many agents ask their clients to sign a separate agency agreement. Having a separate agreement will avoid the problem of foggy memories over other critical issues if differences arise. The Authors Guild reviews its members' proposed author-agent contracts prior to signing to explain their terms and help ensure that they are fair.

The material terms in a typical agency contract, which are discussed briefly below, address the scope of the agent's right to represent you and your work(s), the mutual right to terminate the relationship, commissions and expenses, and the agent's duties to you. Exclusive right of representation means that during the period of representation, if an author enlists the services of a second agent and that agent (or anyone else, including the author) places the work, the author must still pay the first agent a commission. This is fair, considering that agents usually are obligated to use their best efforts to promote the work, and that authors dissatisfied with their agent's efforts or progress typically have (and certainly should have) the contractual right to terminate the agreement (see the following paragraph). Neither a separate contract nor an agency clause should contain the phrase "agency coupled with an interest." The agent does not hold an ownership interest in the work—only the right to fair compensation for his or her work. It is most prudent to begin an agency relationship by allowing the agent to shop one specific work. If the relationship doesn't work out, there will be fewer ties to sever. In addition, this arrangement allows authors, if they so choose, to enlist the services of another agent to market a different work. Be advised, however, that many agents would object to this arrangement, unless you have an objectively good reason for doing so (for example, the works allocated to each agent are of different genres or formats).

Having an at-will termination clause is perhaps the single most important protection you can provide for yourself in an agency contract. This clause states that you may end the agency agreement by giving advance notice (no more than thirty days notice is probably sufficient) whenever you deem it appropriate, without having to give any reason. If the agent has lost interest in representing a work or if you are displeased with the agent's representation, it is in both parties' interest that the agreement end quickly and easily. Keep in mind, however, that an agent is entitled to collect a commission on compensation earned for all works she has placed before the agency ended.

Before giving your agent the right to represent your work in all formats, including nonprint rights (such as film, electronic, merchandising) and foreign sales, question her about the agency's ability to place such rights. Limit the representation to those rights you believe the agent can adequately represent. Be aware, however, that many agents regularly and successfully use subagents to place these rights (providing that the agent and subagent together will collect no more than a 20 percent commission for placement of these rights).

Every agency contract should impose upon the agent the duties to use her best efforts to market your work, to submit all offers to the author (unless you wish otherwise), to attain your permission before signing any contracts, to take reasonable care of your materials, and to forward promptly royalty payments and correspondence to the author.

The agent should get your approval for miscellaneous expenses greater than a certain amount (usually $50 to $100, cumulative), and your reimbursement obligation should be limited to expenses that are specifically listed. Agents who charge a commission of 15 percent sometimes handle ordinary office expenses (postage, telephone, copying, and so on). If you agree to be responsible for such expenses, find out if you can undertake tasks that could save you money, such as providing photocopies of your manuscripts and proposals.

Most contracts and agency clauses provide that the agent will collect all the proceeds for your work from the publisher and oversee the publisher's compliance with the contract. This allows you to avoid administrative chores and spend more of your time writing. The agent's standard practice should be to deduct commissions and expenses, if any, and promptly pay the balance to the writer. According to the Association of Authors' Representatives, to avoid commingling of funds, agencies should segregate payments received for a client from the agency's funds and remit them to the client from a separate bank account.

The agent should examine your royalty statements and, if necessary, obtain corrected versions and payments due from publishers. Royalties can arrive from other sources as well, and the writer should be able to rely upon the agent to check these accountings. Most authors are usually satisfied with receiving the statements sent through the agent from various income-yielding sources. You should have the right to receive an accounting from the agent with respect to funds received and, on reasonable notice, the right to inspect the agent's records relating to your works. As the Association of Authors' Representatives advises, you can expect the agent to keep your financial affairs confidential.

TERMINATION OF THE AGENCY RELATIONSHIP

When the relationship is terminated, the agency clause in a signed publishing contract should not be affected because the agent generally continues to collect her commission on contracts already negotiated, executed, or earning money before (or within a short time after) termination of the agency. The terms governing termination should be set forth in a separate author-agent contract, if you choose to have a written contract. They will not usually appear in the publishing contract. The agency agreement could allow you to limit the number of years following termination of the agency that the agent may collect commissions for the contracts negotiated during the period of representation. Without such a time limit, the agent will argue that you remain obligated to the agent indefinitely for commissions on income from sales she negotiated before termination. Most agents will strenuously object to having any time period placed on their right to receive commissions on contracts they have procured. They point out that the effort expended in placing works that might only yield monetary rewards over time is not worth their while if a time limit is imposed on their right to receive commissions. In many cases of agency termination, commissions might be renegotiated if another agent is retained and further work is required of the new agent to exploit certain rights. The best person to help you with this negotiation is naturally the new agent. After the agency terminates, you should not be liable to it for commissions on income from sales and licenses negotiated by someone else.

SEPARATE PAYMENTS

If you can persuade your agent, add a statement in the "Agency" paragraph in your publishing contract that if either the agent or the author requests, the publisher will send separate checks directly to the author and the agent. This option can give you control over your own earnings and peace of mind, which is especially important if the relationship ends with hard feelings between you and the agent. But be forewarned that this option is currently quite controversial among agents and publishers. Some publishers object because they fear liability to the agent if they send only the commission to the agent and the author currently owes the agent money (agents routinely subtract amounts owed for expenses, etc. from authors' royalty checks). Publishers also complain about having to send two checks and statements when they can satisfy their legal obligation by sending just one. But some publishers do agree to add this clause, especially if the agent asks for it. Agents have raised a number of concerns about the issue of separate payments. Some agents have implemented the clause in their own agency contracts, but others object to what they see as having their hands tied when they are owed for expenses. They have also questioned its effect on the author-agency relationship, which is ideally built on trust. Further, the agent probably has more clout when it comes to demanding late payment from publishers than do individual authors. It is wise to keep all these considerations in mind when deciding whether to ask for a separate payments clause.

CHAPTER 16

COLLABORATION

AGREEMENTS

C*ollaboration*—two writers working together on a single project—presents both challenges and rewards. You might have a great friendship or at least a highly productive relationship with your collaborator(s), but a collaboration agreement is absolutely vital to ensure that these challenges are overcome and the rewards are shared fairly. Thus, the following issues should be addressed in the agreement: ownership and use of the copyright in finished, unfinished, published or unpublished works; allocating the advance and royalties earned; authorship credit; arbitration and mediation clauses; and liability in the event of various types of lawsuits.

COPYRIGHT AND AUTHORSHIP

Under the copyright law, a joint copyright in a work arises when it is prepared by two or more writers with the intention, at the time the work is created, that their contributions be merged into inseparable or interdependent parts of a unitary whole. The term of copyright for a joint work is the life of the last surviving coauthor, plus seventy years. In the United States, either party may license a jointly owned work *on a nonexclusive basis* as long as the proceeds are equally shared, but an *exclusive license requires the consent of all coauthors.* Coauthors own equal shares in the work, regardless of who did the majority of the work. These rules—the ownership of the copyright, the right to license, and the sharing of profits—can all be altered by contract. If they so choose, for example, the collaborators can agree that each retains a distinct copyright in his or her own contributions, or that the work will be considered a "joint work" only if each party completes his or her part. They can provide that the term of the collaboration agreement will be the same as the length of copyright, or they can make the term shorter.

ATTRIBUTION

Authorship credit requires elaboration. The collaboration agreement *and* the publishing contract should include the order, size, and prominence of the names as they will appear on the jacket of the book in each edition, as well as in all promotional materials and advertisements. State whether the work will be "by A *and* B," or "by A *with* B," or "by A, *as told to* B," or something else. The copyright in a coauthored work is usually registered in both authors' names, and that should appear clearly in both contracts. Even if the work is unpublished when completed, it should still be registered as a joint work in the name of both authors, or however they agree.

INCOME AND EXPENSES

The authors, of course, are free to share the advance and royalties in any manner they wish. The usual royalty split is fifty-fifty if the authors are equal partners in the project and in the percentage of work required, although quality may certainly substitute for quantity. The division of the advance and monies from subsidiary rights usually mirrors the division of royalties. In some cases, authors divide various forms of the income earned differently from income for other rights, such as income from electronic or audio rights. In the case of "as told to" works, where one author is doing most of the writing, that person often gets are larger portion of the advance but the other person receives all the royalties earned until each has received the same amount. The issue of which coauthor, or which coauthor's agent, should be the primary recipient of money paid should be resolved up front. Some contracts provide that all funds will pass through one of the authors or agents, to be distributed to the coauthor, but it seems more practical to provide for direct payment to each, if only to circumvent any uncertainties or inconvenience that could arise.

The parties must also devise a system for authorizing and sharing expenses. An easy way to do this is to set a budget that lists specific expenses and allows for some miscellaneous costs. Expenses are usually shared in the same proportion as income from the work is allocated. If expenses are to be shared, the agreement should provide who will own any products that are purchased, such as tape recorders and cassettes, notebooks, and film, as well as the results of such expenditures, such as recordings of interviews, research notes, and photographs. Another common expense involves obtaining permissions to use copyrighted work. Some agreements require each collaborator to pay for the necessary releases for his or her own portion of the work.

CONTROL OF THE WORK

Artistic decisions could be made jointly by the coauthors or they could be assigned to the responsibility of one author. In either case, artistic control—and an orderly plan to complete the work—should be delineated as clearly as possible. The agreement should define the nature of the project and the responsibilities of each collaborator, in as much detail as possible. It should specify a due date for the portions to be contributed by each author. The parties might choose to specify a schedule with a sequence of deadlines for each section. This can help avoid misunderstandings about both the progress and quality of the work being done by collaborators. The contract can give the right to negotiate the licensing of specific rights to specific collaborators, although the other party can and probably should retain the right to veto proposed licenses. In any case, each collaborator should receive a copy of any license or contract that is executed. If each collaborator is allowed to sell his interest in the work, the other party might want to have the first opportunity to purchase the interest on the same terms being offered by outsiders.

The agreement should also deal with the possibility that the work will not be finished or sold to a publisher. What rights will each collaborator have in the work produced if either of these situations arises? The author who completes his or her portion of the work might be better off with the right to finish the work independently or to find another author to complete it. The parties should determine who would own what rights if their contributions to an unsold or incomplete work cannot be separated. One possibility is that the parties could share nonexclusive rights in the inseparable portions. They might include a buyout clause under which one author would have the rights in return for a flat fee or a reduced royalty on future publication of the work. Similar terms could address the situation in which one collaborator becomes disabled or dies. Finally, each author should consider providing for the right to publish his or her contribution to the work independently (if possible) in the event that the joint work is not published or produced after a certain time period.

The collaboration agreement should also address whether the authors may publish works that compete with the collaboration. Often, the parties will decide upon a period of time during which no competing works may be published by either collaborator. A mutual understanding of what "competition" means in the particular case should be reached by all parties and defined in the contract. The best result would protect both parties' interests in the joint work without keeping either from continuing to earn a livelihood from their writing.

Also provide for possible future editions or sequels. What if either party no longer wishes to interact with the other after the project? What if a sequel takes off from sections written by one coauthor but does not use sections written by the other coauthor? This issue of sequels will be especially important if the work creates popular characters.

DISPUTE RESOLUTION

The agreement should provide a method for resolving disputes between the authors, such as a disagreement over which publishers to submit the work to or whether to accept an offer. Disagreements arising between a surviving writer and the estate of a coauthor who has died can be especially thorny. An agreement to mediate or arbitrate disputes can save the parties considerably in both time and legal fees. Through the use of an independent mediator, whose decisions are not binding on the parties, amicable solutions to disputes are often reached.

THE PUBLISHING CONTRACT

The collaboration agreement is not usually incorporated into a subsequent publishing contract. The collaborators must decide whether to enter one publishing contract jointly or to sign separate contracts. If one collaborator is not a signatory to the publishing agreement, the collaboration agreement should refer specifically to the publishing agreement and indicate that the non-signatory has read and approved the contract. The publisher will usually insist that both authors agree to separate warranty and indemnity clauses. If both sign the contract, each coauthor will be liable for breach of contract (although they could agree in the collaboration agreement that a particular party will be responsible for breaches based on particular sections or content).

CHAPTER 17

BOOK PACKAGERS

Book packagers, also known as book producers, book developers, or content providers, are independent companies that produce books to be sold to publishers. The number of packagers listed in the *Literary Market Place* has risen steadily from just over a dozen in 1962 to more than three hundred today. While most of these companies are relatively small operations, they are increasingly becoming full-service operations by making use of advances in digital technology. Packagers are not writers. They need authors to create the content of the works they will market to publishers. As an increasing number "packaged" books are published, packagers are growing into a good source of work for some authors.

Packagers usually work for many different publishers. They take on ideas that publishers do not have the resources or inclination to pursue. As one packager, Steve Ettlinger, put it: "I take half-baked ideas and bake them." The impact of the packager producing the entire book is to eliminate the need for staff involvement at the publishing house. Depending on the contract, the packager may deliver a copyedited manuscript, typeset and designed books, or even the entire print run of books. Often packagers will even design the jacket, although the publisher will usually manifest a strong interest in the end result.

Packagers are particularly useful if the book involves many illustrations or photographs, as in a natural history book or an art book, or when a book requires a great number of permissions, as compilations do, or when it needs a lot of coordination, as does a multimedia project. These kinds of books entail costs that most publishers are reluctant to take upon themselves, although they might be happy to publish the finished product.

The publisher usually pays the packager separately for two things. One category of payment is the production budget, marked up to help cover the overhead of the packaging firm, which has its own staff and might also use freelance editors and graphic designers. The publisher will evaluate the production budget to be sure that it cannot be done cheaper in-house. The other category of payment to the packager mirrors what an author would expect—an advance against royalties pursuant to a publishing contract. In the contract between a publisher and a packager, the packager is effectively the author. If the packager has an agent, money will flow through the agent and commissions will be deducted. If there is no agent, the publisher pays all money owed directly to the packager who, in turn, pays contributing writer(s) and any other freelancers.

As they represent a middleman between author and publisher, packagers typically offer their authors terms inferior to those offered by publishers. They are likely to want to keep a substantial portion of what the author would typically receive from, and through, the publisher. There are many instances of fledgling writers, anxious to be in print for the first time, signing a work-for-hire agreement with a packager in exchange for a flat fee. Some of these books have gone on to sell hundreds of thousands of copies, but the packager, not the author, received the royalties. In other cases, the packager offers a small royalty that escalates if the book sells more than a specified number of copies. In that case, be careful that the contract does not limit the escalation sales to retail or "trade sales," which in many cases will be a small percentage of the market for a packaged work as opposed to book club or foreign sales. Sometimes, the packager will offer a net-based royalty, which would subtract manufacturing cost from receipts. You might end up receiving a typical royalty rate, such as 10 percent, but based on a minuscule "net" (say, 20 percent of the cover price). On a $20 book, that would equal forty cents a book, in contrast to the $2 that you would have received from sales of the same book by a trade publisher. Of course, packagers take on projects that publishers deem too expensive, so a lower royalty is probably an acceptable trade-off for an author who has not been able to sell a project elsewhere. Even so, more experienced writers are often able to negotiate with packagers for higher fees.

Compare the packager's offer with what a publisher might offer for a comparable work. If the advance or royalty is substantially lower, you might want to reconsider your options. If the packager offers a flat fee in return for all rights, it is usually too one-sided. Review the grant of rights and consider whether the packager will have the capacity to deal adequately with the rights it seeks.

Under no circumstances should you work without a firm commitment to pay you. Be wary of situations in which a packager is developing ideas and pitching them to publishers. Your contract should provide for payment even if the project is not placed with a publisher or is later rejected as unsatisfactory by the publisher. Finally, be clear that you will receive appropriate authorship credit on the book, as packagers often wish to be credited as the author.

Carefully review chapters 10 and 11 on negotiating book contracts. Most the issues that arise in dealing with a publisher will also arise when negotiating with a packager.

CHAPTER 18

THE SELF-PUBLISHING

OPTION AND

SUBSIDY PRESSES

Commercial publishers cannot possibly produce and market all the books submitted to them. Although more than fifty thousand new titles are published in the United States every year, that number is a small fraction—approaching 10 percent—of the works that are *written* each year. The fifty thousand titles published include many that are self-published and many done by very small publishers. Based on these numbers, it is obvious that the vast majority of books of all genres make the rounds of the publishing houses only to be rejected in the end. Legends of oft-rejected authors who turned out to be named Grisham and Clancy might be true, but infinitely more stories abound of the writers who never realize their dreams of being published by a major trade publisher. To be sure, many of the rejected works do not have true literary merit, but there are many others, perhaps yours among them, that trade editors think have merit but are unlikely to earn a profit given the resources a publisher must invest in every single book published. Within the next few years, the costs of publishing should decrease dramatically as digital versions continue to replace paper and print. It will surely not stop readers from buying printed books, but it will create a bigger and more efficient marketplace for literature.

Until then, however, many writers continue to face a high number of rejections, and they naturally begin to seek alternatives to commercial publishing. There are several options, including some that are not much easier to break into than commercial publishing (university and nonprofit presses, mid-sized and small specialty presses) and some that are easier to make agreements with (writers' cooperatives; self-publishing; and subsidy, also known as "vanity," presses). University and small presses have similar submission procedures and can be just as slow to respond as commercial publishers. Authors' cooperatives require joining a group and contributing money for publication. The most direct, but also the most costly, route for an author today is to choose self-publication. If you are willing to try digital publishing before making the large investment necessary for traditional self-publishing, review the advice in chapter 14 on e-book contracts. For reasons that this chapter should make clear, even self-subsidized digital publishing, if entered into with proper precautions, is vastly preferable to vanity publishing and could also be a wise first step to take before plunging into traditional self-publishing. If you are going to self-publish, your concerns must be with the quality, price, and speed of the printing job. Once the book is in your hands, you must then figure out how to get it distributed to its audience. The enterprising author can figure out many ways to market and distribute the book. Judith Appelbaum's *How to Get Happily Published* (HarperCollins) has very good advice for self-publishers, and *The Self-Publishing Manual: How to Write, Print and Sell Your Own Book* by Dan Poynter (Self Publishing Manual, 13th ed.) is required reading.

BACKINPRINT.COM

If your work was ever published with an established U.S. publisher and is now out of print, explore Backinprint.com, the Authors Guild's online bookstore for out-of-print books *(www.backinprint.com)*. Through Backinprint.com, readers can easily find and order out-of-print titles online, by mail, or through a toll-free phone number. If you have remainder copies, you can choose the "On Hand Books Service," which lets you list your titles on the Web site and ship some copies to a bookseller that will promptly fulfill orders for your books. You set the prices for your books and receive 55 percent of that price. The On-Demand Books Service is for authors who have obtained a reversion of rights to their out-of-print work and who prefer to have the title reprinted rather than sell their existing stock. Authors are paid 25 percent of the net income (approximately 15 to 25 percent of retail list price) for sales through this service.

SELF-PUBLISHING OPTIONS

Some recent self-published books have achieved widespread success. *The Celestine Prophecy,* by James Redfield, remained on the *Publisher's Weekly* bestseller list for more than a year, and four years after the author self-published, Warner Books licensed it in 1997. It is still ranked in the top 2,500 in sales with a major online bookseller—an extraordinary achievement for any book. Self-publishing, if successful, can lead to big deals with large publishers. Publishing a book that succeeds with the public requires skill and a lot of luck for every publisher. When the major houses see a self-published title resonating with readers, they are often quick to react. Such was the case with Marlo Morgan's self-published *Mutant Message Down Under* for which HarperCollins paid $1.7 million to acquire.

Keep in mind, though, that the cost of self-publishing, in terms of money, time, and effort, is high, and that most writers who do it probably do not earn back their investments. Reaching an audience, however, is well worth the cost to many authors, and they enjoy the added benefit of control over the book's fate. Self-publishing authors choose everything about publication of the book, from what it looks like to how it is marketed and distributed, from what it will cost to how long it will stay "in print." Of course, this freedom is a function of the fact that you are going it alone, and that nobody else is supporting the book financially. Therefore, it is wise to assess the market for the book and the likelihood that you can reach that market before you proceed. Analyze the competition in the specific field and the degree to which grassroots selling, such as bringing books about running to marathon events, or political satires to party conventions, will be effective. Don't worry about others criticizing a book because it is self-published. You might explain some of the venerable history of self-publishing. Anaïs Nin, Virginia Woolf, Stephen Crane, and D. H. Lawrence published some of their great books on their own. If you decide to self-publish, you will oversee the process of designing, printing, and selling the book. In the course of these endeavors, you will probably enter into contracts with a book designer, a printer, and, in some cases, a book distributor, and will also need to fill out and file an application for copyright registration and obtain an ISBN number.

Unless you decide to use one of a variety of desktop-publishing programs, you will need to deal with a book designer, who will lay out and typeset the book. Before you do so, look at samples of the designer's work and talk to prior clients. When you are ready to negotiate a contract with a designer, keep the following points in mind: The contract should state explicitly the name of the book, the specifications, including its dimensions and the number of pages, and whether the designer will work on the cover (front, spine, back, and flaps), the interior, or both. The next issue is the form in which the designer will deliver the finished product. If the designer is going to deliver mechanicals (whether on boards or a computer disk) ready for printing, rather than mere specifications to be followed by another designer or a desktop publisher, the total cost will be lower. Consider whether the designer should be asked to handle the printing and, if so, the proper markup on the printer's bill. Most self-publishers will want to be able to approve the cover design, and even the interior, as the work progresses. The more involved you are in the process, the less likely it is that disagreements will arise. Artistic rights and a stage-by-stage approval process should be clearly spelled out in the contract.

Be certain that the grant to you of rights in the design (and any interior art or photography) includes all uses, including promotional and advertising, that you will need. To the extent that you intend to create promotional items, such as T-shirts, postcards, cups, and tote bags, the contract should specifically include them in the term "promotional uses." If such items will be sold, the designer might ask for a reuse fee. Whatever is included in the grant should be spelled out definitively, and any fees for other uses should be negotiated and included in the contract. The fee for the work must be specified, along with whether tax will be charged (in most states, it is not required on mechanicals or other materials used for book production, because books are produced for resale), and a schedule of expenses, including a maximum amount, that will be reimbursed. Some designers mark up their expenses as much as 15 to 20 percent to cover the interest on the money laid out, the time it takes to obtain the materials, and the paperwork involved. The specific amount or percentage, if any, that will be added to the expenses incurred by the designer should be included in the contract. Retain the option of canceling the contract at any time without being liable for expenses that have not yet been incurred. Revisions that are caused by the designer's errors should be the responsibility of the designer to correct, regardless of how much extra time they take. On the other hand, last-minute changes by you will probably require you to pay additional fees.

You should retain the right to terminate the agreement if the designer fails to deliver a finished product within a specified time. Once the book design is completed, you should be allowed to keep the physical materials necessary to reuse its design. Finally, include an arbitration clause for amounts higher than the limit of your local small claims court.

Contracts with printers are usually less complex than those with designers. Nevertheless, try to learn as much as possible about the printing process before negotiating with a printer. You might want to read *Getting It Printed* by Mark Beach and Eric Kenly (North Light Books). In choosing a printer, you might consult the *Directory of Book, Catalog, and Magazine Printers* by John Kremer (Ad-Lib Publications).

When dealing with a printer, your first concern will be getting the right price. As a first step, send the book's specifications, such as quantity, paper stock, trim size, number of pages, and desired binding, to a number of printers for a price quotation and a length of time for which the quote will be valid. When you have determined the best price, check the quality of the printer. This can be done by examining the printer's camera work, looking at the result of several of the printer's prior jobs, talking to some prior clients, or even hiring a specialist or consultant. If you are happy with the price and quality of a printer, try to lock in that price by pre-scheduling the job and pre-purchasing the paper if the printer will not supply it. Trade custom allows printers a 10 percent "swing" on the press run, meaning that they can print "overs" or "unders" of up to 10 percent of the order. Consider ordering a slightly higher quantity, especially if a significant portion of the intended press run is *pre-sold* (that is, sold prior to publication).

In your contract with the printer, indicate a delivery date, the terms of delivery (for example, who pays shipping and who bears the risk of loss), the price for the quantity ordered, and payment terms. The printer should agree to show you proofs (often called "blue lines") for both the cover and the interior of the book before going to press. Again, retain the option of terminating the agreement at any point before the printer begins work on the project or if the printer fails to meet the production schedule or the quality level. The contract should have an arbitration clause under which the printer's damages should be limited to costs incurred up to the point of termination. Do not allow the printer to limit damages for late shipment, or failure to deliver the books at all, to the cost of the books because there could be significant other losses involved; nor should the printer be allowed to limit the time within which defects or other damages can be reported, because cartons are normally not opened until they are unpacked by bookstores and defects are often not discovered until the books are actually read.

Finally, you might want to find a book distributor with the ability to reach the book's market. The distributor might be a publishing company, preferably one that sells books in the same field, or it might be a distribution company that handles books from a variety of publishers. In either case, seek a company that seems committed to selling the book and will do more than merely list it in its trade catalog. Before entering into a distribution agreement, look closely at the other books distributed by the company to determine both compatibility and competition with your book. In addition, speak with the sales manager for the distributor to get a sense of the type of marketing effort you can expect.

When you decide on a distributor, several issues will arise. The distributor will likely want to buy the books on consignment, meaning that no money will be owed to you unless the books sell, whereas you would be better off selling the books outright to the distributor. The amount paid for the copies is usually in the area of 25 to 40 percent the retail price (which can also be stated as 60 to 75 percent of the net proceeds received by the distributor from its retail accounts), tending toward the lower end if the distributor buys outright and toward the higher end if the books are taken on consignment. If the distributor is buying the books, it will naturally be more cautious about what quantity it buys. As a result, you might have to print fewer copies, and therefore pay higher unit costs, or else bear the burden and expense of storing the books. On the other hand, if the distributor takes large quantities on consignment, you will not see a nickel until books actually sell, and might have all or most of the books returned at some later date.

Whether the contract is for the sale or consignment of books, be careful to limit the grant of rights to the territory within which the distributor sells. If the distributor sells to regular bookstores in the United States, the contract should only give the distributor the right to sell to such retail bookstores in the United States. You would then be free to enter into separate agreements with mail-order companies, foreign distributors, specialty wholesalers, military stores, and the like. You would also be free to sell books for corporate premiums or to book clubs. However, if the distributor has a unique ability to reach other markets, it is wise to grant the right to do so. If the books are to be sold on consignment, the distributor should not have the right to sell them at higher than a specified discount off retail price (perhaps 55 or 60 percent). In fact, the distributor might be allowed a reduced percentage on sales made at higher discounts.

For more information regarding contract negotiations between self-publishers and book designers, printers, or distributors, and for information on other types of contracts you might need, see *Business and Legal Forms for Authors and Self Publishers* by Tad Crawford (Allworth Press). For information on filling out copyright applications, see chapter 3. To get information on obtaining an ISBN number, call Bowker's, a division of Reed Reference Publishing, at (908) 464-6800 and ask to speak to an ISBN agent.

SUBSIDY PRESSES

Subsidy, or vanity, book publishers require the author to underwrite a large part or the total amount of the cost of publishing and promoting the book. Thus, the risk of a given book's failure is practically irrelevant to the vanity publisher's profits, enabling it to accept almost any manuscript a conventional book publisher would reject as a poor investment. Chances are virtually nonexistent that any book published by a typical subsidy publisher will be commercially profitable, even if it is a very good book. The rest of the publishing industry, from distributors and retailers to publishers and literary agents, spurns vanity publishers and the books they bring out.

The lines between self-publishing and subsidizing the publication of a work in digital form are blurring, but it is still not too difficult to tell the difference between respectable ways to get a book to the public and those that cross the line into vanity publishing. One unmistakable signal is the quality of the finished product. Vanity publishers typically take thousands of dollars from the would-be author and turn that money into a badly produced disappointment. If a work has any chance of succeeding by reaching its audience and making the author proud, that chance will suffer if the book is published by a subsidy press. A few exceptional success stories are often repeated to potential authors. But vanity publishers and their operating procedures are well known to distributors and retailers. Books published by vanity presses are recognized as such and are seldom carried by bookstores or distributors.

The typical vanity press contract offered does not spell out what percentage of the fee paid by the author will be used for promotion, nor does it allow the author much control over promotion. It is estimated that about 10 percent of the total paid by the author is the most the publisher pays for promotion. Nor does the agreement obligate the publisher to bind more than a small number of books in the absence of demand in the form of orders.

In fact, the Federal Trade Commission issued restraining orders against several vanity presses several years ago. Those orders required the publishers to refrain from misrepresenting the nature of their services performed for would-be authors. Some of the claims that the FTC considered misrepresentative included: using the word "royalty" because it had the "tendency and capacity to deceive a substantial portion of the purchasing public"; that sales would warrant a second printing; that only manuscripts of literary merit and sales appeal were chosen, that the publisher promotes books aggressively; that libraries commonly purchase large numbers of books from the vanity publishers, and on and on.

If you still are not convinced, and you want to explore the idea of subsidized publishing, make sure that you talk with authors who used a particular vanity press to find out their experiences. Check with a knowledgeable bookseller in your community to see whether he has ever sold books by that publisher or has any in stock in his store. Ask a local printer how much it would charge to print and bind the same number of copies the subsidy publisher is promising to produce. Before giving money to any organization to help you get published, check with the Better Business Bureau in the area where the organization is located.

If you want to look more closely at a subsidy publisher, contact several, compare fees and services offered, and keep the following in mind if you decide to negotiate with one:

- Make sure that you arrange for a schedule of payments that you can meet, with the largest amount due as close to publication as possible or even afterwards.
- Do not grant the publisher any rights to your work except a nonexclusive right to print, publish, and distribute copies of the book.
- Retain all subsidiary rights.
- Negotiate a promotion budget with a detailed account of how it will be spent.
- Make sure that you keep the right to sell books even into markets granted to the publisher.
- Require some editorial assistance, especially copyediting, and ensure you have the right to approve the cover and interior design and to review galleys.
- A very high discount on all copies you purchase is mandatory. This discount should reflect the fact that you already paid for the books once.

Being an author has always been difficult, and in the early twenty-first century, the major houses reject good manuscripts just as they always have, though perhaps for different reasons. Today there are far fewer major publishing houses than there were in the past. If your manuscript has been seen at Random House, Simon & Schuster, HarperCollins, Penguin Putnam and Time Warner Trade Publishing, it has been seen by 80 percent of the market for trade books. The remaining 20 percent offers many more options. Explore them. Find out from other authors how they get themselves published. Authors are, of necessity, an enterprising lot. If you are serious about a writing career, stay away from anyone who asks you for a lot of money to publish your book, when you could do it yourself much better and for less money.

CHAPTER 19

TAXES:

INCOME AND EXPENSES

"To produce an income tax return that has any depth to it, any feeling, one must have Lived—and Suffered." The truth of this quip by author Frank Sullivan might be felt most vividly in April, when many authors scramble to gather the information, and sometimes the funds, to file their income tax returns. Chapters 19 and 20 are written with the intent of enabling you to plan, keep proper records on a regular basis, and pay estimated taxes on time. Sometimes, you can take steps near the end of the year to relieve your tax burden, but more often the end of the year is too late. You need to keep your tax information up-to-date on a regular basis throughout the entire year. If you follow the simple recommendations here, tax preparation should be considerably easier, your tax bill might be smaller, and you will be better prepared to handle an IRS audit. Nonetheless, this and the following chapters are not intended to substitute for the advice or services of a qualified tax advisor. Tax regulations change continuously, and few books can aspire to be completely accurate and current when it comes to income tax rules. The following chapters are an overview based on current tax law, intended to explain the basic concepts most important to authors, so you can prepare and carry out a tax strategy that will make your accountant's job easier in April.

For tax purposes, an author's personal income typically includes fees received for sales of her writing, advances and royalties paid by book publishers and licensees, other wages, prizes, awards, and most kinds of grants. This income is taxed as ordinary income by the federal government and by the state and municipality where she lives. The business expenses incurred by a writer may be deducted from her income, thereby reducing the amount that is subject to taxation.

Professional authors' tax returns must include Schedule C, Profit or (Loss) from Business or Profession, as an addendum to Form 1040. Schedule C is the main form for filing self-employment income and expenses (with the exception of prizes and awards, which you may enter directly on Form 1040 as "Other Income" to avoid self-employment tax on that income). A sample 2001 Schedule C is reproduced at the end of this chapter in order for you to apply the following overview to practical reality.

General guides to federal taxation include IRS Publication 17, *Your Federal Income Tax,* for individuals and IRS Publication 334, *Tax Guide for Small Businesses, for Individuals Who Use Schedule C or C-EZ.* These and other IRS publications can be obtained free of charge from the IRS at *http://www.irs.ustreas.gov.* The IRS also has a Tele-Tax service that allows taxpayers to call to check the status of a refund or hear recorded tax information on many topics. You can also call your local IRS office, but keep in mind that the advice you receive might be erroneous and is not binding on the government. Also be aware that IRS publications and tapes represent the views of the IRS and are sometimes inconsistent with precedent established by tax courts. Tax policy is one of the most potent ways to regulate society, so Congress and the President are frequently amending the tax laws. If you are preparing your taxes without the assistance of an experienced tax advisor, you had better purchase one of the many privately published guides, such as the *J. K. Lasser* acclaimed line of titles, or check into the many tax return software programs available online. Make sure your selection addresses the year of your return.

In addition to personal income tax, you must also determine whether other state or local taxes, such as unincorporated business tax, must be paid. These taxes vary with each state and municipality, so be sure to consult the tax guidelines of your home state and locality.

RECORD-KEEPING

Updating your records on a regular basis makes the task of filling out tax returns much easier come April. All income and expenses generated from your profession as an author should be promptly recorded in a ledger regularly used for that purpose. The ledger entries should specify the date any money was received or paid out, the character of the receipt or payout, the source or destination of the income, and other relevant data, all supported by copies or originals of the checks, bills, and receipts. Consider maintaining separate business checking and savings accounts through which you channel only your professional income and expenses. IRS Publications 552, *Recordkeeping for Individuals,* and 583, *Starting a Business and Keeping Records,* provide details about the "permanent, accurate and complete" records the IRS requires.

The following example illustrates one method of setting up an efficient ledger. The first column is for the date, the second column shows the nature of the income or expense, the third column specifies the check or receipt number, the fourth column shows the amount of income, the fifth column shows the amount of the expense, the sixth and subsequent columns are designated for different expenses based on writers' special needs. This means that each expense is entered twice, once in the expense column and again under the particular expense category into which it falls. If maintained regularly, your ledger will greatly expedite the process of filling out Schedule C and, if you make your expense categories fit easily into the expense categories shown on Schedule C, the task will be even easier. Several computer programs, such as Excel, Quicken, and Quickbook, exist for this kind of record-keeping. Check online or at a bookstore for more options.

Date	Description	Check/ Receipt	Income	Expense	Expense Categories					
					1	2	3	4	5	6 etc.

To illustrate the ease of record-keeping this way, suppose you paid $24 for office supplies on January 8. In your ledger, enter the following: the date, January 8; "office supplies" as the description; a check number if payment was by check as well as an assigned receipt number if you received one (number your receipts to locate them easily). If payments are received from many sources, try creating income categories (such as royalties by book title, articles by name of publication, speaking appearances, and so on).

ACCOUNTING METHODS AND PERIODS

Like any other taxpayer, an author may choose either of two methods of accounting: the cash method or the accrual method. Using the cash method requires that you include all income actually received during the tax year and deduct all expenses actually paid during the tax year. The accrual method, on the other hand, requires that you include all income that you earned and have a right to receive in the tax year, even if you do not actually receive it until the following tax year, and that you deduct expenses when they are incurred instead of when they are paid. The cash method might in a few cases include income not yet actually received, if the income was credited or set apart so as to be subject to the taxpayer's control. For example, income received by an agent for an author will be taxable to the author when received by the agent, unless significant limitations or restrictions exist on when the agent may forward the payment. Most taxpayers, including authors, operate on the simpler cash method, and this chapter will be based on the cash method, and on a tax year of January 1 through December 31.

The tax year for most taxpayers is January 1 through December 31. Theoretically, one could use a different fiscal year, such as July 1 through June 30, but the IRS must accept the reasons given for changing from the calendar year. More information on accounting methods and periods is available in IRS Publication 538, *Accounting Periods and Methods*. One helpful tax-saving technique for any taxpayer using the cash method is to pay as many expenses as possible in December while putting off the receipt of income until January, the new tax year. The idea is to decrease this year's tax bill by offsetting income from the present tax year expenses while deferring income until the following tax year. By the same token, if you anticipate that a significant increase in your income in the next year will put you into a higher tax bracket, or if the tax rate is set to increase in the new year, it makes more sense to receive as much income during the present year as you can, and to defer paying expenses until the following year.

TYPES OF INCOME

An important distinction is made between ordinary income and capital gains income. "Ordinary income" is that which is realized from all the income-producing activities of one's profession, and is taxed at regular income tax rates. "Capital gains income" is that which is realized from the sale of capital assets, such as stocks, bonds, mutual funds, real estate, or precious metals. Capital gains from assets owned for longer than one year are classified as long-term gains and generally receive preferential tax treatment, that is, a lower tax rate than the income tax rate. Copyrights and manuscripts are not considered capital assets and do not receive favorable capital gains treatment. The tax law specifically excludes copyrights, literary, musical, and artistic compositions, letters or memoranda, or similar property held by the taxpayer who created it, from the list of assets qualifying for capital gains treatment. If a writer sells a copyright or a manuscript to someone else, that person will own the work as a capital asset. Another important distinction is the one between ordinary earned income and unearned income. The professional income of an author is considered earned income, but income from stock dividends, interest, rent, and capital gains, for example, is treated as unearned income.

BASIS

The cost of creating a work (or of acquiring a capital asset) is called its "basis" for tax purposes. An author using the cash basis, who deducts expenses when paid, may not deduct expenses from the basis again when a work is sold. In other words, if you deduct expenses currently, then your work has a zero basis and the entire amount of the proceeds from sales will be taxable income.

GRANTS

Grants to writers are usually taxed as earned income. Only degree candidates may exclude scholarships or fellowships from ordinary income and only to the extent the award is used for tuition and course-related fees, books, supplies, and equipment at a qualified educational institution. Nontaxable grants may not include expenses for meals, lodging, or travel. Nor may qualifying scholarships include payments to the grantee for teaching, researching, or any other services that must be rendered in order to receive the scholarship. Nondegree candidates have no right to exclude scholarship or fellowship grants from income. More information on the taxation of grants can be obtained in IRS Publication 520, *Scholarships and Fellowships.*

PRIZES AND AWARDS

Authors must include all monetary prizes as taxable income, unless a recipient assigns an award to a qualified charitable institution. In that case, the prize and the donation are not treated for tax purposes as income and a deductible charitable contribution, but rather as if the award was not received. Should you win a monetary prize, you may choose to enter the amount received on Form 1040 as "Other Income" instead of on Schedule C, and thus avoid paying self-employment tax on the income. On the other hand, if you fear a home-office deduction or hobby loss challenge by the IRS (both of which are explained later), consider entering such income on Schedule C. You should discuss how to treat a money prize with your tax advisor.

PROFESSIONAL EXPENSES

Deductible business expenses, which are listed on Schedule C, include all of the ordinary and necessary expenditures you incur that help you earn income from your writing. They include, but are not limited to, such things as writing materials and supplies, workspace rental, office equipment, professional books and journals, repairs, travel for business purposes, promotional expenses, telephone, postage, agents' commissions, and legal and accounting fees. Expenses claimed must be reasonable and certain kinds of major expenditures, such as computers, may not be fully deductible in the year they are incurred, but must be depreciated over the course of several years.

WRITING SUPPLIES AND OTHER DEDUCTIONS

Items with a useful life of less than one year are typically considered current expenses, fully deductible in the year purchased. They include writing materials and supplies such as paper, ink, pens, erasers, rental of computers, photocopying, stationery, and similar items. You may include sales tax paid in the expense calculation. Postage is deductible as soon as the expense is incurred. The cost of professional journals and books used to prepare specific works is deductible. Dues for membership in professional organizations are deductible, as are fees to attend workshops and programs sponsored by the organizations. Telephone bills and an answering service are deductible in full for a business telephone. As with all expenses, however, if you use the telephone for both personal and business calls, then you may only deduct the portion of the cost attributed to your business use. The IRS will expect very clear and thorough records itemizing both long-distance and local message units expended for business purposes. Educational expenses are generally deductible if they were incurred to maintain or improve skills required to be a writer, but are not deductible if incurred to learn or qualify for a new profession. Consult IRS Publication 508, *Tax Benefits for Work Related Education,* for more information.

Repairs to professional equipment are fully deductible in the year incurred. If you move to a new residence, the pro rata share of the moving expenses attributable to professional equipment is deductible as a business expense. More substantial deductions for reasonable moving expenses can be taken if a self-employed person's new work location is at least fifty miles farther from her former residence than the old job location and certain other requirements are met. This deduction is explained in IRS Publication 521, *Moving Expenses.*

Self-employed people may deduct a large portion of their premiums for health insurance as an expense on Form 1040. This deduction equals 60 percent of the cost of premiums for 2001, 70 percent for 2002, and 100 percent thereafter. It cannot be claimed for any month you are covered by an employer's subsidized health plan, including coverage under the plan of your spouse's employer. The health insurance deduction may not exceed your Schedule C income, but any health insurance premiums that may not be deducted on Form 1040 might be deductible on Schedule A, if you itemize deductions.

WORKSPACE EXPENSES
AND THE HOME-OFFICE DEDUCTION

If you rent workspace at a location different from your home, all of the rent and expenses in connection with that workspace are deductible. However, the tax code has strict rules about business deductions attributable to a home office or home studio. They are allowed only if the self-employed person uses a discrete part of the home on a regular basis as his principal place of business. In a recent case involving a self-employed anesthesiologist, the United States Supreme Court agreed with the IRS that the doctor's home office was not his place of business, despite his spending several hours each day working there and the fact that the hospitals where he worked provided no office space for him. The Court reasoned that some professionals who work in several places might not have any principal place of business, and considered the relative importance of the work done and the amount of time spent at different locations to be the crucial criteria in determining where, and whether, a principal place of business exists. Here, the "principal work" performed by the doctor was done in the hospitals, not in the home office. *Commissioner v. Soliman,* 113 S. Ct. 701 (1994). Even if you have another profession, as long as your home office is the principal place of your writing business and is used for no other purpose, you may take the deduction. If you maintain a separate structure used exclusively and regularly in connection with your writing business, you may deduct fully the expenses attributable to the separate structure. For employees (as opposed to the self-employed), the home-office deduction is available only if your exclusive use of it is for the convenience of your employer, in addition to the criteria described above. IRS Publication 587, *Business Use of Your Home,* explains deductions for and related to work space.

To determine the amount of deductible expenses attributable to a home office, you must calculate what portion of the total space is used as your exclusive workspace. If you rent your home, and one-fifth of the area is used as workspace, 20 percent of the rent is deductible. A homeowner makes the same calculation to find the amount of workspace used, but as a capital asset, the house must be depreciated. A house has a basis for depreciation (only the house—land is not depreciated), which is usually its cost. Depending on when the house was acquired, different systems are used to determine the number of years over which depreciation is taken and the percentage of basis taken as a deduction each year. Depreciating capital assets is explained below. IRS Publication 529, *Miscellaneous Deductions,* and 534, *Depreciating Property Placed in Service Before 1987,* can help in determining the basis and the calculation of depreciation.

You may deduct that portion of expenses for utilities, insurance, and cleaning costs that are attributable to your workspace. Likewise, repairs to maintain the home are deductible on a pro rata basis. Property taxes and mortgage interest are deductible whether or not you claim a home-office deduction, provided you itemize personal deductions on Schedule A of Form 1040. If you do not itemize, the home-office portions of your property taxes and mortgage interest that are deductible business expenses can be entered on Schedule C.

Assuming you qualify to take the home-office deduction, related business expense deductions may not exceed your gross income from writing, reduced by your Schedule A itemized deductions (those incurred outside of business use, such as real estate taxes and mortgage interest). In other words, the tax code disallows any home-office business expense deduction to the extent that it creates or increases a net loss from your writing business. Any disallowed amounts, however, may be carried forward and deducted in future years.

For example, an author earns income of $3,000 in a year from writing, while exclusively and on a regular basis using one-quarter of her home as the principal place of her writing business. She owns her home, and mortgage interest is $2,000, while real estate taxes are $1,600, for a total of $3,600 of deductions that could be taken on Schedule A, whether or not incurred in connection with the business. Other expenses, such as electricity, heat, cleaning, and depreciation, total $8,800. Allocating one-quarter of all these expenses would attribute $900 of the mortgage interest and real estate taxes and $2,200 of the other expenses to the business. The author's gross income of $3,000 must be reduced by the $900 allocated to the mortgage interest and real estate taxes, leaving $2,100 as the maximum amount of her expenses relating to her work space that she may deduct.

Gross income	$3,000
Home-office expenses allocated to the business	
Interest and property taxes	$900
Electricity, heat, cleaning, depreciation	$2,200
Total home-office expenses	$3,100
Expenses of writing business (excluding home-office expenses)	$2,400
Total expenses	$5,500

The author will apply against her gross income (1) deductions for her writing business expenses, excluding expenses allocable to the home office, and (2) the taxes and interest allocable to the business use of the home. Since (1) $2,400, and (2) $900, total $3,300, her gross income of $3,000 would be reduced to a negative figure. A zero or negative figure means that no additional expenses may be deducted, so the other expenses allocable to the home office ($2,200) are lost for the year. She may carry forward the expenses that she may not deduct this year as a deduction in future years when her income is sufficient. Mortgage interest and property taxes would remain fully deductible on Schedule A if she itemized her deductions.

A writer who rents gets to make a simpler calculation, because the deduction for business expenses, which will not include expenses attributable to a home office, may simply be subtracted from gross writing income to determine the limitation amount.

PROFESSIONAL EQUIPMENT

Traditionally, the cost of professional equipment having a useful life of more than one year (cars, computers, homes, and the like) could not be fully deducted in the year of purchase. Its value had to be depreciated over a certain number of years at a certain rate, with corresponding deductions allowed in each year. Over the years, the law has significantly changed the method by which depreciation is determined. The method of depreciation that you must use is based on when the property was placed in service. IRS Publication 946, *How to Depreciate Property,* will aid in the computation of depreciation. Form 4562, *Depreciation and Amortization,* applies for all types of depreciation discussed here. Following is a brief overview of both current expensing and the different relevant time periods:

CURRENT EXPENSING

The tax law allows a certain dollar amount of professional equipment to be deducted in full in the year of purchase. Use caution, however, because the dollar limits of these expenses and the depreciation rules are constantly changing.

1) 1987 to the Present: The Modified Accelerated Cost Recovery System (MACRS) applies to property placed in service from 1987 to the present. MACRS depreciates property using several different depreciation methods. It places assets into different classes with different class "lives." "Five-year property" includes cars; "seven-year property" includes office furniture and fixtures. Residential real property has a twenty-seven-and-one-half year "life." These classifications, and the methods of depreciation, determine how quickly the cost of this property may be expensed. The law restricts the use of MACRS for cars (and other personal transportation vehicles), entertainment and recreational property (such as a television or record player), and computers, unless these types of equipment are used more than 50 percent for business purposes. If they are used less than 50 percent for business purposes, other depreciation rules apply. Form 4562, Depreciation and Amortization, will explain the rules further.

2) 1981 to 1986: Almost all equipment placed in use from 1981 to 1986 must have depreciation computed under the Accelerated Cost Recovery System (ACRS). ACRS provides different categories for depreciation, which depends on the nature of the equipment acquired. Instead of using the ACRS percentages, it is possible to choose an alternate ACRS method, which allows basis simply to be divided out over a specified number of years. Consult IRS Publication 946, and for every depreciation issue, consult your tax advisor.

One alternative to depreciating your big-ticket items over time is to take a one-time deduction, called a "Section 179 deduction," which allows you to take the entire basis of your depreciable business property in one year only. Depending on your situation, a Section 179 deduction might or might not be better for you than depreciating your capital assets. The amount you can deduct under Section 179 is limited to $24,000 for 2001 ($3,060 for a car). IRS publication 946 describes the deduction in detail.

Travel, Transportation, and Entertainment Expenses: Travel, transportation, and entertainment expenses for business purposes are partly deductible, but you must meet strict record-keeping requirements. Travel expenses are defined as the ordinary and necessary expenses, including meals, lodging, and transportation, incurred for travel overnight away from home in pursuit of professional activities. You may deduct such expenses, for example, if you travel to another city to give a lecture series and stay several days to complete your work. If you are not required to sleep or rest while away from home, deductible transportation expenses are limited to the cost of travel. Entertainment expenses, such as business luncheons, parties, or similar, are currently 50 percent deductible. In order to be deductible, meals and entertainment must either be directly related to your writing business or include a substantial business discussion.

If you use a car to make necessary trips for your work, such as travel to interviews or to do research, you may deduct the expenses incurred in connection with the car, including gas, oil, insurance, license and registration fees, parking, tolls, repairs, and so on. Several limitations apply, however. If you claim a home-office deduction, you may not deduct your driving expenses. Costs of commuting to work are not deductible. You may, however, deduct driving expenses between different work locations. If you claim driving expenses, be meticulous about recording every trip, including mileage and its business reason, and keep all receipts. If you use your car solely for business, you can claim all the expenses on Schedule C. If you use it for personal reasons as well, you must prorate the expense deduction according to the percentage of business use. Some taxpayers find that taking a standard deduction based on miles driven more advantageous. You may only do so if you choose that method in the first year of business use of the car. If you deducted actual driving expenses the first year, you must do so from that point on.

Accurate and contemporaneous records detailing your business purposes (and the business relationship to any person entertained or receiving a gift), date, place, and cost are especially important for all these deductions. Get into the habit of writing these details on copies of bills or credit-card charge receipts. IRS Publication 463, *Travel, Entertainment, Gift and Car Expenses,* gives more details, including the current permissible mileage charge. Self-promotional items, such as advertising, business cards, and sending holiday greetings to professional associates, are also deductible expenses.

Commissions, Fees, and Salaries: Commissions paid to agents and fees paid to lawyers or accountants for business purposes are tax deductible, as are the salaries paid to typists, researchers, freelance editors, and other service providers. If you can, it is better to employ and pay people as independent contractors rather than employees, so you can avoid liability for social security, disability, and withholding tax payments. The IRS applies a twenty-factor test to determine who is an employee and who is an independent contractor. It explains these factors in IRS Publication 15-A, *Business Expenses*. If you have any concerns that someone who works for you is an employee rather than an independent contractor, discuss it with your tax advisor. Treating an employee as an independent contractor could result in liability for back taxes and substantial penalties. If you use independent contractors, you must file with the IRS and give to the contractor Form 1099-MISC, Statement for Recipients of Miscellaneous Income, if you paid the contractor at least $10 in a year in gross royalties or at least $600 for services or rental costs.

SCHEDULE C-EZ

Schedule C is not too difficult to complete, especially if you work with a professional tax advisor, but Schedule C-EZ, which is much simpler, is also available for self-employed people who meet a number of requirements: (1) you have one sole proprietorship, (2) you have incurred no net business loss, (3) business expenses are $2,500 or less, (4) you maintain no inventory at any time during the tax year, (6) you use the cash method of accounting, (7) you claim no home-office expense, (7) there is no depreciation to be reported on Form 4562, (8) your business has not previously claimed suspended passive activity losses, and (9) your business had no other employees during the year. If you meet all these requirements, you may use Schedule C-EZ. Again discuss what is best for you with a trusted advisor.

SCHEDULE C (Form 1040) Department of the Treasury Internal Revenue Service (99)	**Profit or Loss From Business** (Sole Proprietorship) ▶ Partnerships, joint ventures, etc., must file Form 1065 or Form 1065-B. ▶ Attach to Form 1040 or Form 1041. ▶ See Instructions for Schedule C (Form 1040).	OMB No. 1545-0074 **2001** Attachment Sequence No. **09**

Name of proprietor	Social security number (SSN)

A Principal business or profession, including product or service (see page C-1 of the instructions) | **B** Enter code from pages C-7 & 8 ▶

C Business name. If no separate business name, leave blank. | **D** Employer ID number (EIN), if any

E Business address (including suite or room no.) ▶ ....
City, town or post office, state, and ZIP code

F Accounting method: (1) ☐ Cash (2) ☐ Accrual (3) ☐ Other (specify) ▶ ....

G Did you "materially participate" in the operation of this business during 2001? If "No," see page C-2 for limit on losses . ☐ Yes ☐ No

H If you started or acquired this business during 2001, check here . . . . ▶ ☐

Part I Income

1	Gross receipts or sales. **Caution.** If this income was reported to you on Form W-2 and the "Statutory employee" box on that form was checked, see page C-2 and check here . . . . ▶ ☐	1	
2	Returns and allowances	2	
3	Subtract line 2 from line 1	3	
4	Cost of goods sold (from line 42 on page 2)	4	
5	**Gross profit.** Subtract line 4 from line 3	5	
6	Other income, including Federal and state gasoline or fuel tax credit or refund (see page C-3) . . .	6	
7	**Gross income.** Add lines 5 and 6 . . . . ▶	7	

Part II Expenses. Enter expenses for business use of your home **only** on line 30.

8	Advertising	8		19	Pension and profit-sharing plans	19
9	Bad debts from sales or services (see page C-3) . .	9		20	Rent or lease (see page C-4):	
				a	Vehicles, machinery, and equipment .	20a
10	Car and truck expenses (see page C-3)	10		b	Other business property . .	20b
11	Commissions and fees . .	11		21	Repairs and maintenance . .	21
12	Depletion	12		22	Supplies (not included in Part III) .	22
13	Depreciation and section 179 expense deduction (not included in Part III) (see page C-3) . .	13		23	Taxes and licenses	23
				24	Travel, meals, and entertainment:	
				a	Travel	24a
14	Employee benefit programs (other than on line 19) . .	14		b	Meals and entertainment	
15	Insurance (other than health) .	15		c	Enter nondeduct-ible amount in-cluded on line 24b (see page C-5) .	
16	Interest:					
a	Mortgage (paid to banks, etc.) .	16a		d	Subtract line 24c from line 24b	24d
b	Other	16b		25	Utilities	25
17	Legal and professional services	17		26	Wages (less employment credits) .	26
18	Office expense	18		27	Other expenses (from line 48 on page 2)	27

28	**Total expenses** before expenses for business use of home. Add lines 8 through 27 in columns . . ▶	28	
29	Tentative profit (loss). Subtract line 28 from line 7	29	
30	Expenses for business use of your home. Attach **Form 8829**	30	
31	**Net profit or (loss).** Subtract line 30 from line 29.		
	• If a profit, enter on **Form 1040, line 12,** and **also** on **Schedule SE, line 2** (statutory employees, see page C-5). Estates and trusts, enter on Form 1041, line 3.	31	
	• If a loss, you **must** go to line 32.		
32	If you have a loss, check the box that describes your investment in this activity (see page C-6).		
	• If you checked 32a, enter the loss on **Form 1040, line 12,** and **also** on **Schedule SE, line 2** (statutory employees, see page C-5). Estates and trusts, enter on Form 1041, line 3.	32a ☐ All investment is at risk. 32b ☐ Some investment is not at risk.	
	• If you checked 32b, you **must** attach **Form 6198.**		

For Paperwork Reduction Act Notice, see Form 1040 instructions. Cat. No. 11334P Schedule C (Form 1040) 2001

Schedule C (Form 1040) 2001   Page **2**

Part III	**Cost of Goods Sold** (see page C-6)		

33 Method(s) used to value closing inventory: **a** ☐ Cost   **b** ☐ Lower of cost or market   **c** ☐ Other (attach explanation)

34 Was there any change in determining quantities, costs, or valuations between opening and closing inventory? If "Yes," attach explanation . . . . ☐ Yes   ☐ No

35	Inventory at beginning of year. If different from last year's closing inventory, attach explanation . .	35	
36	Purchases less cost of items withdrawn for personal use	36	
37	Cost of labor. Do not include any amounts paid to yourself	37	
38	Materials and supplies	38	
39	Other costs	39	
40	Add lines 35 through 39	40	
41	Inventory at end of year	41	
42	**Cost of goods sold.** Subtract line 41 from line 40. Enter the result here and on page 1, line 4 . .	42	

Part IV	**Information on Your Vehicle.** Complete this part **only** if you are claiming car or truck expenses on line 10 and are not required to file Form 4562 for this business. See the instructions for line 13 on page C-3 to find out if you must file.

43 When did you place your vehicle in service for business purposes? (month, day, year) ▶ ..../............/........ .

44 Of the total number of miles you drove your vehicle during 2001, enter the number of miles you used your vehicle for:

a Business ....   **b** Commuting ....   **c** Other ....

45 Do you (or your spouse) have another vehicle available for personal use? . . . . ☐ Yes   ☐ No

46 Was your vehicle available for personal use during off-duty hours? . . . . ☐ Yes   ☐ No

47a Do you have evidence to support your deduction? . . . . ☐ Yes   ☐ No

b If "Yes," is the evidence written? . . . . ☐ Yes   ☐ No

Part V	**Other Expenses.** List below business expenses not included on lines 8–26 or line 30.	
....		
....		
....		
....		
....		
....		
....		
....		
48 Total other expenses. Enter here and on page 1, line 27	48	

Schedule C (Form 1040) 2001

SCHEDULE C-EZ
(Form 1040)

Department of the Treasury
Internal Revenue Service (99)

Net Profit From Business
(Sole Proprietorship)

▶ Partnerships, joint ventures, etc., must file Form 1065 or 1065-B.

▶ Attach to Form 1040 or 1041. ▶ See instructions on back.

OMB No. 1545-0074

2001

Attachment
Sequence No. **09A**

Name of proprietor

Social security number (SSN)

Part I General Information

You May Use Schedule C-EZ Instead of Schedule C Only If You:

- Had business expenses of $2,500 or less.
- Use the cash method of accounting.
- Did not have an inventory at any time during the year.
- Did not have a net loss from your business.
- Had only one business as a sole proprietor.

And You:

- Had no employees during the year.
- Are not required to file **Form 4562**, Depreciation and Amortization, for this business. See the instructions for Schedule C, line 13, on page C-3 to find out if you must file.
- Do not deduct expenses for business use of your home.
- Do not have prior year unallowed passive activity losses from this business.

A Principal business or profession, including product or service

B Enter code from pages C-7 & 8
▶

C Business name. If no separate business name, leave blank.

D Employer ID number (EIN), if any

E Business address (including suite or room no.). Address not required if same as on Form 1040, page 1.

City, town or post office, state, and ZIP code

Part II Figure Your Net Profit

1 **Gross receipts.** Caution. If this income was reported to you on Form W-2 and the "Statutory employee" box on that form was checked, see **Statutory Employees** in the instructions for Schedule C, line 1, on page C-2 and check here . . . . ▶ ☐ | **1** |

2 **Total expenses.** If more than $2,500, you **must** use Schedule C. See instructions . . . . . | **2** |

3 **Net profit.** Subtract line 2 from line 1. If less than zero, you **must** use Schedule C. Enter on **Form 1040, line 12,** and **also** on **Schedule SE, line 2.** (Statutory employees **do not** report this amount on Schedule SE, line 2. Estates and trusts, enter on Form 1041, line 3.) . . . . . | **3** |

Part III Information on Your Vehicle. Complete this part **only** if you are claiming car or truck expenses on line 2.

4 When did you place your vehicle in service for business purposes? (month, day, year) ▶ ...... / ...... / ....

5 Of the total number of miles you drove your vehicle during 2001, enter the number of miles you used your vehicle for:

a Business .... **b** Commuting .... **c** Other ....

6 Do you (or your spouse) have another vehicle available for personal use? . . . . ☐ Yes ☐ No

7 Was your vehicle available for personal use during off-duty hours? . . . . ☐ Yes ☐ No

8a Do you have evidence to support your deduction? . . . . ☐ Yes ☐ No

b If "Yes," is the evidence written? . . . . ☐ Yes ☐ No

For Paperwork Reduction Act Notice, see Form 1040 instructions. Cat. No. 14374D Schedule C-EZ (Form 1040) 2001

Instructions

You may use Schedule C-EZ instead of Schedule C if you operated a business or practiced a profession as a sole proprietorship and you have met all the requirements listed in Part I of Schedule C-EZ.

Line A

Describe the business or professional activity that provided your principal source of income reported on line 1. Give the general field or activity and the type of product or service.

Line B

Enter the six-digit code that identifies your principal business or professional activity. See pages C-7 and C-8 of the Instructions for Schedule C for the list of codes.

Line D

You need an employer identification number (EIN) only if you had a qualified retirement plan or were required to file an employment, excise, estate, trust, or alcohol, tobacco, and firearms tax return. If you need an EIN, file **Form SS-4,** Application for Employer Identification Number. If you do not have an EIN, leave line D blank. **Do not** enter your SSN.

Line E

Enter your business address. Show a street address instead of a box number. Include the suite or room number, if any.

Line 1

Enter gross receipts from your trade or business. Include amounts you received in your trade or business that were properly shown on **Forms 1099-MISC.** If the total amounts that were reported in box 7 of Forms 1099-MISC are more than the total you are reporting on line 1, attach a statement explaining the difference. You must show all items of taxable income actually or constructively received during the year (in cash, property, or services). Income is constructively received when it is credited to your account or set aside for you to use. Do not offset this amount by any losses.

Line 2

Enter the total amount of all deductible business expenses you actually paid during the year. Examples of these expenses include advertising, car and truck expenses, commissions and fees, insurance, interest, legal and professional services, office expense, rent or lease expenses, repairs and maintenance, supplies, taxes, travel, the allowable percentage of business meals and entertainment, and utilities (including telephone). For details, see the instructions for Schedule C, Parts II and V, on pages C-3 through C-6. If you wish, you may use the optional worksheet below to record your expenses.

If you claim car or truck expenses, be sure to complete Part III of Schedule C-EZ.

Optional Worksheet for Line 2 (keep a copy for your records)

a Business meals and entertainment	a	
b Enter nondeductible amount included on line a (see the instructions for lines 24b and 24c on page C-5)	b	
c Deductible business meals and entertainment. Subtract line b from line a	c	
d	d	
e	e	
f	f	
g	g	
h	h	
i	i	
j Total. Add lines c through i. Enter here and on line 2	j	

Schedule C-EZ (Form 1040) 2001

CHAPTER 20

TAXES:

BEYOND SCHEDULE C

$$ $$

Like all self-employed people, you have special tax issues outside of those presented in Schedule C. These issues, while not addressed neatly in one place as income and expenses are on Schedule C, are of great significance to you.

SELF-EMPLOYMENT TAX

Virtually every employed American (with the bizarre exception of our federal lawmakers) contributes from their earnings to, and receives benefits from, the Social Security Administration. Social Security provides retirement and disability income, medical insurance, and benefits to one's dependents in the event of death or disability. Payroll taxes automatically withheld from regular paychecks cover employees' mandatory FICA contributions, as they are called (and employers pay one-half of the tax), but they are not withheld from payments received by the self-employed. All self-employed people, including you, must file a Schedule SE, Computation of Social Security Self-Employment Tax, with Form 1040, and must pay the self-employment tax shown on Schedule SE.

Your self-employment income is basically your net income from writing as reported on Schedule C, subject to certain adjustments. If you have more than one business, your combined business earnings must be totaled on Schedule SE to calculate your self-employment tax. If you receive some income from employers from which social security tax is withheld, you may subtract that amount from your total taxable income to calculate the tax on your self-employment income. If you and your spouse both earn self-employment income, each must file a separate Schedule SE.

To qualify for social security benefits, a worker must have worked and contributed to Social Security for forty quarters (that is, ten full years) during his working life. If the minimum required amount of work credit is established, the worker automatically qualifies for benefits. The amount of one's benefits is based on his average yearly earnings that are covered by Social Security. Therefore, the more one earns, the more one pays into the system, and the larger the benefits from Social Security to which one is entitled.

For all workers, there is a ceiling on the amount of income on which FICA must be paid. The maximum amount of taxed income has steadily increased over the years—from $14,000 in 1975 to $37,800 in 1984 to $80,400 in 2001—and the rate of taxation has also increased from a tax rate of 11.3 percent in 1984 on income to a maximum of $37,800 to 12.4 percent on income up to $80,400, plus an additional Medicare tax of 2.9 percent on all self-employment income in 2001. Fortunately, one-half of your self-employment taxes are a deductible expense on Form 1040.

More information about the computation of self-employment tax can be found in IRS Publication 533, *Self-Employment Tax*. Additional information about the benefits available under Social Security is available at the Social Security Administration's Web site *(www.ssd.gov)* or through its toll free number, 1 (800) 772-1213, including a helpful pamphlet titled *Understanding Social Security* and an information sheet titled *If You're Self-Employed*. Once you have paid into the system for the requisite forty quarters, the Social Security Administration must send you an annual report that explains your earnings history and your projected benefits based on credits earned. If you do not receive this report, contact the Social Security Administration.

ESTIMATED TAX PAYMENTS

Employers withhold both income and payroll taxes from every paycheck of their employees. Self-employed people must pay their income and social security taxes in quarterly installments as computed on Form 1040-ES, Estimated Tax for Individuals. You must mail your quarterly estimated tax payments to the IRS on or before April 15, June 15, September 15, and January 15 (of the year following the taxable year). In most cases, you must file Form 1040-ES if you estimate owing $1,000 or more (for 2001) after subtracting any employment income tax withholding and credits from your total tax (but without subtracting any estimated tax payments). Failure to pay sufficient estimated taxes can expose you to liability for penalties and interest on top of the tax deficiency. To avoid the risk of underpayment, you may pay as estimated tax in the current year what your actual tax bill for the prior year was. Those earning more than $150,000 should pay 110 percent of the previous year's actual tax. IRS Publication 505, *Tax Withholding and Estimated Tax,* gives more detailed information about the estimated tax payments and how to avoid penalties for underpayment.

RETIREMENT PLANS FOR THE SELF-EMPLOYED

A "Keogh" plan permits self-employed people to contribute to a retirement fund and deduct the amount of the contribution from their gross income when computing income taxes. The Keogh deduction is allowed in a given year only if you invest it in one of a specified kind of retirement funds, set forth in IRS Publication 560, *Retirement Plans for Small Businesses.* Even if you are employed by a company with a retirement program, you might still be able to set up a tax-deferred Keogh plan for your writing income. If you have employees, any retirement plan you set up for yourself will probably require contributions for the benefit of your employees.

There are several ways to determine the maximum amount of contributions you may make to a Keogh plan, which are limited by certain caps. As with other tax deferred retirement plans, contributions to a Keogh plan must be made before the filing date of the tax return (usually the following April 15), but unlike other plans, the Keogh plan itself must be set up during the tax year for which your deduction is taken. You must pay a tax penalty for withdrawing from the plan prior to age fifty nine and one-half (unless you become permanently disabled), but no taxes are incurred on the growth of a Keogh fund until the funds are withdrawn. Distributions are taxed when made.

Keoghs are very good for the self-employed. Your tax bracket upon retirement age could be much lower than it is while you are working and making contributions to the funds, so paying income tax on the distributions will cost you less. The funds will have grown tax-free. If you create a trust to hold the Keogh, you can act as trustee and administer the investments. One-participant Keogh accounts less than $100,000 are exempt from any annual filings. More information about Keogh plans can be obtained from the institutions that administer them.

A self-employed person may also create a Simplified Employee Pension (SEP), which cannot be as customized as Keogh plans. SEPs do not need to be set up by the end of the year for which the contribution is made and do not have the same annual filing requirements as some Keoghs. If you want to make the largest possible deductible contributions to your retirement funds, however, the Keogh is preferable to the SEP. IRS Publication 560, *Retirement Plans for Small Business (SEP SIMPLE and Qualified Plans),* helps explain the various plans in more detail.

TRADITIONAL IRAS

Separate from either a Keogh plan or a SEP, you may open a traditional IRA (Individual Retirement Account). By creating an IRA, you may contribute into a retirement fund up to a certain amount per year (assuming that your wages and professional fees amount to at least that much). To qualify to make deductible contributions to an IRA, you must either (1) not be covered by another retirement plan, such as an employer-sponsored 401(k), Keogh, or SEP, or (2) if covered by another retirement plan, not exceed certain limits on adjusted gross income, which increase if you are married filing jointly. The custodial fees charged by a plan administrator may be deducted as investment expenses on Schedule A if these fees are separately billed and paid.

Commissions paid on transactions in your retirement fund are not deductible. Keogh, SEP, and IRA plan contributions are claimed on Form 1040. Check whether you must file additional forms with your plan's administrator.

THE ROTH IRA

Regardless of your participation in other retirement plans, you may also establish and make nondeductible contributions to an individual retirement plan called a Roth IRA. To qualify as a Roth IRA, the account or annuity must be designated as such when it is set up, although you may convert to a traditional IRA to a Roth IRA (and back again) if you are willing to pay income tax on your original contributions to it. Roth IRAs are generally subject to the same rules as traditional IRAs, except that you cannot deduct contributions to your Roth IRA. The great benefit of a Roth IRA is that it grows tax-free, *and* qualified distributions from it can be tax-free when they are made. You may withdraw your original contributions to it at any time without having to pay a tax or penalty (because by definition, you have already paid income tax on them). More information may be obtained from the institutions administering Individual Retirement Accounts, as well s IRS Publication 590, *Individual Retirement Arrangements* (IRAs).

You should also strongly consider setting up a Medical Savings Account, similar in operation to a traditional IRA. If you anticipate medical costs that will not be covered by your insurance, you can save income tax-free to cover them. See IRS Publication 969, *Medical Savings Accounts,* for more details on this excellent new option.

OTHER TAX CREDITS AND DEDUCTIONS

Certain tax credits apply to any individual taxpayer but are explained below because of their prevalence and impact on many authors' tax obligations.

CHILD AND DISABLED DEPENDENT CARE

Payments for child or disabled dependent care might allow you a tax credit. Tax credits, which are subtracted directly from the tax owed, are much better than deductions on income of the same amount. The credit is 20 to 30 percent of the employment-related expenses you pay in order to be gainfully employed. Anyone who maintains a household including either a child under age thirteen or a disabled dependent and must pay for their care in order to gainfully pursue employment or self-employment qualifies for the credit. IRS Publication 503, *Child and Dependent Care Expenses,* describes in greater detail the rules and limitations of this credit.

BAD DEBTS

A common error is the belief that if you write a work under contract and the purchaser never pays, you may take a bad debt deduction. This belief is wrong because the unpaid purchase price is not included as taxable income. As stated in Publication 334, *Tax Guide for Small Businesses (For Individuals Who Use Schedule C or C-EZ),* "Cash method taxpayers normally do not report income until they receive payment. Therefore, they cannot take a bad debt deduction for payments they have not received or cannot collect." Any cash-basis taxpayer can, however, deduct for business or nonbusiness bad debts of a certain type. A loan to a friend that is never repaid, for example, qualifies as a nonbusiness bad debt. (Such a loan must be legally enforceable against the borrower.) Nonbusiness bad debt deductions are taken in the year in which the debt becomes worthless, and may be carried forward to subsequent years' returns, if it exceeds the yearly limit ($3,000 in both 2001 and 2002).

NET OPERATING LOSSES

A self-employed person who experiences a business loss as determined on Schedule C may carry the loss to Form 1040, where it is eventually subtracted from gross income to calculate taxable income. If the loss is large enough to wipe out other taxable income for the year, the excess loss may first be carried back to reduce taxable income in prior years and then carried forward for future taxable years. This type of loss is likely to arise when a professional writer is changing over from salaried employment to full-time writing. One happy result could be a tax refund for previous years' payments and/or a lower tax bill in future years. IRS Publication 536, *Net Operating Losses,* describes the net operating loss deduction in detail. You will most likely need an accountant's help to compute your losses.

AMERICAN WRITERS LIVING ABROAD

American citizens living abroad are taxed by the United States government on all their income earned from anywhere in the world. A relatively new rule offers a tax break to many American citizens living abroad by excluding from U.S. taxation income of up to $76,000 earned from foreign sources. This exclusion can result in substantial tax benefits when the tax rates of the foreign country such as Ireland, where a qualified writer may live tax-free, are lower than the tax rates in the United States. Some or all of the exclusion might be lost if you travel in countries restricted to U. S. citizens under the Trade With the Enemy Act of the International Emergency Economic Powers Act. Check with your local U.S. consulate for more details. Publication 54, *Tax Guide for U.S. Citizens and Resident Aliens Abroad,* explains the guidelines for eligibility for these exclusions. The basic requirements are either a one-year residence or physical presence in a foreign country and earned income created from work done in the foreign country. "Residence" is a flexible concept based on the circumstances of each individual. While the residence must be uninterrupted (for example, by owning or renting a home continually), remaining abroad for the entire taxable year is not necessary. Brief trips to other countries do not affect one's tax status as a resident abroad. "Physical presence" requires the taxpayer to be present in a foreign country or countries for at least 330 days during a period of twelve consecutive months. Regardless of which test is met, the income to be excluded must be received no later than the year after the year in which the income was earned. Certain foreign housing costs might also be excluded or deductible.

Anyone hoping to benefit from the exclusion for income earned abroad needs to consult with a tax lawyer or an accountant about his or her unique situation. If you live abroad, ask your U.S. consulate whether any treaty regarding taxation between the United States and your residence nation affects your tax status. Also, be aware that some income tax paid to a foreign government might be taken as either a deduction or a tax credit, but only on foreign income taxes paid on income that is included as earned income from U.S. taxation. IRS Publication 514, *Foreign Tax Credit for Individuals,* explains these provisions further.

FOREIGN WRITERS IN THE UNITED STATES

Foreign writers who are residents of the United States are generally taxed in the same way as U.S. citizens. Foreign writers who are not residents of the United States are taxed on income from United States sources under special rules. A foreigner who is merely visiting or whose stay is limited by immigration laws is usually considered a nonresident. A foreigner who intends, at least temporarily, to establish a home in the United States and has a visa permitting permanent residence, will probably be considered a resident for tax purposes. For a more extensive discussion of their tax status, foreign writers should consult IRS Publication 519, *United States Tax Guide for Aliens.*

CHAPTER 21

THE HOBBY LOSS RULE

N ot every author is considered by Uncle Sam to be "in the business" of writing. If you do not report an annual profit from your writing on a fairly regular basis, the IRS might someday try to disallow some of your Schedule C deductions by issuing what is known as a "hobby loss" challenge. The hobby loss rule, embodied in Section 183(D) of the Internal Revenue Code, prohibits people from fully deducting their losses if the IRS determines that their activity was in pursuit of a hobby and without the profit motive necessary to qualify it as a business or trade.

If the IRS concludes that you are writing merely as a hobby as opposed to a business, you will only be allowed to deduct your expenses up to the amount of income earned in that year by your writing. On the other hand, an author actively engaged in the business or trade of being an author—one who clearly pursues writing with a profit motive—may deduct all ordinary and necessary business expenses, even if those expenses exceed income earned from writing activity in that year. Obviously, you will need to defend yourself vigorously against a hobby loss challenge from the IRS. The tests, explanations, and examples in this chapter will give you some tools for doing so. Keep in mind that organized record keeping is the key to utilizing these tools. As soon as a hobby loss issue arises in an audit, consult a tax lawyer or your accountant, who can be very helpful in effectively presenting evidence of the factors that favor you at the earliest possible time.

AN INITIAL TEST: THREE YEARS OUT OF FIVE

At the outset, there is an important threshold test in favor of the taxpayer. This test is a presumption that a writer is engaged in a business or trade—and hence is not a hobbyist—if a net profit is created by the activity in question for three of the previous five consecutive years, ending with the taxable year at issue. Many authors who have experienced both good and bad years (and few professional writers can claim otherwise!) can overcome a hobby loss challenge for one of the bad years. This does not mean you are safe from a challenge until you have been writing for five years. The IRS normally may audit individuals' tax returns for only three years after filing, so by definition it need not wait for your business to exist for five consecutive years before it can challenge your losses for any given year. However, if you have not been engaged in writing for five consecutive years, you may file Form 5213 and elect to have the determination as to profit motive suspended until after five consecutive years have passed. The risk of doing so is that if you are then determined to be a hobbyist, the IRS can collect on back taxes owed for all five years. If you anticipate a hobby loss problem and you use the cash basis, you might be able to create some profitable years among five consecutive years by controlling the times you receive income and pay expenses. Instead of having five years of smaller losses, you are much better off reporting three years of small profit and two years of larger losses.

PROFIT MOTIVE: NINE FACTORS

If you do not pass the three-out-of-five-years test, you can still win a hobby loss challenge by showing a genuine profit motive to the IRS. The Internal Revenue Code contains an objective standard to determine profit motive based on all the facts and circumstances surrounding an activity. Therefore, although your claim to be writing with a profit motive is given little weight, other factors evidencing your intent to make a profit will be weighed. The Code lists nine factors used to determine profit motive. Like virtually every legal test that requires the weighing of several factors, the weight of each will vary depending on the facts, and no single factor will trump all the others to determine the issue. Every writer can, to varying degrees, pursue their writing in a businesslike manner, and you should consider these factors the most effective ways to do so:

1. **The manner in which the taxpayer carries on the activity.** To satisfy this requirement, you must demonstrate that you have maintained effective business routines *throughout the life of your business.* Most important, you should be able to present an organized and accurate bookkeeping system under which you have recorded all receipts and expenses. A regularized system for correspondence, submissions, follow-ups, contracts, deadlines, even rejection slips, will also be significant in showing your profit motive.

2. **The writer's expertise, or that of his advisors.** Important indications of expertise can include an author's educational background, publication credits, encouragement by agents or publishers, awards, prizes, membership in professional organizations, recognition in critical publications, and the use of business advisors such as lawyers and accountants who are known to advise writers on a regular basis. Teaching, if the position is at least partially based on writing expertise, can also help.

3. **The time and effort spent on writing.** Can you show that you devote several hours each day on a regular basis to your writing? As most working writers well know, employment in another occupation hardly shows that you lack a writing profit motive, but if you earn a significant amount of overtime income from another job, the IRS might conclude that you do not have enough time to devote to a separate writing business.

4. The expectation that assets used in the activity will appreciate in value. This factor is seldom relevant to writers, because the IRS does not consider your own copyrights to be capital assets.

5. Past business success from other activity, similar or not. Past literary successes, whether financial or critical, can show a present profit motive even if you have been inactive in publishing recently. Oddly enough, you can also demonstrate past business success without your prior business having been related to writing in any way, as long as you can prove that your prior business was regularly profitable.

6. Your dependence on income from writing for your livelihood. This does not mean your writing must support you completely, of course. You should, however, be able to show that a continued failure to make a profit would eventually render you unable to support yourself. Ironically, your failure to realize a profit in the past might actually work in your favor, if you suffered substantially because of your losses.

7. Your losses are either due to circumstances beyond your control or are normal in the start-up phase of the business. Luckily, the IRS expects that a start up business will incur substantial losses in its first year of existence. If you can show a real reduction in your losses over the first five years or so, this factor will weigh in your favor.

8. You change your methods of operation to in an attempt to improve profitability. If a taxpayer continues to use the same business practices and suffers recurring losses, this factor will weigh against him. Conversely, to satisfy this requirement, you have to demonstrate that you made a substantial effort to pinpoint the methods that contributed to your lack of profitability and how you attempted to change them in order to make your writing profitable. If you make too drastic a change, the IRS could see the change of method as a new and distinct business, and weigh this factor against you.

9. Your writing makes a profit in some years, and how much profit it makes. You can satisfy this requirement by demonstrating that your writing generated significant profits in most years, though it also has incurred intermittent smaller losses in between. It will probably not work if you incurred significant losses in most years, interspersed with small profits in fewer years.

THE CASES

A look at some typical hobby loss cases will illustrate the approach of the courts to these factors. These cases are not recent, but the rules that are illustrated still apply. While each case, of course, requires a determination based on its unique facts, awareness on your part of the relevant factors can help you to prevent or defeat a challenge.

CASE I: THE DILETTANTE—NO PROFIT MOTIVE

John Baltis graduated from college in 1948 and commenced work in the newspaper field. In 1967 and 1968, he was a copyeditor for the *San Francisco Chronicle*. During the same two years, he took deductions as a freelance writer—$1,968 in 1967 and $1,974 in 1968. Between 1948 and 1968, he had sold only three articles for a total of $550. Also, many of the claimed items of expense were for family visits. The result: No profit motive could be shown. Significantly, the tax court also pointed out "there was almost a complete failure to substantiate the specific items which the Commissioner disallowed." *John R. Baltis*, 31 T.C.M. 213. Never forget that you must keep accurate records to substantiate deductions.

CASE II: THE WEALTHY SCHOLAR—NO PROFIT MOTIVE

Corliss Lamont, a philosopher who taught at Columbia University, lectured across the country on philosophy, civil liberties, and international affairs. He also wrote numerous books and pamphlets about these subjects. He had independent wealth, so he could afford the continuous losses from his writing over a thirty-year period. The court concluded, "Although continuity and efficiency of operations are criteria which would tend to support the existence of a trade or business . . . the totality of circumstances surrounding Lamont's background, his interest in the wide dissemination of his ideas, his activities and financial status justifies the conclusion of the Tax Court that a profit motive was lacking." *Lamont v. Commissioner,* 339 F.2d 377.

CASE III: THE ESTABLISHED AUTHOR TRAVELING FOR RESEARCH—A PROFIT MOTIVE

A writer of numerous articles and screenplays, a resident of Los Angeles, spent 335 days in New York City during 1965. He had been writing for almost forty years. The author was an expert on the film director D. W. Griffith and spent the time in New York researching Griffith's papers at the Museum of Modern Art. The results of this work provided the basis for an issue of *Film Culture Magazine* published in 1965, and the contents of the magazine were then to be used in a hardcover book scheduled for future publication. Stern received no income from the magazine, but had a contract providing for standard author's royalties on the hardcover book.

The court found a profit motive because the author had "participated in that endeavor with a good faith expectation of making a profit," despite the lack of immediate profits. *Stern v. United States,* 71-1 USTC Par. 9375 at p. 86, 420 (2000). The expense, therefore, was deductible as a business expense.

CASE IV: A WRITING VANDERBILT—PROFIT MOTIVE

Cornelius Vanderbilt, Jr. commenced his writing career in 1919 and pursued it with great success for two decades, despite his wealthy family cutting off his allowance. He published numerous books and articles in addition to founding newspapers and a new service syndicate. Motion picture producers purchased a number of his stories, and he began a successful lecture career in 1929. World War II and health problems curtailed his writing. He resumed his writing and lecturing career after the war and often wrote about travel and current foreign affairs. Much of Mr. Vanderbilt's writing, including several books, was devoted to these topics.

His writing-related activities, especially a substantial amount of travel, caused his deductions to far exceed his writing income. The IRS sought to disallow the entire amount of business deductions claimed in 1951—$30,175.90—on the rationale that Mr. Vanderbilt was not in the business or trade of being a writer in that year, as shown by his large losses over several years, inherited wealth, his inattention to practical business details, and even "his general propensity towards engaging in this field of endeavor whether it resulted in profit or not . . ." *Cornelius Vanderbilt, Jr.,* 16 T.C.M. 1081.

The court disagreed with the IRS's characterization of Vanderbilt's career as bearing "a strong resemblance to that of a romanticist and adventurer." His past commercial success as an author and continued devotion to his writing demonstrated his profit.

CASE V: HEAVY TRAVEL FOR A LIGHT BOOK—NO PROFIT MOTIVE

In another case of large travel expenses in the face of claimed business losses, the key question was whether the taxpayer engaged in the activity with the objective of making a profit, not whether he had a reasonable expectation of making a profit. Even so, sustaining large losses for so many years that there is no realistic possibility of earning enough writing income to offset those losses will likely work against a taxpayer. *Dreicer v. Commissioner,* CCH Dec. 38,948 (1974).

THE BOTTOM LINE

If you are lucky enough to have personal wealth or an independent income, or if your writing expenses are large relative to your writing income over a significant number of years, you are more likely to be ruled a hobbyist. Authors who devote much of their time to their writing, who have demonstrable expertise, or have received recognition for their writing, or for whom the expenses of writing are burdensome, are more likely to be determined engaged in business rather than a hobby. This holds true even more for newer authors who demonstrate that they have made financial sacrifices to begin a writing career. Younger authors are often ruled to have a profit motive, even if other employment is necessary for survival during the difficult early years of their writing careers.

CHAPTER 22

ESTATE PLANNING

FOR

PROFESSIONAL AUTHORS

In 1945, Eugene O'Neill entrusted the original manuscript of *Long Day's Journey Into Night* to his editor, Bennett Cerf of Random House. A written agreement between O'Neill and Random House provided that the play would not be published until twenty-five years after O'Neill's death. Within two years of his death in 1953, O'Neill's widow Carlotta demanded that Random House publish the play. Cerf felt honor-bound not to do so, so Carlotta withdrew the manuscript from Random House and had it published by Yale University Press. As executrix under O'Neill's will, she had every right to do so. O'Neill also left an unfinished manuscript of *More Stately Mansions.* He had told Carlotta shortly before his death that, "Nobody must be allowed to finish my play. . . . I don't want anybody else working on my plays." On a flyleaf placed in the manuscript of *More Stately Mansions,* he had written, "Unfinished work. This script to be destroyed in case of my death!" Despite these admonitions, Carlotta permitted the work to be revised, published, and produced on Broadway as a new play by Eugene O'Neill. Again, as executrix, she had the legal right to ignore the author's wishes because they were not formalized in his will.

Lifetime planning is essential for all authors who want to ensure correct posthumous treatment of the literary works they leave behind. Estate planning should begin during your lifetime with the assistance of a lawyer and, if necessary, an accountant, life insurance agent, or officer of a financial institution's trust department. Like everyone else, you should generally seek to dispose of your assets at your death to the people and institutions of your choice, while reducing the amount of income tax due during life and estate taxes at death. Unlike others, authors have unique concerns in estate planning. This chapter will discuss some general information you should have prior to discussing your estate with your attorney and potential executors. It cannot replace a consultation with an estate-planning expert, who is in the best position to know the relevant state laws governing trust, estate, and tax issues.

BEQUESTS THROUGH A WILL

As an author, the only real opportunity you have to control the use of your literary work after death is through a will. A will is a written document, signed and witnessed under strictly observed formalities, that provides for the disposition of the will maker's (that is, the "testator's") property upon his or her death. Individual states govern the proper drafting and interpretation of wills, as well as the disposition of the property of a person who dies "intestate," that is, without a proper will. If no will is made, property passes at death by the laws of intestacy. These laws vary from state to state, but generally provide for the property to pass to the deceased's spouse and/or other close relatives. An administrator, often a relative, is appointed by the court to manage the estate of one who dies intestate.

A properly drafted will is crucial to any estate plan. A will allows one the opportunity to distribute property to specified persons or institutions. For literary properties such as manuscripts and copyrights, this is usually done by bequest either to specific individuals or to a class. (A "bequest" refers to a transfer of property under a will; a "gift" refers to a transfer of property during the life of the giver.) Under a will, one can provide for: (1) payment of estate taxes by the estate so that bequests are not reduced by tax liability made, (2) uninterrupted maintenance of property insurance policies, and (3) payment by the estate of storage and shipping costs so a beneficiary need not pay to receive a bequest. Estate taxes are usually paid from the "residuary" property, that is, the property of the estate not elsewhere distributed under the will.

In drafting your will, be crystal clear about your literary properties. Specify the person or organization to whom they are granted; the property conveyed (including, but not limited to, any parts of the copyright thereto, whether or not they are currently licensed); the rights conveyed, including their scope and duration; any relevant contracts in force; and your finished and unfinished manuscripts. Avoid ambiguous language, which could subject your will to attack. Failure to bequest specific property rights can result in these rights passing under the will's residuary clause, or, if there is no residuary clause, through partial intestacy laws.

An example of a bequest of manuscripts without copyrights to a specific individual follows:

I give and bequeath all my right, title, and interest in the following manuscripts [describe manuscripts] to my daughter, Jane, if she shall survive me.

An example of a bequest to a class follows:

I give and bequeath to my son, Dick, my daughter, Jane, and my daughter, Sally, or the survivors or survivor of them if any shall predecease me, all my manuscripts [describe manuscripts]. If they shall be unable to agree upon a division of the said property, my son Dick shall have the first choice, and my daughter Jane shall have the second choice, and my daughter Sally shall have the third choice, the said choices to continue in that order so long as any of them desire to make a selection.

If you have a will, it should designate one or more executors, who are charged with administering your will and the assets and liabilities of your estate. All executors you name will bear equal responsibility for your assets. Give careful thought to whom you will appoint to be executors. They are fiduciaries and are obligated to serve the best interests of your estate and its beneficiaries. To avoid conflicts of interest, do not choose an executor who has a personal interest in your estate property. Many people select the trust department of a bank or other financial institution for this important role. One of your executors should be familiar with your work and have some experience in the publishing industry. Some writers divide duties between executors, so that one executor handles general financial matters and another executor handles the disposition of the literary works. Because financial and literary issues are likely to be interwoven, the duties of the so-called literary executor need to be carefully delineated, along with specific provisions to resolve disputes between the primary executor and the literary executor. Such a clause might read as follows:

> I appoint [name executor] to be the literary executor of my estate (hereinafter referred to as my "Literary Executor"), to have custody of, act with respect to, and be empowered to make all determinations concerning the use, disposition, retention, and control of the literary works that I have created or own, my letters, correspondence, documents, private papers, writings, manuscripts, and all other literary property of any kind created by me, whether or not any such items are unfinished or are completed but not yet divulged to the public. Should a dispute arise between Literary Executor and General Executor concerning my literary property, the determination of the General Executor shall be final and binding.

Unless you are very clear in your will that the "literary executor" has the authority to determine how your literary and related property are used after your death, the primary executor will have ultimate control. In fact, it is usually better to allow the primary executor the final decision. An estate's literary works must be assigned a prospective fair market value that might affect the tax bill even when the estate lacks sufficient funds currently to pay taxes. The beneficiaries are better off in this case if the executor's authority to dispose of the assets takes precedence over the literary executor's authority to make decisions about the literary works that are based on aesthetics rather than economics.

An executor has many responsibilities to an author's estate. A preliminary duty is to notify the testator's publishers and licensees that royalties are to be paid to the estate during the probate period. Under the 1976 Copyright Act, an author may not bequeath by will any copyright renewal rights that arise after death. These rights flow directly to the author's spouse and/or children. However, the executor should renew those copyrights if the author's spouse and children, if any, are deceased. Other technicalities exist under the 1976 Act regarding the right to terminate transfers and licenses, which the executor must understand. The right to terminate transfers and licenses does not pass through an author's estate. It passes upon the author's death directly to the author's spouse and children, or if they are deceased, to the author's grandchildren.

You may direct the publication of some or all of your unpublished works in your will. An executor is not responsible to your beneficiaries, however, if he or she fails after diligent efforts to find a publisher for your work. You may, however, restrict certain types of publication and use of your work and provide for a period of time to elapse before posthumous publication. The scope of the executor's duty to dispose of your literary works extends to entertaining offers fairly and granting licenses that would serve your beneficiaries, unless you expressly prohibit that in the will. There is usually no legal requirement, however, that your executor permit others to reproduce your work.

Every estate, large and small, requires that the executor be given delineated powers. The more clear and complete your written instructions to your executor(s) and heir(s), detailing the ideal posthumous treatment of your work, the more likely they are to be followed. After consulting with your executors and advisers, you can decide whether to put the instructions in a separate letter or in your will. You should also clarify whether your instructions are binding on your executor(s) or are merely advisory. In preparing instructions, consider how much posthumous control you really want to exercise over how your literary work is treated. For example, should your unpublished works be published after your death? If they are published, who may edit them? May another author complete your unfinished works? If so, who may decide who will finish them and how may authorship be credited? The publisher, format, the extent to which subsidiary rights may be exploited are all questions that somebody must answer, and all of these creative decisions can impact the estate financially.

You might want to donate copies of books, manuscripts, letters and other personal papers to your local library, university, or another institution. Every institution maintains its own policies on accepting private archives. Many cannot accept all that is offered to them. Be sure to consult with the institution before naming it in your will and identify clearly the works to be donated and the institutions to receive them. You should also state in the will whether or not the institutions should receive the copyright along with the work.

Related issues involve your personal papers. Who, if anyone, will be allowed to publish letters you have written? In what manner should publication be made? Who will have permission to look at your drafts, notebooks, and diaries? Who will have access to letters you received from others? If you designate an official biographer, how will that affect your estate's willingness to make information available to other researchers and the public? The writer who donates manuscripts and personal papers to a university or museum might want to know in advance the treatment the donated materials will receive. What should your executor do if the institution does not treat your papers as promised? You can address all these questions in your will. If you do not, your executor will be operating without knowing what your preference would have been.

TRUSTS

Proper administration of any estate requires funds. If the testator does not set aside enough money to cover costs, the executor might have no choice but to dispose of estate property, even if the will directs otherwise. To avoid these headaches for your executor and loved ones, you could either set aside funds during your lifetime or maintain a life insurance policy for this specific purpose. Another interesting choice is to consider establishing an *inter vivos* revocable trust. Trusts are a valuable estate-planning device under which title to property is given to a trustee who is to use the property (or income from the property) for the benefit of certain named beneficiaries. You may create a trust during your life and/or by will. Trusts created during life can be revocable by the creator of the trust, or irrevocable, in which case the creator

cannot dissolve the trust. Trusts are frequently used to skip a generation of taxes, for example, by giving the income of a trust to children
for their lives and having the grandchildren receive the principal. In
such cases the principal would not be included in the estates of the
children for purposes of estate taxation. The tax law, however, severely
restricts the area of generation-skipping trusts and other similar transfers and it is subject to constant change.

Inter vivos literally means "during life," and an *inter vivos* trust is a
legal instrument in which you transfer title to any of your assets to the
trust while you are alive. As trustee, you control what is done with
those assets. During your lifetime, you are the beneficiary of the trust.
After death, your assets will pass directly to those named in the trust as
beneficiaries. The establishment of an *inter vivos* trust has one great
advantage—the avoidance of probate. Property transferred to the trust
might or might not be included in the gross estate subject to federal
estate tax, but it transfers to your beneficiaries without any of the formalities and delay of probate. Consult a tax specialist or estate planning
attorney on whether an *inter vivos* trust is a good option for you.

ESTATE TAXES

Estate planning allows you to anticipate and control the amount of
estate taxes to be levied by the state (if any) and, more importantly, the
federal government. A writer who lives in more than one state risks
having a so-called double domicile and being taxed by more than one
state, so plan to avoid this result. You will also wish to benefit from a
number of deductions, discussed later, that can substantially reduce the
taxable estate if properly planned. Tax planning is especially necessary
for authors with sizeable estates because copyrights and manuscripts
must be given their fair market value in computing the gross estate.
Thus, the projected earnings of your works, based when possible on
their past earnings, are figured into their fair market value, even though
the earnings have not yet accrued. The valuation process creates uncertainty as to the size of the estate (because the valuation might be high
or low) and raises the possibility that the estate will lack the ready cash
it needs to pay estate expenses and taxes on time.

THE GROSS ESTATE

The gross estate includes the value of all the property in which the testator had an ownership interest at the time of death. Complex rules, depending on the specific circumstances of each case, cover the inclusion in the gross estate of such items as life insurance proceeds, property the testator transferred within three years of death in which he retained an interest, property over which he possessed a general power to appoint an owner, annuities, jointly held interests, and the value of property in certain trusts.

VALUATION

The property included in the gross estate is valued at fair market value as of the date of death or, if so chosen on the estate tax return, as of an alternate date (typically six months after death). "Fair market value" is defined by the Internal Revenue Code as "the price at which the property would change hands between a willing buyer and a willing seller, neither being under any compulsion to buy or to sell and both having reasonable knowledge of relevant facts." Expert appraisers are used to determine the fair market value of copyrights and manuscripts. But whether the estate is large or small, the opinions of experts can exhibit surprising variations. Fair market value is not only important for determining the value of an estate, but also for determining the value of gifts and charitable contributions. Prior to the Tax Reform Act of 1969, writers could donate copyrights or manuscripts to universities or museums and take a charitable deduction for income tax purposes based on fair market value. Since 1969, such a donation by the author of the work would create a charitable deduction based only on the cost of the materials in the work—a negligible amount. (The Authors Guild is supporting legislation that would reverse that regulation.) Currently, anyone who inherits the work from an author's estate may make a charitable contribution and deduct its fair market value.

TAXABLE ESTATE

The executor may calculate the taxable estate by reducing the gross estate with certain deductions. These deductions currently include funeral expenses, some administration expenses, casualty or theft losses during administration, debts and other enforceable claims against the estate, mortgages and liens, the value of property passing to a surviving spouse (subject to certain limitations), and the value of property donated to a qualified tax-exempt nonprofit organization. Regardless of what a will provides, almost every state's laws require that a surviving spouse receive a healthy portion of the estate. Charitable deductions might be of particular interest to an author, because it allows him to bequeath copyrights and manuscripts to tax-exempt charitable or educational institutions. The marital deduction equals the value of property left to the surviving spouse, provided that the value of the property has also been included in the gross estate. Charitable bequests are an excellent way to reduce the amount of one's estate taxes. Also, the intangible benefits, including perpetuating the author's reputation, might outweigh considerations of the precise saving or loss resulting from such bequests. On the other hand, keep in mind that the fair market value of donated works is deducted from the gross estate, so the tax effect is the same as destroying the work before death would be, because the fair market value is added to the gross estate. Even if the estate tax rate were as high as 55 percent, keeping the work would still pass 45 percent of its value to one's heirs. Once the gross estate has been reduced by applicable deductions, what is left is the taxable estate.

UNIFIED ESTATE AND GIFT TAX

If an author makes gifts of copyrights, manuscripts, or other assets while alive, the value of the gross estate at death will be reduced. If, however, you give gifts valued at more than $10,000, a gift tax applies to the amount over $10,000. The government allows everyone a tax credit for gift and estate taxes together. Therefore, any tax credit you use to avoid the gift tax decreases the credit allowed to your estate upon your death. The complexity of the rules in this area makes estate planning and tax advice necessary if you want to ensure that gifts you give are effective for tax purposes.

A progressive federal tax applies to an author's cumulative total of taxable gifts while alive and her taxable estate. The amount of tax on the cumulative total of the taxable gifts and the taxable estate is reduced by a tax credit, so an estate is subject to federal tax only if the cumulative total of taxable gifts and the taxable estate is greater than a set amount. Currently, the tax is levied when the taxable estate is greater than $700,000, assuming no gift tax credit has been previously used. The vast majority of estates are not valued at this amount. Recent legislation purports gradually to eliminate federal estate taxes by the year 2010. Some states also assess estate taxes.

LIQUIDITY

Estate taxes must normally be paid within nine months after death, at the time the estate tax return is filed. For estates that cannot make full payment immediately, it might in special cases be possible to spread payment out over a number of years. One of the best ways to ensure there is cash available to pay estate taxes is to take out a life insurance policy. The proceeds of life insurance payable to the estate are included in the gross estate, as are the proceeds of policies payable to others if the insured retained any ownership or control over the policies. Policies payable to other people and not owned or controlled by the author will not be included in the gross estate. Therefore, if the spouse or children are the beneficiaries under both an insurance policy and the will, they will be able to pay estate taxes from insurance proceeds and preserve the assets of the estate. This arrangement especially helps heirs of creators of intellectual property. Consult with an insurance agent or estate attorney to determine how to obtain life insurance to cover your estate taxes.

CHAPTER 23

HOW TO AVOID

OR RESOLVE DISPUTES

Professional authors begin, maintain, and end many business relationships in the course of their careers. The nature of these relationships can make authors vulnerable to their publishers, agents, collaborators, and other business associates. Sometimes, that vulnerability leads to frustrating misunderstandings, painful disagreements, costly litigation, even to a reputation for being "difficult" among editors and others. As with almost every problem you might encounter along the way to building your career, you can protect your interests with prior investigation and preemptive measures.

As you have seen throughout this book, a well-drafted contract can neatly eliminate potentially complex disputes and foster mutually satisfying and profitable relationships. If you have a publishing contract with a royalty-paying publisher, you owe it to yourself to join the Authors Guild and take advantage of its free contract review services. The Guild legal staff reviews members' publishing and agency contracts, advises in the case of disputes, and holds seminars and symposia on issues of importance to writers. Every member is encouraged to contact the Guild for guidance during contract negotiations. Even a clear, enforceable contract will not always guarantee smooth sailing, however. All too often, people disregard their contractual obligations. You might eventually enforce your contract, but it is obviously better

287

to avoid a problem altogether. The first line of defense, then, is to learn to recognize the warning signs that a dispute could arise and to avoid the situation if possible.

In general, avoid editors who express serious uncertainties about their interest in your project. An editor who is unenthusiastic about a project at the outset is unlikely to be much help to you if difficulties arise down the line. Be wary, too, of editors who do not have at least some experience in the field in which you write, particularly for specialized subject matter or formats. An inexperienced editor can make unrealistic demands of you and of the publisher's employees on which your project depends. Needless to say, her ability to give you the editorial assistance you need could also be lacking.

Stay away from publishers whose budgets are unrealistically low, who display a lack of understanding about the work by setting unrealistic deadlines, or whose contracts are blatantly one-sided. If a publisher who makes you an offer is unknown to you, check with your writing colleagues, authors news groups, editors, or agents you know, even the local Better Business Bureau. The industry is small, and word of dishonorable treatment, payment problems, financial shakiness, and other helpful information usually spreads quickly.

As for agents, avoid signing with one who will only inquire of a limited small number of editors about your work, who does not seem to understand your work, or who is difficult to reach, churlish, or evasive about answering your questions. In fact, you should generally avoid dealing with anyone—editor, publisher, agent, coauthor, or packager—who is reluctant to sign a contract that sets forth your understanding of the transaction you are discussing. Of course, clear, consistent communication between you and the professionals with whom you are working is paramount to avoid misunderstandings and foster good relationships. Be patient with busy editors and agents and always keep your tone cordial and professional.

NEGOTIATING DISPUTES OUTSIDE COURT

What should you do if, despite your precautions and self-education, an irresolvable dispute has arisen between you and a business associate? What if you believe the other party has clearly breached your contract or is otherwise harming your interests? At what point should you consider bringing a lawsuit? In almost every case, the better answer is "not yet." Litigation involves time, energy, and enormous expense, not to mention the almost certain outcome that you will never again be able to transact business with the opposing party. Litigation should be your last resort. The Authors Guild's Contract Services Staff advises more than a thousand authors every year about how to address specific industry issues. A large portion of that work involves guiding authors in cases of disputes, often interceding on their behalf, and finding qualified counsel for referrals when necessary. Never start a lawsuit without consulting industry professionals who are on your side.

Even if you do not join the Authors Guild, you can follow the basic steps the Guild staff employs in legal and business disputes. First, determine what your position is and what exactly you want or need to be satisfied. Then, write a cordial but firm letter to the appropriate person. This person is probably the individual with whom you are having the problem. Set forth clearly and succinctly your version of the relevant events and why a certain course of action is appropriate at this time. Request relief specifically. Carbon copy anyone you think would be interested and helpful to you, but do so carefully. It is better to allow the individual at fault the opportunity to redress the problem privately, as it were, without her supervisor or an outsider knowing about the problem. You can always involve a supervisor later if the first request does not work.

Although in any given case you might be entitled to full relief, be realistic, too. Consider whether any compromise would be acceptable to you. Of course, do not disclose your fallback position in the beginning, but having one can help you stay out of litigation. If it becomes clear that no redress will be forthcoming without pressure, then continue with a systematic barrage of letters, phone calls, faxes, registered letters, and finally a promise to inform the Authors Guild, the Association of Authors' Representatives (for agents), or the Better Business Bureau of the situation. If these actions do not work to obtain relief or a decent compromise, then consider consulting a private attorney.

MEDIATION AND ARBITRATION

Among the advantages of mediation and arbitration are the speed of resolution and the lower expenses than would be incurred in court. Mediation involves an objective and trained third party who actively tries to bring the adversaries to a settlement. Arbitration is more like a trial, but it is presented to a panel of private people, chosen by the adversaries, and is far less formal than a court hearing. No organization, except a court, has the right to force mediation or arbitration on unwilling parties. An arbitration clause in a contract is generally enforceable, thereby requiring both parties to submit to arbitration and its result if either party demands it. In the absence of a provision such as this, arbitration is possible only with the agreement of both parties. The financially superior party might prefer to go to court instead and hope to wear down the other party. Another approach might be to require mediation before arbitration, but this might only prolong the procedure. The speed, relative informality, and enormous savings on legal fees are among the best reasons to consider arbitration. For amounts above the small claims court limit and less than $10,000, it is very difficult to bring a lawsuit because of the likelihood that lawyers' fees will devour any damages that are recovered (or devour the litigant's savings if the case is lost). An agreement to arbitrate ensures that you can seek redress in disputes involving amounts within this problematic range.

Parties need not fear that they will face a hostile arbitration panel. Most arbitration procedures allow for a method by which both sides can avoid or remove arbitrators who are unacceptable in any way. To obtain additional information about mediation and arbitration, contact the American Arbitration Association, the nearest volunteer lawyers group, or a writers organization.

SMALL CLAIMS COURT

If the small claims court in your area is quick and inexpensive, it might be better for you to sue in that venue for amounts up to the maximum allowed. These limits vary from a low of $1500 to $5000 or more in different localities. Call your local bar association or courthouse for information on the location of small claims court, which in turn can advise as to local procedures.

OTHER RESOURCES

AND A LIST OF VOLUNTEER

LAWYERS FOR THE ARTS

Copyright Clearance Center
222 Rosewood Drive
Danvers, Maryland 01923
(978) 750-8400
www.copyright.com

CCC provides licensing systems for the reproduction and distribution of copyrighted materials in print and electronic formats throughout the world. Through their Web site you can get permission to reproduce copyrighted content such as articles and book chapters in your journals, photocopies, coursepacks, library reserves, Web sites, e-mail, and more. Authors can increase their royalty opportunities by licensing copyrighted works through CCC.

Copyright Office
Library of Congress
101 Independence Ave. S.E.
Washington, D.C. 20559-6000
Hotline: (202) 707-9100
Public Information: (202) 707-3000
www.loc.gov/copyright/

The Copyright Office's Web site offers access to all of their key publications, including informational circulars, application forms for copy-

THE WRITER'S LEGAL GUIDE **292**

right registration, links to the copyright law, news of what the Office is doing, including Congressional testimony and press releases, the latest regulations, and a link to the online copyright records database, cataloged since 1978.

InterNIC
www.internic.net

Provides the public with information regarding Internet domain name registration services and is updated frequently.

Martindale Hubbell's Lawyer Locator
www.martindalehubbell.com

The publisher of the most comprehensive directory of the worldwide legal profession.

Reporters Committee for Freedom of the Press
1815 N. Ft. Myer Drive
Suite 900
Arlington, Virginia 22209
(800) 336-4243
www.rcfp.org

The Reporters Committee for Freedom of the Press was created in 1970 at a time when the nation's news media faced a wave of government subpoenas asking reporters to name confidential sources. The Committee has also emerged as a major national—and international—resource in free speech issues, disseminating information in a variety of forms. Academicians, state and federal agencies, and Congress regularly call on the Committee for advice and expertise, and it has become the leading advocate for reporters' interest in cyberspace.

Superintendent of Documents, Government Printing Office
732 North Capitol Street NW
Washington, D.C. 20401
(202) 512-1800
www.access.gpo.gov/

Through the Superintendent of Documents' programs, GPO dissemi-
nates the largest volume of U.S. Government publications and information in the world. Created primarily to satisfy the printing needs of
Congress, GPO today is the focal point for printing, binding, and
information dissemination for the entire Federal community.

LIST OF VOLUNTEER LAWYERS FOR THE ARTS

Arizona
Cahill, Sutton & Thomas
Sam Sutton, Director
Jane Shrum, Office Manager
2141 East Highland Avenue, #155
Phoenix, Arizona 85016
Phone: (602) 956-7000
Fax: (602) 495-9475
Serves both individual artists and
organizations.

California
**Beverly Hills Bar Association
Barristers Committee for the Arts**
Teri R.C. Williiam and Greg
    Victoroff, co-chairpersons
300 South Beverly Drive, #201
Beverly Hills, California 90212
Phone: (310) 553-6644
Fax: (310) 284-8290
E-mail: *mmeadow@ix.netcom.com*

**California Lawyers for the Arts
(Oakland)**
Adrienne Crew, Program
    Coordinator
1212 Broadway, Suite 834
Oakland, California
Phone: (510) 444-6351
Fax: (510) 444-6352
E-mail: *oakcla@there.net*

**California Lawyers for the Arts
(Sacramento)**
926 J Street, Suite 811
Sacramento, California 95814
Phone: (916) 442-6210
Fax: (916) 442-6281
E-mail: *clasacto@aol.com*

**California Lawyers for the Arts
(San Francisco)**
Alma Robinson, Executive Director
Adrienne Crew, Mediation
    Coordinator
Erin Clarke, Program Coordinator
Fort Mason Center, Building C,
    Room 255
San Francisco, California 94123
Phone: (415) 775-7200
Fax: (415) 775-1143
E-mail: *cla@calawyersforthearts.org*

**California Lawyers for the Arts
(Santa Monica)**
Gloria Ruiz, Associate Director
1641 18th Street
Santa Monica, California 90404
Phone: (310) 395-8893
Fax: (310) 395-0472
E-mail: *UserCLA@aol.com*

San Diego Lawyers for the Arts
Law Office of Peter H. Karlen, Esq.
Peter H. Karlen, Director
1205 Prospect Street, Suite 400
La Jolla, California 92037
Phone: (619) 454-9696
Fax: (619) 454-9777

Colorado
Colorado Lawyers for the Arts
Arts Student League of Denver
Lola Farber Grueskin, Executive
    Director
Sandra M. Christie, Legal
    Coordinator
200 Grant Street, Suite 303E
Denver, Colorado 80203
or
P.O. Box 48148
Denver, Colorado 80204
Phone: (303) 722-7994
Fax: (303) 778-6956
E-mail: *cola@artstozoo.org*

Connecticut
**Connecticut Volunteer Lawyers
for the Arts**
Linda Dente, Senior Program
    Associate and Staff Coordinator
Connecticut Commission on
    the Arts
One Financial Plaza
Hartford, Connecticut 06103
Phone: (860) 566-4770
Fax: (860) 566-6462

District of Columbia
**District of Columbia Volunteer
Lawyers for the Arts**
Joshua Kaufman, Esq., Executive
    Director
Jeffrey Kleinman, Esq., Associate
    Director
918 Sixteenth Street NW
Washington, D.C. 20006
Phone: (202) 429-0229
Fax: (202) 293-3187

**Washington Area Lawyers
for the Arts**
Elena M. Paul, Esq., Executive
    Director
Paige Conner Totaro, Esq., Director,
    Legal Services
815 15th Street NW, Suite 900
Washington, D.C. 20005
Phone: (202) 393-2826
Fax: (202) 393-4444
E-mail: *ptotaro@thewala.org*

Florida
**ArtServe, Inc./ Volunteer
Lawyers for the Arts**
Andrea Pinson, Executive Director
    of Artserve
Suzanne Jarvis, VLA Chair
Martha Smith, Program
    Coordinator
1350 East Sunrise, Suite 100
Ft. Lauderdale, Florida 33304
Phone: (954) 462-9191
Fax: (954) 462-9182

**Volunteer Lawyers for the
Arts/Western Florida**
A division of Business Volunteers
    for the Arts
14700 Terminal Boulevard, Suite 229
Clearwater, Florida 33762
Phone: (727) 507-4114
E-mail: *bkotchey@co.pinellas.fl.us*

Georgia
Atlanta Lawyers for the Arts
Executive Director: Charles J.
    Driebe, Jr., Esq.
152 Nassau Street N.W.
Atlanta, Georgia 30303
Phone: (404) 524-0606
Fax: (404) 524-0607
E-mail: *sealc@altavista.com*

Georgia Volunteer Lawyers for the Arts

c/o Bureau of Cultural Affairs
City Hall East, 5th Floor
675 Ponce de Leon Avenue NE,
  Suite 5150
Atlanta, Georgia 30308
Phone: (404) 873-3911
Fax: (404) 817-6827
E-mail: *georgiavla@hotmail.com*

Illinois

Lawyers for the Creative Arts

Timothy S. Kelley, Esq., Executive
  Director
213 West Institute Place, Suite 401
Chicago, Illinois 60610
Phone: (312) 944-ARTS
Illinois only: (800) 525-ARTS
Fax: (312) 944-2195

Kansas

Mid-America Arts Resources

c/o Susan J. Whitfield-Lungren, Esq.
P.O. Box 363
Lindsborg, Kansas 67456
Phone: (913) 227-2321

Kentucky

Lexington Arts & Cultural Council

Dee Fizdale, Executive Director,
  ArtsPlace
161 North Mill Street
Lexington, Kentucky 40507
Phone: (606) 255-2951
Fax: (606) 255-2787
Serves individual artists and arts
organizations; organizations must be
Council members and artists must
live in Lexington-Fayette County.

Louisiana

Louisiana Volunteer Lawyers for the Arts

c/o Arts Council of New Orleans
Mary Kahn, Associate Director, Arts
  Council of New Orleans
225 Baronne Street, Suite 1712
New Orleans, Louisiana 70112
Phone: (504) 523-1465
Fax: (504) 529-2430
LVLA is sponsored by the Arts
Council of New Orleans and the
Louisiana State Bar Association.

Maine

Maine Lawyers and Accountants for the Arts

Caroline Greenleaf, Executive
  Director
Elizabeth Spencer Adams, Esq.,
  Director
43 Pleasant Street
South Portland, Maine 04106
Phone: (207) 799-9646
or
4 Dane Street
Kennebunk, Maine 04043
Phone: (207) 799-9646
Fax: 207/846-1035

Maryland

Maryland Lawyers for the Arts

Cheryl Hay, Executive Director
218 West Saratoga Street
Baltimore, Maryland 21201
Phone: (410) 752-1633
E-mail: *imani2@msn.com*

THE WRITER'S LEGAL GUIDE **296**

Massachusetts
**Volunteer Lawyers for the Arts
of Massachusetts, Inc.**
Carolyn Rosenthal, Director
P.O. Box 8784
Boston, Massachusetts 02114
Phone: (617) 523-1764
Fax: (617) 523-4005
or
Office of Cultural Affairs
Boston City Hall, Room 716
Boston, Massachusetts 02201
Bar Referral Service: (617) 123-0648
In Massachusetts only: (800) 864-0476
E-mail: *VLA@world.std.com*

Minnesota
**Resources and Counseling
for the Arts**
Chris Osgood, Director of Artists'
 Services
308 Prince Street, Suite 270
St. Paul, Minnesota 55101
Phone: (612) 292-4381 or
 (800) 546-2891
Fax: (612) 292-4315
E-mail: *RCA@Gold.tc.umn.edu or
 Chris@RC4Arts.org*

Missouri
**St. Louis Volunteer Lawyers and
Accountants for the Arts**
Sue Greenberg, Executive Director
3540 Washington
St. Louis, Missouri 63103
Phone: (314) 652-2410
Fax: (314) 652-0011
E-mail: *vlaa@stlrac.org*

Montana
**Montana Volunteer Lawyers
for the Arts**
c/o Joan Jonkel, Esq.

P.O. Box 8687
Missoula, Montana 59807
Phone: (406) 721-1835
Fax: (406) 728-8905

New Hampshire
**Lawyers for the Arts/
New Hampshire**
Joan Goshgarian, Executive
 Director
New Hampshire Business
 Committee for the Arts
 (NHBCA)
One Granite Place
Concord, New Hampshire 03301
Phone: (603) 224-8300
Fax: 603-226-2963
E-mail: *Joan_Goshgarian@
 BCBSNH.COM*

New York
**Albany/Schenectady League
of Arts Inc.**
Doug Pace, Executive Director
19 Clinton Avenue
Albany, New York 12207
Phone: (518) 449-5380
E-mail: *artsleague@aol.com*

**Volunteer Lawyers for
the Arts**
Amy Schwartzman, Executive
 Director
1 East 53rd Street, Sixth Floor
New York, New York 10022
Phone: (212) 319-2787
Art Law Line: (212) 319-2910
Fax: (212) 752-6575
E-mail: *vlany@busy.net,
 vlany@vlany.org*

North Carolina
North Carolina Volunteer Lawyers for the Arts
Daniel Ellison, Esq., President
P.O. Box 26513
Raleigh, North Carolina 27611
or
P.O. Box 25005
Durham, North Carolina 27702
Phone: (919) 990-2575
Fax: (919) 683-1204

Ohio
Volunteer Lawyers and Accountants for the Arts— Cleveland
113 Saint Clair Avenue
Cleveland, Ohio 44114
Phone: (216) 696-3525

Toledo Volunteer Lawyers and Accountants for the Arts
Arnold N. Gottlieb, Esq., Director
608 Madison, Suite 1523
Toledo, Ohio 43604
Phone: (419) 255-3344
Fax: (419) 255-1329

Oregon
Northwest Lawyers and Artists
Oregon Lawyers for the Arts
Kohel Haver, President
621 SW Morrison Street Suite 1417
Portland, Oregon 97205
Phone: (503) 295-2787
E-mail: *Artcop@aol.com*

Pennsylvania
Philadelphia Volunteer Lawyers for the Arts
Dorothy R. B. Manou, Executive Director
Paul Sheehan, Assistant Director
Ray Bruckno, Business Manager

Myra Reichel, Artspace Coordinator—(215) 985-1730
251 South 18th Street
Philadelphia, Pennsylvania 19103
Phone: (215) 545-3385
Fax: (215) 545-0767
E-mail: *pvla@libertynet.org*

Western Pennsylvania Professionals
P.O. Box 19388
Pittsburgh, Pennsylvania 15213
Phone: (412) 268-8437

Rhode Island
Ocean State Lawyers for the Arts
David M. Spatt, Esq., Director
P.O. Box 19
Saunderstown, Rhode Island 02874
Phone and Fax: (401) 789-5686

South Dakota
South Dakota Arts Council (SDAC)
Jocelyn Hanson, Assistant Director
230 South Philips Avenue, Suite 204
Sioux Falls, South Dakota 57102
Phone: (605) 339-6646
In State: (800) 423-6665
Fax: (605) 773-6962
or
800 Governers Drive
Pierre, South Dakota 57501
Phone: (605) 773-3131

Texas
Artists' Legal and Accounting Assistance
Michelle Polgar, Executive Director
P.O. Box 2577
Austin, Texas 78751
Phone: (512) 476-4458
E-mail: *mpolar@bga.com*

Lawyers and Accountants of North Texas for the Arts (LANTA)
P.O. Box 2019
Cedar Hill, Texas 75106
Phone: (972)291-9010

Texas Accountants & Lawyers
Kelly S. Herron, Manager
2917 Swiss Ave.
Dallas, Texas 75204
Phone: (214) 821-1818
Fax: (214) 821-9103

Texas Accountants & Lawyers for the Arts
Jane Lowery, Executive Director
Annabel Shull Levy, Staff Attorney
   and Director of Professional
   Services
Alice Fernelis, Staff Attorney and
   Director of Mediation Services
1540 Sul Ross
Houston, Texas 77006
Phone: (713) 526-4876
Fax: (713) 526-1299
E-mail: *info@talarts.org*
San Antonio and El Paso offices:
contact TALA at Houston office.

Utah
Utah Lawyers for the Arts
Phyllis Vetter, Contact Person
P.O. Box 652
Salt Lake City, Utah 84110
or
P.O. Box 4530
Salt Lake City, Utah 84145
Phone: (801) 482-5373

Washington
Washington Lawyers for the Arts
Richard Hugo House
1634 11th Avenue
Seattle, Washington 98122
Phone: (206) 328-7053
Fax: (206) 568-3306
E-mail: *director@wa-artlaw.org,*
   info@wa-artlaw.org
www.wa-artlaw.org/

INTERNATIONAL

Canada
Canadian Artists' Representation Ontario (CARO)
★Artist's Legal Advice Services
   (ALAS)
183 Bathurst Street, First floor
Toronto, Ontario M5T 2R7
Canada
Phone: (416) 340-7791
Fax: (416) 360-0781 Tuesday and
Thursday 5:00 to 7:30 P.M.

Australia
Arts Law Centre of Australia
Ian Collie, Director
Rochina Iannella, Legal Officer
The Gunnery, 43 Cowper Wharf
   Road
Woolloomooloo, Sydney NSW 2011
ACN 002 706 256
Phone: (02) 356-2566 and
   (008) 221-457
Fax: (02) 358-6475

SELECTED

BIBLIOGRAPHY

Allen, Moira Anderson. *The Writer's Guide to Queries, Pitches, and Proposals.* New York: Allworth Press, 2001.

————. *writing.com.* New York: Allworth Press, 1999.

Alpern, Andrew. *101 Questions About Copyright Law.* Mineola, N.Y.: Dover Publications, 1999.

Appelbaum, Judith. *How to Get Happily Published.* New York: Harper-Collins, 1998.

Appleton, Dina and Daniel Yankelevits. *Hollywood Dealmaking: Negotiating Talent Agreements.* New York: Allworth Press, 2002.

Baker, John F. *Literary Agents: A Writer's Introduction.* New York: Hungry Minds, 1999.

Balkin, Richard. *A Writer's Guide to Book Publishing.* New York: Plume, 1994.

Beach, Mark and Eric Kenly. *Getting It Printed: How to Work with Printers and Graphic Imaging Services to Assure Quality, Stay on Schedule and Control Costs,* 3d Ed. Cincinnati, Oh.: North Light Books, 1999.

Bell, Patricia J. *The Prepublishing Handbook: What You Should Know Before You Publish Your First Book.* Eden Prairie, Minn.: Cat's-Paw Press, 1992.

Blanco, Jodee. *The Complete Guide to Book Publicity.* New York: Allworth Press, 2000.

Bowker, R. R. *Literary Marketplace.* New Providence, N.J.: R. R. Bowker, 2002.

Bowerman, Peter. *The Well-Fed Writer: Financial Self-Sufficiency as a Freelance Writer in Six Months or Less.* Atlanta, Ga: Fanove Publishing, 2000.

Breimer, Stephen F. *The Screenwriter's Legal Guide,* 2d Ed. New York: Allworth Press, 1999.

Brinson, Diane J. and Mark F. Radcliffe. *Multimedia Law Handbook.* Menlo Park, Calif.: Ladera Press, 1994.

Bunnin, Brad and Peter Beren. *The Publishing Law Handbook.* Reading, Mass.: Addison–Wesley Publishing, 1998.

Cole, David. *The Complete Guide to Book Marketing.* New York: Allworth Press, 1999.

Clausen, John. *Too Lazy to Work, Too Nervous to Steal: How to Have a Great Life as a Freelance Writer.* Cincinnati, Ohio: F&W Publications, 2001.

Crawford, Tad. *Business and Legal Forms for Authors and Self-Publishers.* New York: Allworth Press, 1999.

Curtis, Richard. *Beyond the Bestseller: A Literary Agent Takes You Inside the Book Business.* New York: Plume, 1990.

———. *How to Be Your Own Literary Agent: The Business of Getting a Book Published.* Boston: Houghton Mifflin Company, 1996.

———. *This Business of Publishing: An Insider's View of Current Trends and Tactics.* Allworth Press, 1998.

Doyle, Robert P. *Banned Books.* Chicago: American Library Association, 1995.

DuBoff, Leonard. *The Law (in Plain English) for Writers.* New York: John Wiley & Sons, Inc., 1992.

Fishman, Stephen. *The Public Domain: How to Find and Use Copyright-Free Writings, Music, Art and More.* Berkeley, Calif.: Nolo.com, 2001.

Goldfarb, Ronald and Gail E. Ross. *The Writer's Lawyer.* New York: Times Books, 1989.

Greco, Albert N. *The Book Publishing Industry.* Needham Heights, Mass.: Allyn & Bacon, 1996.

Herman, Jeff. *Writer's International Guide to Book Editors, Publishers, and Literary Agents.* Roseville, Calif.: Prima Communications, 1999.

Holm, Kirsten, ed. *2002 Writer's Market: 8,000 Editors Who Buy What You Write.* Cincinnati, Ohio: F&W Publications, 2001.

Jassin, Lloyd J. and Steven C. Schecter. *The Copyright Permission and Libel Handbook: A Step-by-Step Guide for Writers, Editors, and Publishers.* New York: John Wiley & Sons, Inc., 1998.

Kahin, Judith. *Internet Publishing and Beyond: The Economics of Digital Information and Intellectual Property.* Cambridge, Mass.: MIT Press, 2000.

Kirsch, Jonathan. *Kirsch's Handbook of Publishing Law.* Los Angeles: Acrobat Books, 1995.

Kozak, Ellen M. *Every Writer's Guide to Copyright and Publishing Law.* New York: Henry Holt & Company, 1997.

Levine, Mark Lee. *Negotiating a Book Contract: A Guide for Authors, Agents and Lawyers.* Wakefield, R.I.: Moyer Bell, 1988.

Litwak, Mark. *Contracts for the Film and Television Industry.* Los Angeles: Silman-James Press, 1994.

———. *Dealmaking in the Film & Television Industry,* Los Angeles: Silman-James Press, 1994.

Lyon, Elizabeth. *Nonfiction Book Proposals Anybody Can Write: How to Get a Contract and Advance before You Write Your Book.* Portland, Oreg.: Blue Heron Publishing, 2000.

Mason, Peter and Derrick Smith. *Magazine Law: A Practical Guide (Blueprint).* New York: Routledge, 1998.

Mettee, Stephen Blake, ed. *The Portable Writer's Conference: Your Guide to Getting and Staying Published.* Sanger, Calif.: Quill Driver Books, 1997.

Multimedia and the Law. New York: Practising Law Institute, 1994.

Norwick, Kenneth and Jerry Simon Chasen. *The Rights of Authors, Artists, and Other Creative People.* Carbondale, Ill.: Southern Illinois University Press, 1992.

Owen, Elizabeth. *Selling Rights.* New York: Routledge, 1997.

Perkins, Lori. *The Insider's Guide to Getting an Agent.* Cincinnati, Ohio: F&W Publications, 1999.

Perle, E. Gabriel and John Taylor Williams. *The Publishing Law Handbook.* New York: Prentice Hall Law and Business, annual supplement.

Pinkerton, Linda F. *The Writer's Law Primer.* New York: Lyons & Burford Publishers, 1990.

Poynter, Dan. *The Self-Publishing Manual 13th Ed: How to Write, Print, and Sell Your Own Book.* Santa Barbara, Calif.: Para Publishing, 2001.

Ross, Tom and Marilyn. *The Complete Guide to Self-Publishing.* Cincinnati, Ohio: Writer's Digest Books, 1994.

Scott, Michael. *Multimedia Law Practice.* Englewood Cliffs, N.J.: Prentice Hall Law and Business, 1993.

Sedge, Michael. *Marketing Strategies for Writers.* New York: Allworth, 1999.

_____. *Successful Syndication.* New York: Allworth, 2000.

Stim, Richard W. *Getting Permission: How to License and Clear Copyrighted Materials Online and Off with Disk.* Berkeley, Calif.: Nolo.com, 1999.

Winokur, Jon. *Advice to Writers: A Compendium of Quotes, Anecdotes, and Writerly Wisdom from a Dazzling Array of Literary Lights.* New York: Vintage, 2000.

Woll, Thomas. *Selling Subsidiary Rights: An Insider's Guide.* Tucson, Ariz.: Fisher Books, 1999.

INDEX

BOOKS FROM ALLWORTH PRESS

The Journalist's Craft: A Guide to Writing Better Stories edited by Dennis Jackson and John Sweeney (paperback, 6 × 9, 240 pages, $19.95)

Making Crime Pay: The Writer's Guide to Criminal Law, Evidence, and Procedure by Andrea Campbell (paperback, 6 × 9, 304 pages, $19.95)

The Writer's Guide to Queries, Pitches & Proposals by Moira Anderson Allen (paperback, 6 × 9, 288 pages, $16.95)

writing.com: Creative Internet Strategies to Advance Your Writing Career by Moira Anderson Allen (paperback, 6 × 9, 256 pages, $16.95)

Marketing Strategies for Writers by Michael Sedge (paperback, 6 × 9, 224 pages, $16.95)

Writing for Interactive Media: The Complete Guide by Jon Samsel and Darryl Wimberly (paperback, 6 × 9, 320 pages, $19.95)

Business and Legal Forms for Authors and Self-Publishers, Revised Edition by Tad Crawford (paperback [with CD-ROM], 8½ × 11, 192 pages, $22.95)

The Writer's Guide to Corporate Communications by Mary Moreno (paperback, 6 × 9, 192 pages, $19.95)

How to Write Articles That Sell, Second Edition by L. Perry Wilbur and Jon Samsel (hardcover, 6 × 9, 224 pages, $19.95)

How to Write Books That Sell, Second Edition by L. Perry Wilbur and Jon Samsel (hardcover, 6 × 9, 224 pages, $19.95)

Writing Scripts Hollywood Will Love, Revised Edition by Katherine Atwell Herbert (paperback, 6 × 9, 160 pages, $14.95)

So You Want to Be a Screenwriter: How to Face the Fears and Take the Risks by Sara Caldwell and Marie-Eve Kielson (paperback, 6 × 9, 224 pages, $14.95)

The Screenwriter's Guide to Agents and Managers by John Scott Lewinski (paperback, 6 × 9, 256 pages, $18.95)

The Screenwriter's Legal Guide, Second Edition by Stephen F. Breimer (paperback, 6 × 9, 320 pages, $19.95)

Please write to request our free catalog. To order by credit card, call 1-800-491-2808 or send a check or money order to Allworth Press, 10 East 23rd Street, Suite 510, New York, NY 10010. Include $5 for shipping and handling for the first book ordered and $1 for each additional book. Ten dollars plus $1 for each additional book if ordering from Canada. New York State residents must add sales tax.

To see our complete catalog on the World Wide Web, or to order online, you can find us at *www.allworth.com*.